URBAN DESIGN STUDIES

Volume 3

URBAN DESIGN STUDIES

ANNUAL OF THE UNIVERSITY OF GREENWICH URBAN DESIGN UNIT

Editor

MEHRDAD SHOKOOHY

VOLUME 3

1997

SCHOOL OF ARCHITECTURE AND LANDSCAPE, THE UNIVERSITY OF GREENWICH

LONDON

1997

URBAN DESIGN STUDIES

ANNUAL OF THE UNIVERSITY OF GREENWICH URBAN DESIGN UNIT

Editor:

Mehrdad Shokoohy

Editorial Board:

Martin Eyre (Assistant Editor), Evan Fergusson (*Book Reviews*),
Robert Holden, Frank Linden, Philip Stringer, Catherine Teeling

NOTE TO CONTRIBUTORS

Urban Design Studies will consider articles on all aspects of urban studies. Some issues may be devoted to specific themes, but most will include articles concerning any topic relevant to urban design. Articles must be the result of original work and unpublished previously. They should be limited to 30-35 double-spaced pages, preferably including the footnotes. Illustrations, up to a maximum of 15, should be in black and white, and be of a quality that can be enlarged to A4 size or be reduced to fit a quarter of A4 size paper. Before sending your manuscripts please ask the Editor to send you a copy of the *Guide-lines for Contributors*, adhering to which will minimize editorial interference with your manuscript.

Urban Design Studies will also consider books for review on all aspects of urban studies, planning and design.

All articles and books for review should be sent to: The Editor, *Urban Design Studies*, School of Architecture and Landscape, University of Greenwich, Dartford Campus, Oakfield Lane, Dartford, Kent DA1 2SZ England.

© The University of Greenwich

School of Architecture and Landscape, Dartford Campus, Oakfield Lane, Dartford, Kent DA1 2SZ, England

Published for the School of Architecture and Landscape, University of Greenwich by
Araxus Books, 130 St. Julian's Farm Road, London SE27 0RR, England

First published in Great Britain 1997

ISSN 1358-3255
ISBN 1 870606 05 1

British Library Cataloguing-in-Publication Data
A catalogue record of this book is available from the British Library

Printed by J. W. Arrowsmith Ltd, Bristol.

TABLE OF CONTENTS

Urban Design Studies, Volume 3, 1997

RELIGION AND THE CITY:
THE CATHOLIC CHURCH IN DUBLIN 1691-1878

HUGH CAMPBELL

Each new historical era mirrors itself in the picture and active mythology of its past or of a past borrowed from other cultures. It tests its sense of identity, of regress or new achievement against that past. [1]

For fourteen successive Sundays in 1826, a large procession made its way around four Catholic churches in Dublin. Beginning at St. Michael and John's chapel on Essex Quay, the procession moved onto Bridge Street chapel, then to Adam and Eve's Franciscan chapel off Cook Street before crossing the river and making its way up Sackville Street to the new St. Mary's church on Marlborough Street. The chapel, known also as the Metropolitan, and more recently as the pro-Cathedral, had been consecrated just a few months previously on the feast of Laurence O'Toole. Along the route of the procession were banners representing the various parishes and confraternities involved. Hymns were sung, incense hung in the air. The priests and members of religious orders were in their finest vestments.

This procession was called The Unity, and it formed the centre-piece of the celebrations of the 1826 Jubilee, inaugurated by Archbishop Daniel Murray in the Metropolitan on 8th March. The Jubilee was a period of dedication and prayer which commemorated the handing of the keys of the church to St. Peter. It had been celebrated in Rome the previous year, the first of Leo XII's reign, for the first time in fifty years. In the intervening period the Catholic Church had seen its authority and power increasingly questioned and undermined throughout Europe. The Jubilee offered an opportunity for regrouping and consolidation.

For the Irish hierarchy, the Jubilee could not have come at a more opportune time. Since 1780, successive Relief Acts had restored to Catholics many of the rights they had previously been denied. Subsequently, the Act of Union between Britain and Ireland was endorsed by the Catholic middle-class on the basis that it would lead to full emancipation. And although this was not the case, it did open the way for a more broadly based, democratic protest movement against the continuing inequities. This movement was spearheaded by Daniel O'Connell whose massive rallies around the country transformed the Catholic population into a potent, politicised force. The celebration of the Jubilee could tap into this new political energy.

It would also encourage increased observance of the sacraments and more frequent attendance in church. The ceremonies were, after all, commemorating the foundation of St. Peter's church. Thus, they would offer an ideal opportunity to highlight the recent advances made in providing fitting places of Catholic worship in the capital. Furthermore, the ceremonies would allow Irish Catholics to feel part of a wider religious community — to put their heads over the parapet and look at the world.

The Unity procession embodied these ideas. Organised by Father Henry Young, a Roman-trained priest, it spoke of a desire to unify Dublin Catholics and to unite them with the Roman church. Its route traced the journey from the obscurity of the 18th century penal chapels to the new centre of Irish Catholicism: the Pro-Cathedral. It also sought to connect 19th century Dublin Catholics to the pre-reformation city — consciously echoing the guild processions which were a prominent feature of that time.

In *Flesh and Stone*, Richard Sennett notes the importance of ritual in uniting people and place — linking flesh and stone. He discusses its potential value for people alienated from power and privilege:

'Ritual is one way the oppressed can respond to the slights and contempt they otherwise suffer in society, and rituals more generally can make the pain of living and dying bearable. Ritual constitutes the *social* form in which human beings seek to deal with

1

denial as active agents rather than as passive victims.'[2]

The Unity marked a turning point for the Irish Catholic Church, whereby it transformed itself from 'passive victim' to 'active agent'. It was an open, public response to a long period of oppression, a celebration of imminent new freedoms. It also demonstrated the central role the city could play in strengthening a resurgent religion. In *Ulysses*, James Joyce portrayed the city as a structure overlaid with myths and memories and with the traces of everyday life: a shifting kaleidoscope which might provide a myriad of different readings. Citizens could feel a sense of ownership and belonging in such a city. *Urbs* and *civitas* could happily unite. The Unity procession promised just such a sense for the Catholic population of Dublin. It enacted a reconnection with the urban fabric, setting the tone for a period during which Catholicism would remake the city in more tangible ways, and it also revived a fragment of the urban past. Its resonances were temporal as well as spatial, symbolising and legitimising the passage of the Catholic Church from mediaeval to modern times.

RELIGION IN DUBLIN UNTIL 1691

BEGINNINGS

The map of mediaeval Dublin shows a city dominated by religious settlements. The walled city was divided into ten parishes, each with its own church. Beyond the walls, the approaches to the city were marked by the religious settlements of the various orders which began to arrive in Dublin in the 12th century. To the north were the extensive lands held by the Cistercians of St. Mary's Abbey. The western approach was dominated by St. Thomas Abbey and St. John's Hospital, both run by the Augustinians. To the south, there was the Franciscan friary of St. Francis, St. Patrick's Cathedral and the Carmelite St. Mary's Priory. The orders also occupied ground to the east of the city. Clustered around Hoggen Green, where the parliament sat at the Thingmount were the Holy Trinity Friary, All Saints Priory and St. Mary deHogges Abbey.

As James Lydon notes: 'the very existence of so many churches and religious houses is an indication of the importance of religion in the life of mediaeval Dubliners. From birth to death they lived in the embrace of the church'.[3] Religious institutions were the sole providers of alms to the poor. Attached to each church and religious house was a guild to which many parishioners belonged. Through the guilds, the religious orders effectively oversaw the education and welfare of their community and became woven to the fabric of daily life. The powerful craft guilds also had religious affiliations, with each guild having a chapel in a parish church. Trade, commerce and religion were inextricably linked. The church did not stand aloof from the messy business of urban living. Nor did it neglect its own worldly interests. By the end of the 15th century most of the churches owned extensive property in their immediate surroundings. The outlying abbeys in particular tended to own substantial lands as well as estates elsewhere in the country. Often these regular houses were associated with wealthy landed families who would sponsor their activity, perhaps seeing the religious houses as an acceptable conduit through which to acquire property.

This state of affairs persisted until about 1530, when the Reformation began to alter the religious landscape of Dublin. As Lennon describes: 'The dissolution of the religious houses in the late 1530s caused the single greatest topographical upheaval of the period'.[4] Within twenty years, Anglicanism was established as the official state religion of Ireland, with Catholicism facing an uncertain future. While most parish churches were adapted to the redefined religious requirements, the monasteries, friaries and abbeys were sold off. All Hallows, for instance, became the site for Trinity College; the Earl of Meath bought most of the St. Sepulchre Liberty; St. Mary's Abbey was acquired by the Jervis family. The handover had a decisive and far-reaching effect on the development of the city. However traces of the pre-reformation city continued to have an influence on Dublin's evolving religious geography.

UPHEAVAL

By 1563 the Catholic presence in Dublin reached its lowest ebb. All known Catholic places of worship had been seized and either turned over to the Established Church or sold on for other uses. However, it is clear from research that even at this difficult time, the sacraments continued to be observed. A letter from the Protestant Archbishop of Dublin to Queen Elizabeth in 1575 indicates that the houses of Catholic gentry were being used as refuges for the clergy and for the celebration of mass. A letter to the Queen from the Lord Deputy in 1592 notes that:

> 'Through the whole realm, yea in the English pale, there are Jesuits and Seminary priests, all labouring to ... in many places

openly maintained and followed, and in some place — namely the English pale — secretly maintained in the houses of some noble persons, and in many gentlemen's houses partly disguised in apparel of serving men'.[5]

In 1618, in the reign of James I, an official document was issued — 'A Government List of the Catholic Clergy in 1618' — which detailed a number of the private houses used as mass houses at the time:

> 'The places of most public note, whereupon the priests resort for Mass in Dublin are:
> The Baker's hall, in the College, adjoining St Audoen's chancel
> A back-room of Brown, near Newgate
> A back-room of Mr. Plunkett in Bridge Street
> A back-room of Nicholas Quietrot's in High Street
> A back-room of Cary in High Street
> A back-room of Widow O'Hagan in High Street
> Shelton's beyond the bridge, at the corner of the so-called Hangman-Lane' [Hammond Lane][6]

The 'college' had been established by the Jesuits a few years previously. It was the only institutional trace of the Catholic Church. Every other place of worship was a back-room, removed from the gaze of officialdom. The Church had gone underground.

Charles I acceded to the throne in 1625, and his reign marked the beginning of a more conciliatory attitude towards Catholics, if only because they were willing 'to constantly pay an army of five thousand foot and five hundred horse provided they might be tolerated in the exercise of their religion'.[7] To win the wars on the continent England was prepared to tolerate Catholicism on its doorstep. Donnelly describes how 'the result of this tacit toleration was immediately visible ... warehouses, outhouses, stables, buildings of any kind that were more or less spacious were rented to be converted into temporary chapels'.[8] The Superior of the Carmelites praised the improved religious climate: 'Now ecclesiastics publicly perform their sacred functions and prepare suitable places for offering the Holy Sacrifice. With open doors they now preach to the people, say Mass, and discharge all their other duties without being molested by anyone'.[9]

However this freedom was short-lived. In 1629, in response to pressure from the Privy Council, a Proclamation was issued against the Catholic clergy, who had, it accused, 'dared to assemble in public places ... to erect edifices called public oratories, colleges, Mass-houses, and convents of friars, monks and nuns'. The Proclamation commanded that all clergy 'desist from preaching or performing any rite in any public chapel or oratory, and that all owners of such houses and schools should apply them without delay to other uses'.[10] The clergy responded by simply closing the doors of the chapels and admitting the congregation through hidden passages.

On St. Stephen's Day, Archbishop Bulkeley, with a group of soldiers, invaded the Francis Street chapel. Within a few days ten chapels and mass-houses had been closed. Bulkeley subsequently drew up a report on the mass-houses in his diocese, naming among them 'St Michael's chapel at the rere of George Taylor's House between High Street and Back Lane; St. Michan's in Patrick White's house; St. Catherine and St. James over Charles Carroll a victualler on Thomas Street'.[11] The Council of Trent (1545-64) had urged the accurate plotting of counter-reformation parishes.[12] Perhaps in response to this, Bulkeley's report gave Catholic places of worship the more formal title 'chapel', each one representing a particular parish.

With the arrival of Oliver Cromwell in Ireland in 1649, Catholicism once again almost completely disappeared from the capital. At one point only two priests remained in the city. However, the restoration of the monarchy in 1660 allowed Catholics to regroup. It was in this period that a number of the mass houses from the early part of the century were updated and improved or, in some cases replaced with more suitable buildings. By the end of the 17th century, Catholicism had regained some lost ground, but its presence in the city remained marginal and precarious.

ENDURANCE 1691-1782

endure: 1. undergo (a difficulty, hardship etc.); 2. remain in existence, last.

Following King William's victory at the battle of the Boyne in 1691, a series of Acts, which became known as the Penal Laws, codified the continuing discrimination against Catholics. In 1697 'An Act for banishing all Papists exercising any ecclesiastical jurisdiction, and all regulars of the popish clergy out of the kingdom' decreed that:

> 'All popish archbishops, vicars general, deans, Jesuits, monks, friars and all other regular popish clergy and all Papists exercising ecclesiastical jurisdiction, shall depart out of this kingdom before the 1st of May, 1698. If any of the said ecclesiastical

persons shall be at any time after the said 1st of May, 1698, within the kingdom, they and every of them shall suffer imprisonment, until he or they shall be transported beyond the seas; and if any person so transported shall return again into this kingdom, they and every of them shall be guilty, of high treason, and suffer and forfeit as in case of high treason' [i.e. death and forfeiture of goods].[13]

For the Catholic clergy merely living in Ireland was now an offence and in the wake of this Act all but two of Ireland's bishops left the country, most of them never returning. However, almost immediately, this draconian regime was relaxed somewhat. In 1704 a Registration Act was passed by Queen Anne which required all priests in the country to register their names in court. Those who did were free to celebrate mass and carry out all their normal functions without penalty. The Act could be exploited to allow most priests to remain active. As Maureen Wall describes: 'Dublin city, which during the century consisted of nine parishes, had 33 registered priests. Old mediaeval parishes were revived and priests, many of them regulars, were registered for these parishes, and carried out the duties of curates'.[14] Bishops remaining in the country registered themselves as parish priests.

Paradoxically, the Act had actually been designed to bring about the collapse of Catholicism in Ireland. As the registered priests died off, none would be available to replace them (priests not being allowed to re-enter the country). In 1709 an Act was introduced obliging all clergy to take an Oath of Abjuration swearing allegiance to Queen Anne and disavowing the right of the Catholic James III to the throne. However, there was a widespread refusal to take the oath and the act was never enforced. This failure to enforce the Act soon became part of a generally more tolerant approach. Within a few years it became apparent that the penal laws, though sanctioning discrimination, could never succeed in eradicating Catholicism. As Thomas Bartlett comments:

'It is clear that, whatever their original purposes may have been, they did not lead to the elimination of Catholicism, nor did they bring about the mass conversion of Catholics, nor did they keep Catholics poor... by the 1730s Protestants in general were content to see the penal laws remain in the statute books as an earnest of their good intentions rather than as a blueprint or strategy for transforming the religious geography of Ireland.'[15]

In fact, the Catholic church was continuing to exert an influence, albeit a marginal one, on the religious geography of Dublin. In 1731 the Protestant Archbishop of Dublin sent a report on the 'state of popery' to the Government, summarising the position in the capital:

'The Archbishop of Dublin returns, from the account sent him by his country clergy, fifty-eight Mass houses, twenty-four of them built since the first year of King George I; sixty-one priests besides a friar that officiates in a private family at Ballrothery and several regulars and seculars that are unsettled and stroll from place to place; four private popish chapels and twenty-nine popish schools.

By the return made by the clergy of the City of Dublin in his Grace's diocese it appears that there are in the city and liberties of Dublin sixteen Mass houses, four whereof have been built since the reign of King George I; one hundred and two popish priests; three private popish chapels; two nunneries, but the number of nuns is uncertain; and there are forty-five popish schools'.[16]

The report reveals the extent to which Catholics in Dublin, despite being in a minority, and being subject to an antagonistic Protestant dominated Corporation, were managing to weather the storm. In fact, paradoxically, their numerical strength was actually increasing. The presence of a number of private chapels bears witness to the support of the remaining Catholic gentry. The large number of schools demonstrates a determination on the part of the clergy to retain a central role in the urban communities, ministering to secular as well as religious needs as their medieval counterparts had done. Pre-reformation traditions were being sustained in dramatically altered circumstances.

A far more detailed report on the state of Catholicism in Dublin was drawn up in 1749.[17] When read in conjunction with John Rocque's map of the city, published in 1756, the report gives quite a complete picture of the practice of Catholicism in the 18th century city (fig. 1.1). It also demonstrates a conscious effort by the authorities to regulate and control Catholicism. Recognising their inability to stamp out Catholic practice, the authorities instead sought to survey it accurately. As a policy of eradication gave way to one of tacit toleration and containment there was a greater need for control. For this to be possible, accurate information about the Catholic places of worship was needed.

fig. 1.1 Extract from John Rocque's map of Dublin, 1756, showing positions of Protestant churches and Catholic chapels.

The 1749 Report gives details of nineteen chapels in Dublin: nine parish chapels, five regular chapels and four nunneries. It identifies the location of each chapel, describes its interior and fittings and gives some its history. From the report it is possible to trace the Catholic Church's impact on, and engagement with, Dublin's urban geography (figs. 1.1 and 1.3).

LOCATION

The chapels were mainly located in the south-western part of the city, within the old walls and in the Liberties. In 1749 this was still the main commercial and entertainment district of the city. It contained the Tholsel and market which formed the centre of commercial life. Although by the mid 18th century the wealthier citizens were beginning to move to the new developments to the east such as the Aungier Estate, and St. Stephen's Green, the western districts remained prosperous, with a higher Protestant than Catholic population. Of the chapels listed, 11 were in the south-west; four of the nunneries were on the north-west bank, as were two parish churches. Only the Liffey Street chapel of St. Mary's ventured east of Essex Bridge on the north side. Only Hawkins Street chapel of St. Andrew's lay east of the castle on the south side (although there is evidence of a Carmelite presence on Whitefriar Street, part of the Aungier estate). Catholics were unable to respond to the shift eastwards because of their lack of resources and the difficulties of acquiring sites in the new developments. As David Dickson notes, the only land made available for non-residential use in the large scale developments was earmarked for the Established Church.[18] This mitigated against a large Catholic presence. In the liberties, tenants were generally more free to make their own changes and alterations. This was obviously more suitable for the Catholic Church. By contrast, the new developments were quite rigidly zoned and controlled. There was, also, a natural inclination to hold onto what was already serving, at least adequately, as a place of worship. As Nuala Burke puts it:

> 'In congested areas, once premises had been acquired, it was usually easier to remain on the same site and gradually enlarge the premises rather than move to a new site. Moreover the clergy attempted to acquire property near the site of pre-Reformation churches which were all in the older parts of the city, keeping old dedications, and thus the parallel network of parishes developed'.[19]

This parallel network allowed greater numbers of priests, but also maintained a memory of the mediaeval city. St. Mary's parish corresponded with the lands of St. Mary's Abbey, St Nicholas chapel was sited on the grounds of the Franciscan Friary, and so on. The area around St. Audoen's (fig. 1.7), reputedly the site of Colmcille's Church, and thus a potent icon for the Celtic church, was home to between 40 and 50 priests at the time. The religious community seemed to gain strength and resolve by remaining close to its historical roots. Thomas Butler writes of Edmund Byrne establishing the John's Lane chapel in 1703:

> 'Designedly or not, he had chosen a site, under the shadow of the old tower of St. John's Hospital, historically associated with the Augustinian order... This was the most Augustinian spot in Dublin since 1188. The wheel had come full circle, Here at last the order came home to roost'.[20]

SITING

Almost all the chapels documented were located away from main thoroughfares and were accessed by lanes. Sometimes they had a frontage on a minor street or lane, particularly in the newer, less populous parts of the city. The Franciscan chapel off Cook Street was typical. It was known as Adam and Eve's because the sign for a tavern of that name also marked the lane which led to the chapel entrance. The chapel itself was buried deep in the centre of a dense mediaeval city block. By law, Catholic churches were forbidden to front onto main thoroughfares. They could not signal their presence with anything like the power of the Established Church buildings of the time, such as St. Mary's, completed in 1697 by William Robinson, which formed part of the formal grid layout of the Jervis estate, and had an extensive graveyard. No parish in Dublin had a Catholic graveyard during the 18th century, and burials had to be made in Protestant grounds, sanctioned by amenable priests.

LAYOUT

The chapels normally dated from the early 18th century. Though generally an improvement on the mass-houses of the 17th century, they were still somewhat irregular and makeshift (fig. 1.2). If not actually adaptations of existing buildings, they tended to be built on tight, awkward and irregularly shaped sites. Inevitably this meant that the plan form of the chapels was quite varied. In

fig. 1.2 St. James's Street Chapel (Irish Catholic Annual, 1932).

almost all instances the chapels are described as being galleried. These galleries served to maximise the churches' capacity, reflecting the need to accommodate as many people as possible. The simple, galleried box was also a standard type for contemporary Anglican churches in Dublin — as in St. Mary's and St Mark's on Pearse Street (1729). Their Catholic counterparts seem to have drawn on similar sources, albeit in a less formal manner. The Rosemary Lane chapel is described as having three galleries, as are Hawkins Street and St. Mary's Lane. The contingent nature of much of the planning is exemplified by Rosemary Lane, whose F shaped configuration was unusual enough to prompt the compiler of the report to sketch it in the margins.[21] Galleries were also useful for ancillary functions: they served as confessionals and sometimes as sleeping quarters for priests.

INTERIOR

In many cases, the interiors of these chapels revealed a different world. What resources were available were used internally, many of the interiors being assembled from various bequests and donations made by the wealthier parishioners. The churches on Francis Street and Liffey Street seem to have been the most elaborate, and merit detailed description in the report. Liffey Street has a gilt leather altar, a gilt tabernacle and 'a neat oak pulpit'.[22] In Francis Street 'the altar-

piece, four pillars and the steps, are all of Kilkenny marble', while 'the decorations are the same as in the chapel of Liffey Street'.[23] Up to 1737 St. Nicholas parish had been the mensal parish (the seat of the archbishop) a status which transferred to the recently created St. Mary's parish. These churches would therefore have acted as standard-bearers for the whole city and as locations for special masses.

This patronage is reflected in the provision of 'several pews for the better sort'[24] (the remaining members of the dwindling Catholic gentry and the increasingly powerful Catholic merchants). The laws forbidding ownership of property had prompted Catholics to invest in trade and industry. In 1641, 59% of Irish land was Catholic-owned. In 1703 this figure was 14%, and by 1776 it had dropped to 5%. By contrast, in 1780 approximately 35% of Dublin merchants were Catholic. Bequests and gifts to the church were one way in which these prosperous merchants could invest their money back into the community, and ensure their continuing pre-eminence. They could secure a place in heaven and a good seat at Mass. This creation of hierarchies within the laity mirrored Anglican practice.

The 18th century Catholic church remained invisible or at best anonymous on the exterior, only to reveal a richly appointed interior, echoing its social and political position. Hidden from public view it survived and even flourished, with new parishes created in response to the shifting

7

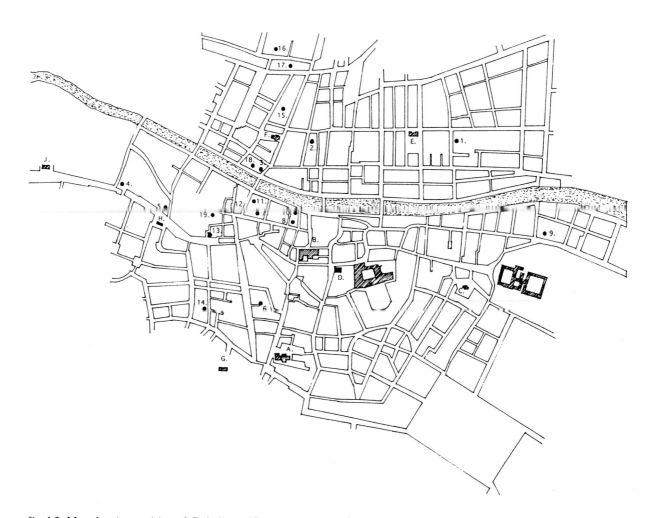

fig. 1.3 Map showing position of Catholic and Protestant places of worship in Dublin 1750.

Key

Catholic Chapels from 1749 Report

1 Liffey Street	11 Bridge Street, Dominican
2 St Mary's Lane	12 Wormwood Gate, Carmelite
3 Arran Quay	13 St. John's Lane, Augustinian
4 St. James's Street	14 Ash Street, Carmelite
5 Dirty Lane	15 Curch Street, Capuchin
6 Francis Street	16 Channel Row, Dominicans
7 Cook Street	17 King Street, Poor Clares
8 Rosemary Lane	18 Arran Quay, Carmelites
9 Hawkins Street	19 Mullinahack, Augustinian
10 Adam and Eve, Fransiscan	

Principal Protestant Churches

A St. Patrick's
B Christ Church
C St. Andrew's
D St. Werburgh's
E St. Mary's
F St. Michan's
G St. Nicholas's
H St. Catherine's
J St. James's

and growing population. Theological disputes continued, but behind closed doors. Just as the Establishment was becoming used to the continued presence of Catholicism, so the Catholic church was adapting to its situation, shaping itself to meet the demands and strictures of the time.

'Frequently during the seventeenth century the Catholic bishops of Ireland had hoped for a restoration of the church to its ancient position — for a return of confiscated lands and church buildings, and all the pomp and ceremony and dignity which went with them'.[25]

However, by the 18th century, as Maureen Wall explains, that pre-reformation richness seemed farther away than ever. The Church seemed less willing to dwell on the past and more determined to set down markers for the future. The past was still used as a source for siting, decoration and imagery, but there was little wallowing in unreflective nostalgia.

Between the 1st and 4th centuries AD, the Christian church in Rome moved from being one among many obscure cults operating underground to becoming the official religion of the city, and subsequently the empire. In *Building God's House*

8

in the Roman World,[26] White outlines how the era breaks down into three distinct periods. In the first (roughly 50-150 AD) the Christians had no formal settings for worship and meetings took place in the homes of wealthy church members. In the second period, lasting till about 250 AD, the growing community had more complex demands, but concomitantly greater resources, and houses began to be modified to serve as places of worship; rooms were adapted, altars erected. This was the *domus ecclesiae* — the house of God, which still retained its domestic character, betraying nothing externally, but becoming internally a setting for new rituals. Between 250 and 313 AD the Christians gradually moved from these domestic adaptations to larger scale buildings to accommodate their growing numbers, often in existing buildings, stables and factories lying away from the main thoroughfares.

The parallel with the trajectory of Catholicism in Dublin is striking. From the early 17th-century back rooms to the first mass-houses, through the larger chapels of the mid-18th century, each Roman stage finds its equivalent in Dublin. This Roman parallel did not go unnoticed in penal times, with Catholics often portraying themselves as latter-day versions of the Christians in the catacombs.

In 313 AD Constantine had built the Lateran Basilica — the first of a type which was to become the model for early Christian churches — marking the beginning of a period during which Christianity became increasingly powerful and increasingly visible in Rome. In Ireland, the gradual abandonment of the penal laws from the 1780s onwards signalled the beginning of a new era for the Catholic faith. As in Rome, a new scale and order of church-building was required to reflect the religion's new position.

EMERGENCE 1782-1823

emerge: 1. come up or out into view esp. when formerly concealed; 2. come to light, become known; 3. become recognised or prominent; 4. survive with a specified result

On 8th August 1781, the foundation stone of the new Custom House was laid by John Beresford. The building of the Custom House crystallised the altered profile of Ascendancy Dublin, setting 'the two poles of James Gandon's neo-classical city'.[27] It was the clearest statement to date of the desire to escape the dense, unhealthy atmosphere of the mediaeval city and create a splendid new city to the east. Its effect was also to further polarise the religious communities. By and large, the Protest-

ant community moved east, while the Catholics stayed in the west. Consequently most Catholic development remained rooted in the older parts of the city. Notwithstanding this, the position of Catholics was changing. Between 1778 and 1793, a succession of Catholic Relief Acts were introduced, allowing Catholics the right to long-term leases, the right to vote and other basic rights. This freed the wealthier Catholics to invest openly in property and to partake more fully in professional and political life.

Agitation for Catholic Relief had been forcefully supported by Luke Gardiner, one of the most powerful developers in the city, who saw Catholic investment as vital to the continuing success of his new estates north of the river.[28] William Stevens wrote:

'Numbers of the middling Catholics, who had idle money, so soon as they could take satisfactory leases, ran on house building; and many of the more rich were induced by the security of tenure [since the 1778 Relief Act] to lay out large sums for their own accommodation'.[29]

A number of the wealthier merchants moved to Gardiner's developments in the north-east, encroaching into Ascendancy territory. The lines of religious division, though retaining a certain topographical clarity, became somewhat less constrictive.

In 1782 a new chapel for St. Catherine's parish was built on the east side of Meath Street in the Liberties. The building was facilitated by the friendship between Archdeacon Bermingham, the parish priest and the Earl of Meath, who owned the whole liberty. As Myles Ronan explains, 'the first departure from the penal time model was made, and the new church on Meath street was created on a spacious site and in a continental style'.[30] While it is not certain what Ronan means by a continental style, it is clear that this church marked a decisive change from what had gone before. It had a hexagonal form, galleried on five sides with the altar on the sixth, the whole being contained within a plain brick box. The church did not address the street directly, but sat behind the new priest's house which fronted onto Meath Street.[31] Its plan form clearly displays the continuing dichotomy between the interior and external expression — here taken to a more formal level, with two geometric figures superimposed. Although the church was not yet able to address the street directly, the priest's house asserted a public presence. Ronan stresses the relative spaciousness of the site: the building was not constrained by the surrounding fabric; it found its own coherent form. Clearly, the Catholic Church's circumstances were improving. No longer had it to contend with the contingencies of unsuitable, irregular sites. It was now only hampered by the strictures of Government legislation. Its future form begins to take shape on Meath street.

Following St. Catherine's at least two other purpose built chapels appeared: St. Michael and John's on Essex Quay, and St. Michan's on North Anne Street. Both were of a very similar neo-Gothic style. They appear to imitate the restrained style of the 18th century Anglican church. The plan was a simple rectangle with a deep gallery to the rear. The continuing importance of the Catholic gentry in funding these early churches is witnessed by the coat of arms of Captain Bryan of Kilkenny which appears over the Anne Street entrance to St. Michan's. St. Michael and John continued the tradition of acquiring and adapting existing buildings: in this case a whisky storehouse which had housed the Smock Alley Theatre since 1790. The site was bought for £1,600 in 1811. St. Michael and John housed the first Catholic church bell to sound since the reformation. It was also home to Father Henry Young, a Roman-trained priest who was highly influential in harnessing Catholic energies in the city. To finance the church-building, Young collected a weekly average of £22 through penny-a-week contributions from parishioners. Church building was becoming more fixed and formal, being identified more strongly with the people of the parish.

The period was also marked by efforts at reform and improved organisation within the Church. Archbishop Troy (1739-1826) took office in Dublin in 1786, serving as archbishop of the diocese until three years before his death in 1826. 'Troy ruled and reformed his archdiocese with an iron hand'[32] comments Emmet Larkin. His reforms included a conscious effort to eradicate what he perceived as the less appropriate rituals which had grown up around Catholic practice.

Given the shortage of places of worship, wealthier parishioners offered their houses for the celebration of Mass. The mass moved from house to house over the year. This tradition was known as the 'stations', and was still widespread at the end of the 18th century. The practice led to suspicions of favouritism and corruption. The 'pattern' (a corruption of 'patron') involved a procession to a holy site, usually a well. The assembled pilgrims generally made several rounds of the well or landmark, reciting prayers. Often they were barefoot. Small tokens were left at the site, and pilgrims usually bathed in or drank the holy water. A great many of these assemblies were dedicated to St. John (the Baptist) and took place on St. John's Eve — the midsummer festival. In Dublin they took place on Watling Street. Though important to the community, the pattern had no place within Troy's doctrinaire conception of Catholicism. He looked on such customs as being contrary to the correct principles of the faith. A contemporary biographer reports that Troy 'felt it necessary to prohibit the celebration of these public festivals called "patrons" and "Mayballs" which, although they had originated in the piety of the faithful, were frequented with a spirit utterly conflicting with devotional exercises and closed in riot, intemperance and vice'.[33]

Troy also began to stamp out the local favouritism which had traditionally governed the appointment of bishops and parish priests. He looked directly to Rome for guidance on such matters. 'He laid the basis for Reform in the rest of Ireland by his influence over episcopal appointments at Rome'.[34] Troy had studied in Rome and acted as rector of San Clemente before becoming bishop of Ossory in 1776. This Roman experience must have been influential. San Clemente was a 12th-century church, built over the remains of a 4th-century basilica, one of the earliest Christian churches in Rome. Troy may have felt the desire to bring Irish Catholicism into a similarly grand setting.

In the first year of his reign, he relocated the mensal parish from St. Nicholas to St. Mary's and soon afterwards took up residence near the Liffey Street chapel. This move seems to have been an effort to keep up with the shift of the powerful and wealthy citizens to the north-east quarter which formed part of St. Mary's parish. To further reinforce this move, Troy embarked on his most ambitious and significant project: the building of the new parish chapel which was to become the pro-Cathedral (fig. 1.4).

In 1803, Lord Annesley's mansion on Marlborough Street, abandoned after the Act of Union, was bought for £5,755 (all but £250 of this was paid off by 1810). A house for the archbishop was built on the north edge of the site, and the next step was to build a church 'harmonising somewhat in style and dimensions with the dignity of the residence and with the superior wealth and respectability of the inhabitants'.[35] The architectural requirements of the site clearly marked a significant advance on what had gone before.

A competition was held and in 1814 John Sweetman was appointed as architect. Sweetman was a little known architect who had been

fig. 1.4 The Pro-Cathedral (Metropolitan Chapel of St. Mary) on Marlborough Street (photo: T. de Paor).

involved in the 1798 uprising and had subsequently fled to Paris, from where he submitted his entry. He had obviously been influenced by the neoclassical basilica type churches (in particular Chalgrin's St. Phillipe du Roule) which were being built in France. Troy's co-adjutor archbishop, Daniel Murray, had spent time in Paris between 1810 and 1812, and would have been familiar with the neo-classical splendour of St. Geneviève and the Madeleine. This may have influenced the choice of design.

Perhaps because of Sweetman's inexperience, a board of advisors was convened to expedite the design. There is evidence that Richard Morrison, a Protestant, and John Keane, a Catholic architect were both involved in the committee, which oversaw substantial changes to the original design. A dome was introduced at the crossing of the nave and transept, disrupting the sophisticated scheme of clerestory lighting. It was presumably meant to give the church a stronger urban presence.

Interestingly, even at this new scale, there was still a schism between internal and external treatment: inside the Roman splendour of St. Phillipe du Roule, outside the powerful Greek Doric of Paestum. It is also striking that, though to some extent imitating the strategies of the Ascendancy, the church drew inspiration from other sources: 'The interior ... seems to derive from continental models ... rather than from English examples. Indeed for its date there would have been few British examples to offer as an appropriate model for a Catholic congregation'.[36]

In the genesis of the design, Troy's Roman experience would also have had a decisive influence. The early Roman basilicas, like San Clemente, sought to insert a Christian function into a public building type, and the same might be said of the Metropolitan chapel. It sought to assert a massive, simple public presence, consciously echoing the temple-like quality of 18th-century buildings like the Four Courts, the Royal Exchange and the Customs House. The church's separation from the street on a podium reinforced the impression. It tried to fit in with the grand public scale demanded by the occasion — to live up to its surroundings (fig. 1.4). The Rev.

11

Willaim Meagher reports, no doubt apocryphally, that a Protestant gentleman passing the new church was heard to exclaim: 'How vain to fight against destiny! The men who projected and carried out this work will not submit long to their bondage!'[37] Moreover, the Metropolitan exhibited little concern for its immediate antecedents. While remnants from the Liffey Street chapel (pillars, altar-rails and statues) found their way into the new church, they did little to influence its overall design.

In 1815, the foundation stone was laid. The vaults were completed the following year and leased temporarily as a whisky storehouse to help defray costs. Work continued over the following thirty years. Though the debts were paid off and the bell hoisted only in 1844, by that stage the church had been functioning, and acting as a potent symbol of Catholic strength, for nearly twenty years. Troy died in 1823 before seeing his most ambitious project completed. It was left to his predecessor Daniel Murray to open the church, and to usher in a new era for the Catholic faith in the city.

CONSOLIDATION 1823-1852

consolidate: 1. make or become strong or solid; 2. reinforce or strengthen (one's position, power etc.) 3. combine (territories, companies, debts etc.) into one whole.

Archbishop Daniel Murray (1768-1852) was educated initially in Dublin under Doctor Betagh and subsequently at the University of Salamanca in Spain 'as an alumnus of the ancient Irish ecclesiastical college in that city'.[38] He was ordained in 1790 and served as parish priest in St. Paul's in Arklow where he remained till 1798, when he was removed to Dublin. On 30th November 1809 he was advanced as co-adjutor archbishop of Dublin by Archbishop Troy, under the title Archbishop of Hierapolis. Following Troy's death, Murray became archbishop of Dublin, a position he held till his death in 1852.

Murray officially dedicated the Metropolitan chapel on 11th November 1825, the feast day of St. Laurence O'Toole, patron saint of Dublin. The occasion marked the beginning of a new period in Irish Catholic history when, as William Meagher, Murray's biographer, put it, 'as was said of her in the tenth century, religion began throughout the land to array herself once more in the garments of glittering purity and brightness'.[39]

The Metropolitan was of a scale and splendour hitherto unthinkable to Dublin Catholics. It was, in Meagher's opinion, 'one of the most matchless architectural gems that has been wrought in any Christian capital for centuries'[40] It bore witness to the continuing vitality of Catholicism. 'It tells in its, for that time, amazing beauty and amplitude, how brightly the aspirations of Christian art still burned amongst a people, that for centuries beheld nothing encircling their altars but lowliness and depravity'.[41] It also signalled the beginning of a huge upsurge in church building during Murray's reign: 'He built up this glorious Cathedral pile, impressing us with conception of what, if possible, Christ's earthly residence should be; and in every town, and village, and hamlet of his Archbishopric the suggestion was caught up, and our Lord now finds everywhere a befitting home'.[42]

Despite all the euphoria, however, there seemed to be a feeling that the church was still selling itself short — resisting the temptation to adorn itself fully in 'purity and brightness'. Following his extravagant praise, Meagher wrote that 'It need scarcely be added that these remarks apply almost exclusively to the interior. Notwithstanding its noble porticoes the Church outside ... is a very inferior thing'.[43] The Church remained unwilling, or unable, to reveal itself fully. A few months later however, an opportunity presented itself for the church to consolidate its position on the streets of the city. On the 8th of March 1826, the Metropolitan chapel formed the setting for the opening of the Jubilee (described above) by Archbishop Murray:

'The Jubilee celebrations in the city parishes were ... providential and awakened the citizens to the necessity of personal sanctification. The various parish societies had been doing heroic work to effect it, but it required the call from Rome and from the Archbishop of Dublin to make the people realise the meaning and the grandeur of their faith and that they were an important portion of the Catholic church spread throughout the world. It was a new vision to the people of the city and of the Liberties that they meant anything beyond their own struggle for existence in difficult times and in squalid surroundings. Most of the penal-time chapels were still in use; the lack of proper accommodation had, no doubt, something to say to their neglect of the sacraments. It was the first time the people were called upon for nearly three hundred years to proclaim that Catholic Dublin was still, in spite of those centuries of oppression, a living part of the Church of Christ'.[44]

For Murray, the Jubilee offered an opportunity to

cement his relationship with his flock and to attract faltering sinners back to the fold:

'You will have observed, beloved brethren, how much the ample powers granted on this occasion to all approved confessors, respecting censures and reserved cases, facilitate now the conversion of those sinners who may have been deterred by fear or shame from approaching the tribunal of penance. May they enter, at length, at the door of mercy which is open to them. Awakened by the zeal of the Supreme Pastor to a sense of their miseries, and animated with courage by his moving exhortation to make their peace with heaven, may they return to the House of their Father, which they had wickedly forsaken. May they throw themselves at the feet of their offended God in sentiments of sincerest compunction, and now that the whole Church is in supplication along with them, his paternal bosom will be more than ever open to receive them'.[45]

Murray emphasised the fact that it was now easier to 'return to the house of their Father' than ever before. The more commodious and comfortable churches which were starting to be built were testament to this — an explicit demonstration that the whole church could now be 'in supplication' together.

The celebration of the Jubilee was, according to contemporaries, a huge success, sparking an increased observance of the sacraments and bringing thousands of Catholics into contact with church buildings and church rituals — many quite possibly for the first time. William Meagher's effusive account of the period is worth quoting at length:

'At all periods of the day, from dawn to a late hour at night the work of sanctification ... was going on. The public devotions commenced each morning at 7 o'clock, consisting of prayers and instructions from the pulpit, and were renewed again at mid-day, and a third time in the evening. On the week-days, the celebrated Father Kenny harangued the people continually on their duties, in those effusions of commanding eloquence which never failed to achieve the most signal victories over sin: while on Sundays His Grace addressed them with the same gratifying results. Meanwhile the sacred Tribunals were crowded almost without interruption by unprecedented multitudes. Every rank without exception, and every age and sex sent their penitent throngs in unbroken succession to these fountains of propitiation, so

that on the first morning of general Communion, a spectacle such as Dublin never before, it is probable, had witnessed, was presented in the Church of the Conception. The sacred edifice was thronged to complete repletion, and of the numbers congregated, it was deemed that there was not one who did not partake of the sacred synaxis. The renovation of baptismal vows terminated the glories of that memorable morning. It was conducted by Father Kenny, who upon beholding the sight that met him as he ascended the pulpit, burst forth into such strains of jubilation and thanksgiving, as made his overflowing audience almost beside themselves, while with uplifted hands and streaming eyes they literally shouted aloud their eternal renunciation of Satan and his works. It was indeed a Jubilee that morning in Dublin — a bright epoch in the lives of many a wanderer, who never before had knelt at the holy table, and thence forward never strayed away from their father's house. And yet all this was the beginning merely of the blessings which marked those days of Salvation. During the entire period of the jubilee which had to be extended again and again scenes of excited devotion were continually witnessed in almost every parochial and every conventual church within the city and in several throughout the rural districts. The archbishop renewed in person the same imposing ceremonies in each church as those with which he opened the holy times in his cathedral. The attachment of the metropolitan Catholics to the observance of their religion had been for a long time anything but edifying. To the fidelity with which the graces of the holy year were husbanded is due the amazingly increased frequentation of the sacraments, which has now for so long a time distinguished the faithful of our city'.[46]

The Jubilee was also marked by the Unity — the procession of the Catholic faithful through the streets of Dublin. The route of the Unity, from St. Michael and John's to the Metropolitan, told the story of the Catholic Church's development in the city: from its roots in the walled, mediaeval city to its new offshoot in the heart of the Ascendancy quarter. Thus, it recalled the past and looked to the future. The route described not only the emergence of Catholicism but also the extension of the city. Dublin's eastern trajectory was assimilated into Catholic ritual and experience. As Ronan notes, the processions also harked back to the guild processions of pre-reformation days. 'The infidel ... and the sectarian smiled scornfully at the attempt, as they called it, to engraft on the enlightenment of the nineteenth century the inanities and follies of the twelfth', writes Meagher.[47] But the revival of this ritual allowed Catholics to connect themselves to their faith and to the city and to understand the links between the two. They could feel connected to Dublin's remote past, but also to its most recent history. In what was to become a recurring 19th century theme, they began to assert a sense of ownership and belonging beyond their own immediate experience. The Unity clearly implied that, for the first time, the whole city was, potentially, Catholic.

The Catholic Church was obviously willing to engage with the city, to use its own burgeoning urban presence as a rallying call to the faithful. This theme of linking the church to its physical surroundings was to continue throughout the century. Murray's term of office saw the consolidation of the church in the city centre, a strong marking of territory in the west, the spreading of offshoots into the newer eastern parts of Dublin and the beginnings of parish organisation and church building in the suburbs.

Though a conciliatory moderate by nature, Murray was determined to continue the reforming work begun by Troy. In 1825, soon after taking office, he convened the bishops of the diocese and issued a document, *The Pastoral Instruction to Clergy and Laity in Ireland*, which stressed the need for the 'vigilant administration of the holy sacraments':

> 'Nothing can excuse you from the discharge of this duty; nothing can exempt you; not labour, not fatigue, nor watching, nor hunger nor thirst, nor heat, nor cold; you can have no just cause of delay when pressed by an obligation so strict and so important'.[48]

The thrust of the document was clear: it was an attempt to codify and consolidate the rituals of the church. Further on, in an interesting turn, Murray became surprisingly political:

> 'Whilst you study to have peace with all men, do not forget, that you are watchmen on the towers of the city of God to detect the ambuscades of her enemies...'[49]

In 1825 Daniel O'Connell's influence was everywhere. The Catholic Association had been founded two years previously and the campaign for emancipation was gathering force. Church buildings were widely used for Association meetings (Clarendon Street church in Dublin in particular). Priests often used the pulpit to exhort parishioners to vote. The church, almost unavoidably, was becoming politicised. The parish unit became the unit of organisation for the Association, the parish priest a sort of chargé d'affaires for the O'Connellites. As Oliver McDonagh explains, 'the fact that the structure of parish organisation and the weekly mass could be used, immediately and unchanged, for the formation of the political branches, the raising of revenue ... and the promotion of public meeting and demonstrations of numerical strength' were all central to the success of the campaign.[50] Where previously the Irish bishops had acquiesced to the Act of Union on the promise of emancipation, and had threatened excommunication for those involved in the 1798 rebellion, now they were becoming far more independent-minded.

At about the same time, the Established Church was embarking on a campaign of proselytism to combat increasing Catholic power. Opposition to the Union had been strongest among Protestants, but by the 1820s they were beginning to see it as their best hope of survival. Where previously Protestant privilege had contrasted sharply with Catholic oppression, the two religions now stood on a more equal footing, battling for the right to be seen as the one true church in Ireland.[51]

It was in this context that Murray made his remarks. Speaking specifically to a Dublin audience, he conjured the image of 'watchmen on the towers of the city of God'. It is easy to see the churches built during Murray's reign as just such sentinels — marking and watching over Catholic territory, eyeing warily any encroachments or 'ambuscades of her enemies'. In the fifteen years after Emancipation was finally granted in 1829, six important new churches were built in the centre of the city: Adam and Eve's Franciscan Church on Merchants Quay (1830); St. Francis Xavier's on Gardiner Street (1832); St. Nicholas of Myra on Francis Street (1832); St. Paul's on Arran Quay (1835) (fig. 1.5); St. Andrew's on Westland Row (1837) (fig. 1.6); and St. Audoen's on High Street (1841-6) (fig. 1.7).

Of the six, both William Bolger's St. Andrew's and John Keane's St. Francis Xavier's may be seen as an attempt to consolidate the growing Catholic presence in the east of the city, a process begun by Troy's move to Liffey Street 40 years previously. The Catholic population of the northeast, particularly around Mountjoy Square, was accommodated by St. Francis Xavier's, while St. Andrews catered to those Catholics who could afford a fashionable address on Fitzwilliam or Merrion Square (and also to the many Catholic

fig. 1.5 St. Paul's Church, Arran Quay, 1835 (photo: T. de Paor).

fig. 1.6 St. Andrew's Church on Westland Row, 1837 (photo: T. de Paor).

fig. 1.7 St. Audoen's Church, 1841-6, seen from the rear (photo: T. de Paor).

servants employed by the area's wealthy inhabitants). The Catholic Church could not be as bold as its Protestant counterparts in these areas: St. Francis Xavier's insertion into the terrace of Gardiner Street has none of the grandeur of the Hardwicke Place set-piece which fronted Francis Johnson's St. George's; St. Andrew's position on Westland Row (fig. 1.6) is low-key compared with St. Stephen's termination of the Mount Street vista. During his time as archbishop, Murray became quite a respectable member of Dublin society. Though invited to serve on many committees and to attend numerous functions, he was blackballed from the Royal Dublin Society. Similarly, these two churches seem like guests in a society of which they will never fully be part — slightly ill at ease and anxious not to offend the host. In the west of the city there would be less reason for discomfort.

Of the four churches built in the west, three were the work of Patrick Byrne (1783-1864).[52] He also had some involvement in the completion of St. Nicholas, adding the cupola and portico to John Leeson's design. In all these churches common concerns and strategies can be detected. The surroundings were dominated by simple, forceful statements which engaged the topography and which often emerged from existing patterns of use. St. Audoen's church (fig. 1.7) may be seen as an expression of the Catholic pre-eminence in this section of the city. From the river, the massive block dominates the hillside site. While in the 18th century, a number of small churches had permeated the dense fabric, here that accumulated energy was compacted and released in a single concerted burst. Yet the church also operated at a more domestic scale and retained a certain reticence about exposing itself. It sat back from High Street, approached through a small entrance court (rather like the traditional atrium). Its portico compounded this domestication, lending scale to an otherwise unarticulated mass.

St. Nicholas of Myra follows much the same pattern. Seen from the rear, it looms large over Francis Street's surroundings, where the 18th-century chapel would have been practically invisible. On Francis Street itself, however, the church remains hidden until one is almost upon it. Suddenly a space in the street opens, forming a forecourt terminated by the portico and cupola.

Similarly, Adam and Eve's Franciscan Church on Merchants Quay, also by Byrne, had its main entrance away from the main thoroughfare, like its 18th-century predecessor. It was originally approached through a garden which linked Cook Street to the river. Yet the church's bulk and its shallow dome announced its presence at the urban scale.

Of these early churches, only Byrne's first commission, St. Paul's on Arran Quay (fig. 1.5), addresses the street directly. The church is a simple rectangular box lit at clerestory level. In a reversal of the usual pattern it is given urban scale by its portico and cupola. They lend grandeur to the modest nave. The church's siting on the river increases this significance. With the building of Gandon's Customs House and Four Courts, the potential of the Liffey as the site of major public monuments had been realised. After the relative failure of the Pro-Cathedral to engage directly with the Ascendancy city, St. Paul's may be seen as the first classical urban monument of the Emancipation era.

Our Lady of Refuge in Rathmines was Byrne's last major commission, and a vitally important one. The parish, which had been separated from St. Nicholas in 1823, stretched from Harold's Cross to Milltown. Its population continued to grow over the next 25 years and in 1854 the parish priest, Dean William Meagher determined that a new church was required. A forceful and influential man, educated in Rome, Meagher consistently brought his continental experience to bear on Irish matters. He wrote extensively, publishing letters, sermons and of course his encomium of Daniel Murray. Meagher, rather than Byrne, was the presiding spirit of Rathmines. He felt himself uniquely qualified to pronounce on the form and style of the new church:

> 'Accustomed myself from earliest youth, to devote a rather unusual share of attention to the study of ecclesiastical architecture, and having enjoyed lengthened opportunity of maturing my ideas in the subject by familiarity with the great masterpieces of the art scattered over the Catholic countries of the continent; feeling also, that, when prepared by suitable previous reflection, a clergyman is, in general, the person most likely to comprehend aright the requirements of the divine worship in any particular locality and best fitted to devise the properest [sic] means of providing them'.[53]

The Greek Cross plan, the massive scale and the rich decoration of Our Lady of Refuge all bear witness to Meagher's close involvement in the design. Though the present dome dates only from 1922, the original saucer dome must still have had a dramatic impact on the Dublin skyline, forcefully marking the Catholic presence in a suburb whose municipal affairs were Protestant-dominated and visually linking the suburb back across the canal to the city. Four statues presided over the crossing of the nave: S. Filippo Neri, St. Francis Xavier, St. Vincent de Paul and S. Charles Borromeo. Meagher dubbed Murray the 'Borromeo of Dublin' and may have intended the statue as a direct tribute to the archbishop. Borromeo had been archbishop of Milan during the counter-reformation and had built a number of that city's great churches. For Meagher, Murray was presiding over a similar era in Dublin: countering the proselytising of the Established Church and inserting Catholic monuments into the urban and suburban fabric.

In some ways, however, the triumphalist ethos of Rathmines seems slightly alien to Murray. Described as 'the sheet anchor of the moderates', the archbishop was loath to be too outspoken or radical, avoiding involvement in the campaign for Repeal and taking a non-sectarian approach to the education question. As Oliver McDonagh portrays him, 'Murray, although freed from the timorousness of the *ancien regime*, was still a pre-emancipation bishop, and bore to the end the very mark of his generation, deference to British power, but cisalpinism in the face of Roman'.[54] A quiet-spoken man, he could never adapt his voice to the scale of the post-Emancipation churches, having begun his preaching in the tiny Townsend Street chapel. Completed in 1854, Our Lady of Refuge seems to herald the beginning of a more triumphant era in Catholic history. On Murray's death in 1852, Paul Cullen was translated from Armagh to become primate of Dublin. It is his spirit more than Murray's which is captured in the Rathmines church. Over the following 26 years, he would preside over what Emmet Larkin has called a 'devotional revolution'.

EXPANSION 1852-1878

expansion: 1. increase in size or bulk or importance 2. give a fuller description or account 3. become more genial or effusive; discard one's reserve.

Cardinal Archbishop Paul Cullen (1803-1878) was born in County Kildare and educated at Shackleton's Quaker School, Ballstore, at Carlow College and at the Urban College of the Propaganda in Rome. He was ordained in 1829. In 1831 he became rector of the Irish College in Rome, returning to Ireland as Archbishop of Armagh in 1849. He was translated to Dublin in 1852. In 1866 he became the first Irish cardinal, and continued to preside over the Dublin diocese until his death in 1878.

Just as Murray began his term with the celebration of the Jubilee in 1826, so Cullen opened another Jubilee in the Metropolitan in 1852:

> 'We have the 40 ore at Marlboro St. with great pomp and magnificence. The Church is ornamented with damask, a great machine erected and what is better crowds of people are attending. The devotion will be continued through the entire three months of the jubilee'.[55]

The Metropolitan was again the setting for the celebration, but this time it was covered in rich decoration, clothed in the trappings of ritual and devotion. Again, the Jubilee proved a great success, a rallying point for the city's Catholics. Cullen wrote two months later: 'The Jubilee has succeeded beyond all hope. All the churches are crowded with people trying to go to confession. Were the priests ten times as many as they are they could not hear them all'.[56]

In 1850, while still bishop of Armagh, Cullen presided over a general synod in Thurles. It was the first such assembly since 1618. The most immediate concern for the Synod was the question of Catholic education. Following the establishment of the Queen's Universities in 1845, the hierarchy, and Cullen in particular, was anxious to create a Catholic University. The eventual outcome of the Synod's deliberations was the establishment of the Catholic University in 1854 under the guidance of Cardinal Newman.

As part of the University's accommodation a College chapel was built on St. Stephen's Green. The chapel, designed by Newman and John Hungerford Pollen, was an amalgam of various Roman sources. Most notably, its apse was a copy of that in San Clemente in Rome. The basilica, home to the Irish Dominicans, was well-known to the Irish hierarchy. The mosaic of the apse dates from the 12th century when the church was rebuilt, but its style and themes date back to 4th and 5th century models.[57] San Clemente's 12th century rebuilding signalled a fresh resurgence of Christianity in Rome. Its being chosen as a model for the University Church was therefore particularly appropriate. The apse was a 19th century copy of a 12th century adaptation of a 4th century original. Irish Catholicism was connected back to Rome and through Rome to the very origins of Christian architecture.

The Thurles Synod also sanctioned the top-down reform of the church organisation. Central to this policy was an emphasis on the importance of the church building. There was a redoubled effort to stamp out the vestiges of older practices like the stations which still persisted in some areas. Dublin, under Cullen's leadership, led the way in this reform. In 1853, Cullen boasted that:

> 'In this diocese of Dublin all marriages and baptisms are celebrated in the churches. In the city and in the towns all the confessions are heard in the churches. In all the mountainous places where there are no churches nearby, if the distance is not too great, I told the priest to find every means of transporting the people to those distant churches — but if that were not possible to hear the confessions in private houses (except in case of illness), if the church is not more than two miles away'.[58]

The church was seen as the only appropriate setting for the administration of the sacraments. It was also portrayed as exerting a 'holy influence' over its immediate surroundings (at least within a two-mile radius). This marked a definitive shift from 18th century convention, whereby the church, particularly in rural areas, was regarded as only intermittently sacred, often serving other, secular purposes during the week.

> '[Cullen's] emphasis on the church building as the centre of worship, apart from stimulating a building boom, permitted participation in services very lax before the famine, if only because of lack of accommodation, to increase sharply. The emphasis on the physical primacy of the church building concentrated the specialised functions hitherto diffused as status symbols among the private names of the more affluent members of the community, who suffered with ill-concealed chagrin Cullen's insistence on the equality of Catholics before God'.[59]

Joe Lee points up the paradoxical nature of Cullen's ideology. While stressing the authoritarian structure of the Church, and while sanctioning lavishly ostentatious church building, Cullen was also keen to see the democratisation of the Catholic Church. He sought to eradicate the favouritism and corruption which still persisted. Cullen marshalled the Catholic clergy and laity into coherent shape and gave them churches as concrete symbols of this order. He saw the value of spectacle and ostentation; of making the church the most splendid building in any area, the better to focus people's attention on it. To further intensify this focus he oversaw the introduction of a myriad of devotional practices and devotional aids:

'The new devotions were mainly of Roman origin and included the rosary, forty hours, perpetual adoration, novenas, blessed altars, *Via Crucis*, benediction, vespers, devotion to the Sacred Heart and to the Immaculate Conception, jubilees, triduums, pilgrimages, shrines, processions and retreats. These devotional exercises, moreover, were organised in order to communalize and regularize practice under a spiritual director and included sodalities, confraternities such as the various purgatorial societies, the Society of St. Vincent dePaul, and Peter's Pence as well as temperance and altar societies. These public exercises were also reinforced by the use of devotional tools and aids: beads, scapulars, medals, missals, prayer books, catechisms, holy pictures, and *Agnus Dei*, all blessed by priests who had recently acquired that privilege from Rome through the intercession of their bishops. Furthermore, this was the period when the whole world of the senses was explored in these devotional exercises, and especially in the Mass, through music, singing, candles, vestments, and incense'.[60]

This, then, was the 'devotional revolution'. The Jubilee of 1826 was a mere foretaste of the religious world described here. And, crucially, the focus of all this regulation, adoration and devotion was the church building itself. It became the true centre of the community, much like the mediaeval religious houses, offering not only the sacraments but also education, recreation and social functions.

Most of these new practices were of Roman origin. Throughout his career, Cullen 'considered himself merely the Pope's chief whip in Ireland'.[61] He was in constant contact with Propaganda, replacing the Gallican tendencies of some pre-emancipation bishops with a fervent ultramontanism. While despising the violent republicanism of the Fenians, he saw himself as a nationalist and established the National Association in 1864 to promote links between nationalism and Catholicism. However in aligning himself with the constitutional party of nationalism, Cullen was careful not to affect the temporal concerns of the church. In this he followed O'Connell's dictum: 'Our religion from Rome, our politics from Ireland'.

To advance the cause of the Catholic Church and to continue the campaign of religious build-ings, Cullen needed funds. In a cruel twist, the famine proved providential in this regard. Between 1845 and 1851 Ireland lost two million people through death and emigration. The great majority of these were from the poorer sections of the Catholic community. This haemorrhaging of the Catholic population left the church with a smaller but substantially richer laity. The effect was twofold. In 1840 there was one priest for every 3,000 Catholics. By the year 1850 the ratio was 1:2,100 and by 1871 it had reached 1;1,560.[62] This meant that contact between laity and clergy became easier and more regular. Secondly, because the surviving congregations were richer, Catholic resources increased, enabling more ambitious building programmes to be undertaken. By 1880, the bishop of Armagh could write that 'the condition of the people is on the whole improving, and there is hardly a diocese in Ireland in which there are not two or three magnificent Churches in the course of erection, not to speak of the convents and schools which are rapidly spreading in every direction over the land'.[63]

Perhaps the most significant undertaking of this kind in Dublin was the building of St. Augustine and John church and priory on Thomas Street (figs 1.8-1.10). Begun in 1862, the church was substantially completed by 1874 but it took another three years, between 1892 and 1895, to finish the exterior. The cost of the building was £60,000, a huge increase on the £8,500 spent on the nearby St. Nicholas of Myra thirty years previously. The site on Thomas Street was bought for £4,000 by Dr. Dominic Corrigan in 1854. Corrigan was a famous and wealthy physician who lived on Thomas Street, (demonstrating the continuing prosperity of the area). He donated the site to the Augustinians, who had been using a chapel on John's Lane, an enlargement of that mentioned in the 1749 report. The site corresponded almost exactly with that of the 12th century John the Baptist hospital, the first Augustinian presence in the city. The belfry tower stood on the site of the hospital tower, which had survived until 1800. 'For over six hundred years this eighty foot high, square tower, created as a fire-proof building to house sacred vessels, was a conspicuous landmark on the western end of the city'.[64] By placing the 93 foot bell tower on this spot, the architects, Pugin and Ashlin, were forging a cultural link with the 12th century (fig. 1.9); restating the continuity of Catholicism in the city in forceful, dramatic terms. The design also included a priory and school to the rear of the site (fig 1.8), accessed through a courtyard — another echo of the site's monastic beginnings.

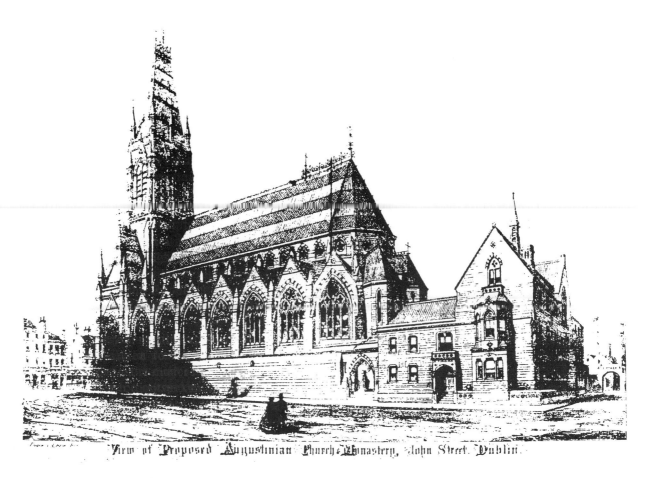

'View of Proposed Augustinian Church & Monastery, John Street, Dublin.'

fig. 1.8 St. Augustine and John's, Thomas Street, proposed church and monastery, Pugin and Ashlin, Architects (Irish Builder, December 15th 1861).

The church also became associated with the nationalist sentiment which had always characterised the area. The rebels of 1798 had held regular meetings on Thomas Street, which was also the scene of Robert Emmett's aborted revolution and his subsequent execution. Many of the builders who worked on the church were Fenians:

> 'It may come as a surprise to learn that [the church] was built, stone by stone, by men whose aspirations and thoughts were focused on revolution. Many of the young men, who worked by day as builders' labourers, met by night at the house of their foreman, Denis Cromien, in Pimlico or in some back room, to drill in the use of arms and learn the ways of revolution'.[65]

At the time the association was well known and St. Augustine and John quickly became known as the Fenian Church. The connection is further strengthened, if only anecdotally, by the fact that Padraig Pearse's father was responsible for the large statues on the spire (fig. 1.10).

A glance from St. Audoen's on High Street to St. Augustine and John's clearly demonstrates the differing priorities of Murray's and Cullen's respective reigns. Beyond the obvious shift from an unadorned classicism to an elaborate French Gothic, the church's siting bears witness to the growing power of Catholicism in Dublin. Where St. Audoen's sits back from the street and respects the scale of its surroundings, St. Augustine and John's comes right to the street line, its yawning entrance dwarfing the domestic fabric. From the river, its copper-roofed nave towers over the area. Its spire is omnipresent in the tangle of surrounding streets, confronting the inhabitants at every turn. The bulk of the church disappears from the south side, but the spire is constantly visible, a beacon for the whole city. The perspectives made by Pugin and Ashlin reinforce the idea of the church as a massive, discrete form in the city. The side streets pull away to reveal misleading views of the eastern elevation. Pugin and Ashlin build right to the street line — there is no attempt to hide the building's size. Neither is there any humility or self-effacement about the external treatment — the church is decked out in all its finery.

St. Augustine and John's typifies the ostentatious confidence which characterised the Cullen era. None of the reticence or politeness of the earlier 19th century is evident. Instead, there was a conviction that grandeur, scale and floridity could help consolidate the Catholic faith. John Ruskin who, as Butler puts it, 'was no mean judge of architecture' pronounced the church a 'poem in stone'. The influence of Ruskin and of Pugin is as evident in Thomas Street as in the concurrent work of Deane and Woodward. The use of the Gothic style further emphasised the connection to the pre-reformation church and to the site's own history.

St. Augustine and John acted as a focus for the whole area, and indeed for the western half of the city. It displayed its wealth openly through rich materials and abundant decoration. Through its style and siting and construction, it established continuity with the past and with the traditions of the parish. It stood as a formidable fortress of the faith.

While the Thomas Street tower rose throughout the 1870s George Street was engaged in the restoration and enlargement of Christ Church Cathedral. The local inhabitants were witnessing a battle between the two churches to dominate the city's mediaeval high ground. The work on Christ Church followed hard on Sir Arthur Guinness's restoration of Dublin's other cathedral — St. Patricks which was completed in 1865. With its disestablishment in 1869, the Church of Ireland lost many of its traditional privileges. The restoration of the two cathedrals can be seen as a last-ditch attempt to assert Protestant supremacy in Dublin. St. Augustine and John's was the definitive Catholic response.

RELIGION AND THE CITY

Troy, Murray and Cullen. It is tempting to see this triumvirate embodied in the architecture of their respective reigns: Troy's Roman reform expressed in the unadorned mass of the pro-Cathedral; Murray's quiet determination perhaps best mirrored by the poised composition of St. Paul's on Arran Quay; Cullen's grandiloquence reflected in the dramatic power of St. Augustine and John's. The Thomas Street church ends this lineage, but also leads back, ritually, to its beginning: to Ailread Palmer's hospital on the edge of the 12th century city. Religion has come full circle, from being the dominant urban archetype, through a period where it became virtually invisible, only to emerge again as the principal type of public building in Dublin. Though there is some dispute as to the nature and extent of 19th century reform in the Irish Catholic Church, it is abundantly clear that, over the course of the century, it redrew the urban and rural geography of the nation.

fig. 1.9 Proposed church of St. Augustine and John's, Thomas Street, Pugin and Ashlin, Architects (Irish Builder, December 15th 1861).

In *The Body in Pain*, Elaine Scarry discusses the ways in which religion makes itself manifest to the faithful. An essentially abstract concept, it requires concrete symbols to make itself meaningful. Scarry outlines the circular logic whereby humanity creates religion, religion creates God, and God creates humanity.[66] Following this pattern, as the Catholic church created public architecture in its name, so this architecture seemed to confirm, if not create, the Catholic community.

One of 19th century Dublin's central themes is about religion making itself manifest, and the consequences which flow from that manifestation. Emmet Larkin hints at one such consequence: that the industrialisation which marked other Victorian cities did not, to any great extent, happen in Dublin:

'The contributions made by the Catholic middle classes in terms of both money and personnel explain to some extent at least,

21

fig. 1.10 The spire of St Augustine and John's, Thomas Street (photo: T. de Paor).

why there was no Industrial Revolution in Dublin and Cork as there was in Belfast — they chose to put their resources into a religious establishment rather than an industrial machine'.[67]

Though the truth of Larkin's theory has been questioned, it does lead to a more fundamental realisation. While Catholicism went from strength to strength in Ireland, throughout most of the western world religion was losing its pre-eminence. As Eric Hobsbawm puts it:

> 'Religion, from being something like the sky, from which no man can escape and which contains all that is above the earth, became something like a bank of clouds, a large but limited and changing feature of the human firmament'.[68]

Secular and materialist ideologies took over as the mainstays of cultural and social change. 'With the American and French Revolution major political and social transformations were secularised'.[69] These twin catalysts set in motion the process which Owen Chadwick has called the 'secularisation of the European mind', Where religion did flourish, it was in 'its most uncompromising, irrationalist and emotionally compulsive forms'.[70] Sects, cults and proselytising groups sprang up around Europe and especially in America. This trend was echoed in Ireland's devotional revolution which 'consisted of the gradual addition of emotional "devotions" to the straightforward moralistic religion... It would seem to be an offshoot of contemporary romanticism, emphasising emotional rather than rational aspects of religion'.[71]

In Ireland however, this 'emotional' religion was no mere marginal cult. It increasingly formed the cornerstone of an Irish identity, and, as the century continued, it played a greater role in the political, social and cultural life of the majority of the population. Karl Marx famously wrote that: 'Religion is the sign of the oppressed creature, the heart of a heartless world, the soul of a soulless environment. It is the opium of the people'.[72] In formulating his alternative ideology, Marx saw the attractions of religion. For Irish Catholics who, though by no means uniformly poor, did include almost all the poorer members of society, it offered a means of coping with the present and hoping for the future.

It has been suggested that after the disaster of the Famine, there was a new mood of fear and uncertainty among the Irish people: a vacuum waiting to be filled. The Catholic Church filled that vacuum, offering a steady, recognisable belief system to counter instability and loss. As

Hobsbawm puts it: 'religion might create social and sometimes educational and political institutions in an environment which provided none, and among politically undeveloped people it gave primitive expression to their discontents and aspirations'.[73] Religion gave a focus to people's lives, and engrained itself into their daily existence. In all this, the architecture of the institution played a vital role. It made the strength of the connection between church and community tangible. Further, and perhaps less consciously, it strengthened the connection between the community and the city. As more people became more resolutely Catholic, Catholic monuments became more prevalent and prominent in Dublin. By the end of the century the city could appear, at least through Catholic eyes to be a representation of a resurgent religion; a stronghold of the Catholic faith.

At a time when Irish nationalism was becoming increasingly anti-urban, this process is worth stressing. Though the urban environment might sometimes be portrayed as an immoral place, hardly conducive to a pious life, the Catholic Church could not afford to reject the city outright. In the struggle to establish Catholicism's pre-eminence, the capital had consistently been in the vanguard. While mass-houses and mass rocks and inadequate cabins still formed the architecture of the 18th-century church in rural areas, in the city more fitting places of worship were already appearing. The first post-emancipation churches were built in the capital. And Dublin was foremost in the subsequent boom in church building. Certainly, Rome recognised Dublin's importance: on Murray's death, Cardinal Cullen, faithful Roman servant, was immediately translated from Armagh to the capital to spearhead the continuing Catholic revival.

Rome's role in the rehabilitation of Irish Catholicism was important. Beyond its influence in Episcopal appointments and church organisation, it seems to have provided the inspiration for the church's architectural strategy. The parallels between what Krautheimer calls the 'Christianisation of Rome' and what might equally be termed the 'Catholicisation of Dublin' are striking. Troy, and later Cullen, returned from Rome with the image of the San Clemente basilica and the history it embodied firmly implanted in their minds. As the Christians moved from the *domus ecclesiae* to the Lateran basilica, so might Irish Catholics emerge from penal chapel to pro-Cathedral.

In an effort to justify the lack of Christian churches in Rome, it had been claimed that 'Christians pass their time upon the earth, but they have their citizenship in heaven'. Such sentiments may have given solace to Irish Catholics in penal times, but by the late 19th century, they could justly claim to have their citizenship in Dublin.

Hugh Campbell
University College Dublin

ACKNOWLEDGEMENTS

The author would like to thank Dr. John Olley for his continued enthusiasm and insights during the research and preparation of this work; as well as colleagues and students at University College Dublin for their contributions; and Helen Blake for her support, encouragement and help with the preparation of the text.

NOTES

1 George Steiner, *In Bluebeard's Castle, or some notes towards a re-definition of culture*, (first pub. 1971), London, 1989, 13.
2 Richard Sennett, *Flesh and Stone*, London, 1994, 80.
3 James Lydon, 'The Medieval City', in Art Cosgrove (ed.), *Dublin Through the Ages*, Dublin, 1988, 42.
4 Colm Lennon, '"The Beauty and Eye of Ireland" — the sixteenth century', in Art Cosgrove op. cit., 49.
5 N. Donnelly, Introduction to *State and Condition of Roman Catholic Chapels in Dublin both Secular and Regular, A.D. 1749*, Dublin, 1904, 4.
6 Ibid., 5.
7 Ibid., 5.
8 Ibid., 6.
9 Ibid., 6.
10 Ibid., 8.
11 Archbishop Bulkeley, *Report on Popish Activity*, Dublin, 1630, M.SS. in Trinity College Dublin.
12 See Conchubhair O'Fearghail, 'The Evolution of Catholic parishes in Dublin City from the sixteenth to the nineteenth centuries', in Kevin Whelan (ed.), *Dublin, City and Country from Prehistory to Present*, Dublin, 1992, 63-71.
13 Quoted in Maureen Wall, 'The Penal Laws, 1691-1760', in Gerard O'Brien (ed.), *Catholic Ireland in the Eighteenth Century — Collected Essays of Maureen Wall*, Dublin, 1989, 9.
14 Ibid., 31. This also allowed the building of more chapels. Looking back to pre-reformation times was already helping to strengthen the Catholic position in Dublin.
15 Thomas Bartlett, 'The Origins and Progress of the Catholic Question in Ireland, 1690-1800', in T. P. Power and Kevin Whelan (eds.), *Endurance and Emergence, Catholics in Ireland in the Eighteenth Century*, Dublin, 1990, 2.
16 Maureen Wall, op. cit., 'The Penal Laws, 1691-1760', 39.
17 N. Donnelly, op. cit.
18 David Dickson, 'Large-scale developers and the growth of the

18th century Irish cities', in P. Butel, and Cullen, L. M. (eds.), *Cities and Merchants: French and Irish Perspectives on Urban Development, 1500-1900*, Proceedings of the fourth Franco-Irish Seminar of Social and Economic Historians (Department of Modern History, University of Dublin), Dublin, 1986, 95.

19 Nuala Burke, 'A hidden Church? The structure of Catholic Dublin in the mid-eighteenth Century', *Archivium Hibernicum*, XXXII, 1974, 81-92.

20 Thomas C. Butler, Johns Lane, *A history of the Augustinian Friars in Dublin, 1280-1980*, Dublin, 1983, 80.

21 N. Donnelly, op. cit., 14.

22 Ibid., 11.

23 Ibid., 13.

24 Ibid., 12.

25 Maureen Wall, op. cit., 'The Penal Laws, 1691-1760', 27.

26 L. M. White, *Building God's House in the Roman World.*

27 Edward McParland, 'Strategy in the planning of Dublin 1750-1800', in L. M. Cullen and P. Butel, op. cit., 104.

28 See David Dickson, op. cit., 89.

29 William Stevens, *Hints to the People, especially to the Inhabitants of Dublin*, Dublin, 1799, 25.

30 Myles Ronan, *An Apostle of Catholic Dublin*, Dublin, 1944, 25.

31 Information on churches and parishes is compiled from a number of sources, principally: Richard Bowden, 'Church building in the Diocese of Dublin 1880-1916', 1916, M.S.S. in Dublin Diocesan Archive; Peter Costello, *Dublin Churches*, Dublin, 1989; Maurice Craig, *Dublin 1660-1860*, (first pub. 1952) London, 1992; Nicholas Donnelly, *A Short History of Dublin Parishes*, I-XII, Dublin, 1911; Niall McCullough, *Dublin, an Urban History*, Dublin, 1989; Myles Ronan, *An Apostle of Catholic Dublin*, Dublin, 1944; M. Ronan, Collected MSS. in Dublin Diocesan Archive.

32 Emmet Larkin, 'Church and State in Ireland in the Nineteenth Century', in *Church History*, XXXI, 1962, 294-306.

33 John D'Alton, *The Memoirs of the Archbishops of Dublin*, Dublin, 1838, 485. Although other evidence, particularly in Sean Connolly, *Priests and People in Pre-Famine Ireland, 1780-1845*, Dublin, 1982, 137-138 suggests that the pious nature of the pattern is a later addition to what began as a pagan celebration.

34 Emmet Larkin, op. cit., 301.

35 Rev. William Meagher, *Notices of the Life and Character of His Grace Most Rev. Daniel Murray*, Dublin, 1853, 95.

36 Alastair Rowan, 'Irish Victorian Churches; denominational distinctions', in Raymond Gillespie and Brian P. Kennedy (eds.), *Ireland: Art into History*, Dublin, 216.

37 W. Meagher, op. cit., 98.

38 Ibid., 13.

39 Ibid., 95.

40 Ibid., 96

41 Ibid., 95.

42 Ibid., 149.

43 Ibid., 96.

44 Myles Ronan, op. cit., 208.

45 Quoted in W. Meagher, op. cit., 105.

46 Ibid., 106-107.

47 Ibid., 102.

48 Quoted in John D'Alton, op. cit., 489.

49 Ibid., 489.

50 Oliver MacDonagh, 'The politicization of the Irish Catholic Bishops, 1800-1850', *Historical Journal*, XVIII, no. 1, 1975, 37-53, particularly 42.

51 Debate raged over whether St. Patrick was the founder of the Church of Ireland or by rights a Catholic. See for instance Matthew Kelly, *Dissertations on Irish Church History*, Dublin, 1864, in which he counters the claims of Henry J. Monck's 1846 treatise, *The Testimony of St. Patrick against the false pretensions of Rome to primitive antiquity in Ireland.*

52 On Patrick Byrne, see C. P. Curran, 'Patrick Byrne: Architect', *Studies*, June 1944, 193-203; Patrick Raftery, 'The last of the Traditionalists, Patrick Byrne 1783-1864', *Irish Georgian Society Bulletin*, 1964, 61-67.

53 Patrick Raftery, op. cit., 63.

54 Oliver MacDonagh, op. cit., 51.

55 Quoted in Emmet Larkin, 'The Devotional Revolution in Ireland, 1850-1875', *American Historical Review*, LXXVII, 1970, 645-646.

56 Quoted in ibid., 646.

57 See Richard Krautheimer, *Rome, Portrait of a City*, Princeton, 1980, 163.

58 Emmet Larkin, op. cit., 647.

59 Joe Lee, *The Modernisation of Irish Society, 1848-1918*, (first pub. 1973), Dublin, 1989, 49.

60 Emmet Larkin, op. cit., 645.

61 Joe Lee, op. cit., 43.

62 Figures from N. Donnelly, op. cit., 35.

63 Quoted by Emmet Larkin, 'Economic Growth, Capital Investment, and the Roman Catholic Church in Nineteenth Century Ireland' *American Historical Review*, LXXII, 1967, 864.

64 Thomas C. Butler, *A history of the Augustinian Friars in Dublin, 1280-1980*, Dublin, 1983, 135.

65 Ibid., 142.

66 Elaine Scarry, *The Body in Pain: the making and unmaking of the world*, New York, 1985, 21.

67 Emmet Larkin, 'Church and State in Ireland in the nineteenth century', *Church History*, XXXI, 1962, 302-3.

68 E. J. Hobsbawm, *The Age of Revolution*, (first pub. 1962) London, 1977, 267.

69 Ibid., 279.

70 Ibid.

71 Desmond Keenan, *The Catholic Church in Nineteenth Century Ireland*, Dublin, 1983, 242.

72 Karl Marx quoted in Owen Chadwick, *The Secularisation of the European Mind in the Nineteenth Century*, (first pub. 1975) Cambridge, 1993, 49.

73 E. J. Hobsbawm, op. cit., 280.

Urban Design Studies, Volume 3, 1997

CITY TEXTURE AND MICROCLIMATE

KOEN STEEMERS, NICK BAKER, DAVID CROWTHER,

JO DUBIEL, MARIA-HELENI NIKOLOPOULOU, CARLO RATTI

The urban microclimate and urban form are interrelated. The importance of this relationship is increasing, with growing proportions of the global population and energy use occurring in cities, and with problems such as airborne pollution and the urban heat island effect receiving increasing attention.

As well as the effect of microclimate on outdoor conditions, its influence on the internal climate is also of interest, especially in passive low energy buildings. The potential for natural ventilation, for example, is influenced not only by morphological properties of the building under discussion, such as plan depth, but also by conditions immediately adjacent to the building in terms of air movement, atmospheric pollution and noise. These conditions are themselves dependent in part on morphological parameters. We know that the urban texture offers varying degrees of isolation from the free-flowing climate. In some cases this isolation may be an advantage, as in the moderation of extreme temperatures, but in other cases a disadvantage, for example in reducing dilution of pollutants by the prevailing wind.

Whilst the modelling of internal environmental conditions in buildings is now well advanced, the modelling of conditions around buildings in an urban context remains a problem. This is partly due to the spatial complexity and partly due to ill defined boundary conditions. The usual approach to modelling is by detailed simulation, for example using the computing techniques of computational fluid dynamics (CFD) or radiosity algorithms, but these models require a detailed dimensional description of the urban tissue and thus make heavy demands on input and computing time. In addition, the dynamic interaction between a building and its urban environment is not easily modelled using current techniques.

Rather than approaching the problem with a precise description of urban topography, we are looking for generalised parameters which, once derived, could be used to predict environmental performance using simplified models. For example, the mean surface area to volume ratio tells us something about the average plan depth of buildings, and hence the potential for natural ventilation. The rate of reduction of built floor area with height above ground level indicates the openness of the city to the sky. This in turn indicates the daylight conditions in the street, on building facades, and hence the potential for the use of daylight in buildings. The same parameter will indicate useful solar gains, and in conjunction with the mean surface reflectance, the potential to capture solar gains in the spaces external to the buildings. Certain city plans have strong directionality which in relation to wind direction and solar orientation, would influence pollutant dispersal, temperature, and the general street microclimate.

This paper explores the nature of the relationship between urban form and environmental characteristics. The aim is to establish links between various urban 'textures' and their impact on the availability of solar radiation (direct and diffuse), the effects on air and airborne pollutant movement and the consequences for energy use. Each of these environmental parameters is modelled using appropriate techniques available to the research team, involving both computer and physical modelling. Part of the purpose of this project is to demonstrate the possible roles of such techniques. The modelling is carried out for a series of simplified generic urban forms, then for three real urban sites in Europe, described below.

We then propose mathematical techniques to produce simple descriptions of complex urban form, derived from an analysis of its solid geometry and its pattern of pores and fissures. We are aiming to develop a series of 'urban form parameters' which can be used to characterise those aspects of the form's morphology which are

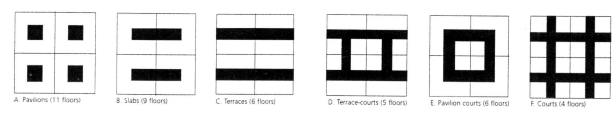

A. Pavilions (11 floors)   B. Slabs (9 floors)   C. Terraces (6 floors)   D. Terrace-courts (5 floors)   E. Pavilion courts (6 floors)   F. Courts (4 floors)

fig. 2.1 Generic urban forms.

fig. 2.2 Plan diagrams showing a 400 x 400m. area at the same scale of the three study sites in London (top), Toulouse (middle) and Berlin (bottom).

likely to affect its environmental and energy performance. This part of the work is described in the section of the paper on these parameters.

Relationships between the microclimate and urban form parameters are then discussed. Our ultimate aim is to develop an urban 'porosity' model that relates form parameters to indices of overall environmental performance. The use of such a simplified model would be to extend the level of precision for the modelling of energy, daylight, natural ventilation currently available at the single building scale, to an intermediate urban scale of blocks, streets, squares and parks.

DEFINING THE SIMPLIFIED FORMS

To initiate the investigation, a number of simplified urban arrays were analysed. The reasons for choosing simplified forms are that modelling techniques and calculations are made easier and can be tested before tackling the complexity of real examples. More importantly, the links between urban form and the resultant environmental characteristics are more easily established. Six generic forms were chosen (fig. 2.1), based on previous work[1] at the predecessor of the Martin Centre, the Centre for Land Use and Built Form Studies, University of Cambridge. They are based on three original forms, the pavilion or tower, the street and the court, and are capable of being replicated to create various urban arrays. For this study, the building height and width has been adjusted so that all forms have the same plot ratio of total floor space to site area. The number of parameters is further reduced by making the ratio of 'passive' to 'non-passive' area the same throughout ('passive' being the area within 6m. of an outside wall — which is thus potentially capable of being daylit and naturally ventilated). In this way, the observed differences in environmental performance are due solely to variations in form or urban texture.

THE THREE URBAN SITES

Three urban sites of dimensions 400m x 400m were chosen for the study, in the central areas of London, Berlin and Toulouse. The sites were chosen for their apparent variation of urban texture. These differences are shown in the three case study sites shown in the street plans in figure 2.2,

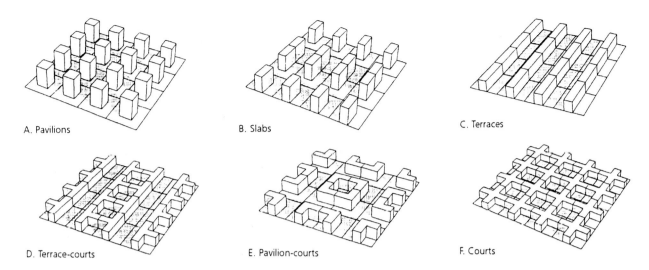

A. Pavilions   B. Slabs   C. Terraces

D. Terrace-courts   E. Pavilion-courts   F. Courts

fig. 2.3 Generic urban forms tested with Shadowpack.

which are drawn to the same scale. The London site is orthogonal in plan but quite random in the third dimension. Toulouse is random in plan but less so in terms of building heights. Berlin has a large grid pattern with a limited variation of building heights (through planning legislation).

ENVIRONMENTAL CHARACTERISTICS

The following environmental characteristics were modelled, and are discussed here:
— Availability of solar radiation: computer simulation using SHADOWPACK software.
— Wind conditions at ground level: wind tunnel analysis with polystyrene beads.
— Clearance of airborne pollutants by wind: wind tunnel analysis with smoke.
— Effect of geometry on absorption of solar radiation: laboratory photometric studies and computer simulation using RADIANCE software.
— Energy consumption: analysis using the LT method.

SOLAR RADIATION ANALYSIS

Solar radiation analysis was performed for all of the generic forms (fig. 2.3) and for the London site. The SHADOWPACK computer software was employed to calculate the total annual solar radiation incident on ground and building surfaces, taking account of both obstructions and first reflections. Real climate data, the Test Reference Year for Kew, was used, combining both direct and diffuse radiation. The surface reflectances were assumed to be 40% for the walls and 20% for the ground. A summary of the results for the generic studies is shown in Table 2.1, from which a number of interesting points arise. The array

with the highest total incident radiation on building surfaces and ground is the pavilion. This form has the largest free ground area and relatively unshaded vertical surfaces. The array receiving most on its building surfaces is the court, 21% more than the slab (on a N-S axis), which receives least. Of this, more than half falls on the roof. Conversely, it receives the least on vertical surfaces, 32% less than pavilion arrays. The form most strongly affected by orientation in the slab. Of relevance to the microclimate of urban spaces, pavilions allow the most solar radiation to reach the ground, 24% more than courts. However, this is largely because of their smaller footprint (384 as opposed to 1056 m^2). In terms of solar radiation per square metre of open ground, courts actually receive more solar radiation, that is, less of its open ground area is in shadow.

Form	All building surfaces		Vertical surfaces		Ground only		Total	
Pavilion	6.79	91%	5.35	100%	6.88	100%	13.67	100%
Slab (W-E)	6.17	83%	4.56	85%	6.55	95%	12.72	93%
Slab (N-S)	5.89	79%	4.28	80%	6.17	90%	12.06	88%
Court	7.48	100%	3.65	68%	5.22	76%	12.70	93%
Surface reflectances - walls: 40%; - ground: 20%								

Table 2.1 Comparison of annual incident solar radiation (direct and diffuse) for three of the generic forms (TJ).

These results suggest that the court form is particularly suitable when considering solar collection on the roof, for example with photovoltaics. The fact that it receives the least radiation on vertical surfaces further suggests its suitability for hot climates, as a way of minimising solar gain through facades. This strategy is exemplified by vernacular architecture in hot desert regions, where the courtyard is a recurring feature. The results also demonstrate the value of putting photovoltaics on the facades of free-standing pavilions. With respect to public urban space, both pavilions and courts perform well in different ways for solar radiation received at ground level. According to context, either form could be relevant for climates where sunshine is important for promoting outdoor activity. In overall terms, the N-S aligned slab receives least solar radiation, although all the arrays receive substantially more radiation than a flat horizontal plane of the same site area (with reference to Table 2.2, such a plane would receive 9.02TJ in total).

Quadrant & plot ratio	All building surfaces		Vertical surfaces		Ground only		Total	
NW 1.95	1.87	100%	1.08	100%	1.02	100%	2.88	100%
SW 2.03	1.64	88%	0.88	81%	1.02	100%	2.66	92%
NE 2.25	1.57	84%	0.92	85%	0.31	30%	1.88	65%
SE 2.26	1.56	84%	0.76	70%	0.88	86%	2.44	85%
ave 2.15	1.64	88%	0.88	81%	0.8	78%	2.43	84%

Surface reflectances - walls: 40%; - ground: 20%

Table 2.2 Incident annual solar radiation (direct and diffuse) for London (GJ/m^2).

FORM	Wind direction	Area of beads (sqm)	Ground coverage
A. Pavilions	0°/90°	1152	14%
	45°	812	10%
B. Courts	0°/90°	2516	44%
	45°	3184	55%
C. Slabs	0°	1796	22%
	45°	1212	15%
	90°	960	12%
D. Court-terrace	0°	3072	46%
	45°	2252	34%
	90°	1424	21%
E. Terraces	0°	2564	36%
	45°	960	13%
	90°	416	6%
F. Pavilion-courts	0°/90°	1192	17%
	45°	1304	18%

Table 2.3 Wind tunnel results for the generic urban forms.

Solar radiation for the London site

The incident solar radiation for the urban blocks in the London site was consistent with the patterns established by the generic studies. For ease of input and manipulation, the area was split into four quadrants, and the results are summarised in Table 2.2. The two eastern quadrants (NE and SE) of the site have a plot ratio of about 2.25, compared to about 2.0 for the western quadrants. This is inversely related to the energy incident on the buildings per square meter of floor area. Thus for an average plot ratio of 2.25 the average energy is 1.56 GJ/m^2, and for a plot ratio of 2.0 it is 1.76 GJ/m^2. As the density reduces, the solar access has the potential to increase — a reassuring general result for a complex situation.

The low vertical solar exposure of the southeast quadrant is particularly noteworthy. This is likely to be due to the fact that this quadrant happens to have a disproportionate number of long thin blocks aligned N-S. As the generic studies show, urban forms of this shape tend to receive least incident solar radiation (such as the slabs aligned N-S in Table 2.1).

WIND ANALYSIS

Wind conditions in the generic urban spaces were studied using 1:250 scale models in a wind tunnel, at three orientations (0° parallel, 45° and 90° at right angles to the main street axis). The aim was to gain insights into wind conditions at ground level, linked with issues of human comfort and airborne pollution dispersal, which in turn are linked with natural ventilation and health.

Wind analysis using expanded polystyrene beads

Expanded polystyrene beads were used for the results presented here. Being small (about 500mm. high at 1:250) and light-weight, they are very sensitive to air movement and can provide clear indication of the scouring effect of wind. On the other hand, they form clumps and get trapped in confined spaces in dissimilar ways to airborne pollutants in reality. Nonetheless, we can obtain patterns that indicate reasonably well those areas at street level subject to high air movement (where beads are absent) and those subject to low air movement (where beads remain). For outdoor comfort, which of these conditions is preferable will depend on climate and season. For pollutant dispersal, high air movement is always likely to be preferable.

The most noticeable findings (summarised in Table 2.3) are that in general, continuous open streets aligned with the wind (0°) are cleared most quickly. However, cross currents and turbulence can reinforce or disrupt this pattern. For

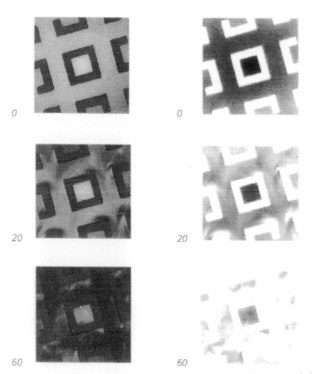

0

0

20

20

60

60

fig. 2.4 Original and processed images of smoke in model of the pavilion-court form at 0, 20 and 60 seconds. In the original images (left) smoke is white and in the processed image (right) the darker areas indicate the presence of smoke.

pavilions, the turbulence created at 45° clears the array more effectively than 0/90°, despite the less direct air paths. For slabs, the turbulence reinforces clearance at 90°, but tends to disrupt it at 0°. The most efficient form for clearing beads overall is the pavilion, with continuous streets in both axes, supplemented by turbulence at 45°. Conversely, enclosed areas are much less disturbed. Thus courts have by far the largest area remaining covered. For both this form and terraces at 90°, the resultant pattern is independent of wind duration. Note that more pollutants, as from vehicles, are likely to be generated in streets than in courts; thus the clearance of courts is less significant.

SMOKE ANALYSIS

The porosity of the urban texture will affect the dispersal by wind of airborne pollutants generated or trapped in the city. This process will have a directional variation, depending on how the wind relates to the axes of streets and other open areas, as well as variation with the openness of the urban texture. This may be investigated using Computational Fluid Dynamics, but to avoid this very computationally intensive method, an innovative experimental technique was developed. This was based on wind tunnel modelling of smoke dispersal, followed by analysis of video images of the tests. It should be noted that this models only the wind-driven effects of air movement, which are dominant over thermal effects except in conditions of very low wind speed.

EXPERIMENTAL PROCEDURE

All three urban sites and the generic forms were included in these tests, using the same scale models at 1:500 and 1:250 as in the bead tests. A fixed quantity of smoke was introduced into each model at street level, and filmed and lit from above so that the smoke appeared white against the black model. At the start time of the test, the wind tunnel fan was started. The smoke was filmed as it gradually dispersed, taking one to three minutes. An image was also taken of the model with no smoke present. The air velocity used in the tests was low, at around 0.2 ms -1. The vertical velocity profile was adjusted to a typical urban profile by the use of slats in the incoming air, and by adjusting the roughness of the ground on the upwind side of the model.

ANALYSIS

The video images were 'frame-grabbed' to produce a series of frames at regular intervals (3 to 5 seconds) for each test, with each frame being a grey-scale digital image with pixel values in the range 0 to 255. Some examples are shown on the left of fig. 2.4, with the corresponding images on the right having been processed to show the location of smoke as dark pixels. The software used to produce and process these images was the public domain program NIH Image.[2] By using the smoke-free background image as a reference and the varying pixel values to indicate smoke density at any point, each image was image-processed to produce a value representing (but not necessarily linearly related to) the quantity of smoke present. After scaling to 100% at the start of each test, these values were plotted as time series showing smoke decay (figs. 2.5-2.7). Each test is further characterised by the reciprocal of the fraction of smoke left after a set time, which represents the clearing efficiency of the form, with higher numbers indicating a more porous form which clears more quickly.

CLEARING EFFICIENCY OF GENERIC FORMS

The above procedure was carried out with models of the generic forms. Forms which were not

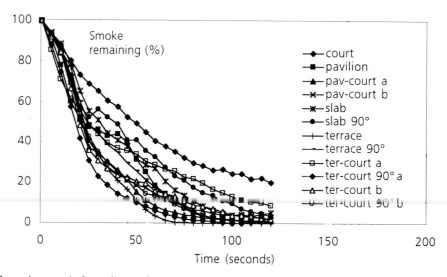

fig. 2.5 Smoke decay in generic form dispersal tests.

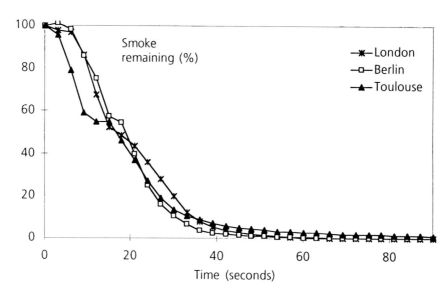

fig. 2.6 Smoke decay in dispersal tests for London, Toulouse and Berlin sites.

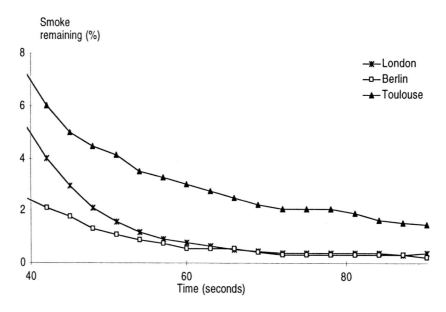

fig. 2.7 Detail of fig. 2.6 showing smoke decay from 40 seconds onwards in dispersal tests for London, Toulouse and Berlin sites.

fig 2.8 Unprocessed images of London, Toulouse and Berlin models, showing the areas trapping smoke as white. Wind is from the prevailing direction, at the top of each image.

Clearing efficiency rank (1 = best)	Form (b=courtyards blocked from smoke, a=courtyards open to smoke)	Smoke left after 60s (%)
1	Terrace	3.5
2	Terrace-court at 90°, a	6
3	Pavilion-court, a	8.2
4	Terrace-court at 90°, b	13.7
5	Pavilion-court, b	14.5
6	Terrace-court, b	15.6
7	Terrace at 90°	17.3
8	Pavilion	18.4
9	Slab	27.3
10	Terrace-court, a	28.8
11	Slab at 90°	32.8
12	Court	40.8

Table 2.4 Ranking of generic forms in order of clearing efficiency

symmetrical were also tested after rotation through 90°, and forms which included courtyards were tested with and without the courtyards being filled with smoke at the start. Rather than using a wind direction parallel or orthogonal to the edges in the highly orthogonal forms, it was thought to be more representative to use a wind direction at 15° to these edges. Figure 2.4 shows the typical smoke location in each form after 35 seconds. Figure 2.5 shows the resulting smoke decay curves for these tests, and Table 2.4 shows the ranking of the forms in order of clearing efficiency, using the percentage of smoke left after 60 seconds. As might be expected, the terraces aligned with the wind are quickest to clear, and the court form the slowest. The terrace-court and pavilion-court forms are also quick to clear, and the slab forms are slow.

CLEARING EFFICIENCY OF THREE URBAN SITES

A similar procedure was carried out with the models of the three urban sites, using the pre-vailing wind direction for each location. In this case, the models were filled with smoke from above. This produced a less even smoke density and led to some extraneous smoke drifting across the images, so the results are not so clear-cut as for the generic models. However, it is still useful to compare the results from the three cities (figs. 2.8 and 2.9). While Toulouse was the quickest to clear initially, the most interesting part of the graph is after the initial extraneous smoke has disappeared at around 40 seconds. After this point, Toulouse has the most smoke left, followed by London, then Berlin. Figure 2.8 shows the three cities after similar lengths of time, showing those areas which trap smoke.

EFFECT OF VARYING WIND DIRECTION

The porosity of the urban layout, as measured by these tests, might be expected to vary with direction, depending on the alignment of streets and other open areas. This was investigated with the London model, which had a strong directional quality. A series of 24 smoke clearance tests following the procedure described earlier was carried out with the model rotated by 15° in the wind tunnel each time. The clearing efficiency was calculated in this instance as 100/(percentage of smoke left after 30 seconds). The resulting values for each compass direction were plotted on a polar diagram (fig. 2.9). It can be seen that some directions were considerably more efficient at clearing (shown as larger values) than others. It should be remembered here that 0° North in the London site is not aligned with the street grid, but is approximately 34° clockwise of the vertical in the site chosen. Thus the peak in clearing efficiency at 330° NW occurs when the longest streets are aligned with the wind, with their openings on the upwind side of the model where wind can enter at ground level. The other peaks in clearing efficiency at 180° S and 270° W, both

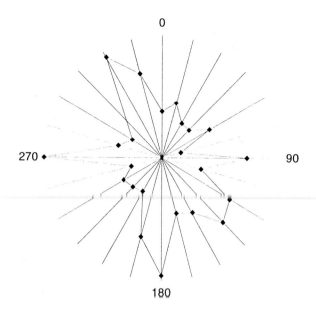

fig. 2.9 Clearing efficiency of London model for different wind directions.

about 34° off the two prevailing urban directions. The extra turbulence generated in the streets by this slight angle, particularly if the streets are not open-ended in the model, could account for the increased clearing efficiency. The directions of poor clearing efficiency are the South-West, which is a prevailing wind direction in London, and the north-east.

DISCUSSION AND CONCLUSIONS
TO SMOKE ANALYSIS

Two of the most crucial parameters for accurate wind tunnel modelling are the wind velocity vertical profile and the wind velocity relative to the scale of modelling. The vertical profile was adjusted to a typical urban profile, as already described. Flow patterns around sharp-edged obstacles, as used here, are relatively insensitive to wind velocity, so the low wind velocities used in these studies should not be of concern. However, in spite of these two most important criteria being satisfied, a number of questions remain regarding whether the movement of smoke in the wind tunnel is representative of the movement of pollution in real streets. It is difficult to model turbulence and gustiness in a wind tunnel. Turbulence in particular could affect the vertical movement of pollution out of street canyons. Local surface roughness also could be important, and is not considered here. At low wind velocities thermal effects could become important. Using a finite sample area for the model results in edge effects which affect both flow patterns and

smoke escape. Problems may also occur in the areas of particularly dense and deep layers of smoke. The visibility of smoke in the areas of interest — at street level — is partly obscured by the opacity of smoke higher up. The measured clearing efficiencies would reflect more what is happening above street level, particularly at the initial stages of the tests when smoke is most dense. Such problems have been minimised by controlling the total amount of smoke in the model. Also, the key findings have been related to results taken at the latter stages of smoke depletion (e.g. after 40 seconds). Although there are additional inaccuracies related to uneven smoke distribution and wind velocity, nevertheless, the flow patterns are grossly correct. The particular value of the technique is in assessing the clearing efficiencies and permeabilities of different urban configurations relative to each other.

In summary, the technique shows promise as a way of assessing the relative permeability of urban textures as a measure of the ease of pollutant dispersal by wind, and of high-lighting particular problem areas where pollution might be trapped. However, there are a number of issues where more confidence would be desirable, so the technique would benefit from more development and preferably validation, and should be regarded as experimental until this is done.

REFLECTANCE ANALYSIS

One of the ways in which urban texture influences indoor and outdoor climate is as a result of the fact that different city layouts absorb different proportions of solar energy. This can occur simply because of differences in inter-reflection in cavities such as street canyons and courtyards. The effect may be expressed as a decrease in the hemispherical reflectance of the urban texture when compared with a flat plane of the same material and same surface reflectance (hereafter referred to as the 'paint' reflectance). This

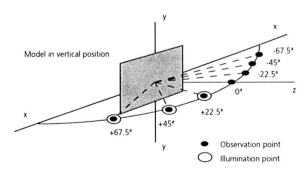

fig. 2.10 Model set-up for reflectance experimental measurements.

decrease is an effect of the extra geometrical complexity as well as the 'paint' reflectance for the radiation band concerned. Thus the effect can be applied at any wavelength. However, our investigations are chiefly concerned with visible wavelengths, containing around 50% of the energy of the solar radiation reaching the Earth's surface. This fractional decrease in reflectance represents the radiant energy that is absorbed and converted to heat, rather than being reflected back out to the sky. There may be occasions when this extra heat may be beneficial in saving energy, for example in colder climates and seasons. However, over large parts of Europe it will be a hindrance because of the need for additional cooling and because of the contribution to the urban heat island effect. In order to maximise energy saving and minimise pollution, it is important to quantify the potential for this type of energy capture.

The decrease in reflectance may be expected to vary with solar altitude, with orientation in relation to sun position, and with the 'paint' reflectances of the city components. It will also depend on characteristics of the urban geometry, which we have termed the 'urban texture'. For example, a city with a complex structure of cavities would be expected to trap more radiation than an open city with large blocks of deep-plan buildings. To study these effects, the generic forms and three urban sites were investigated using laboratory measurements of photometric reflectance, in parallel with computer simulations which allow the estimation of total extra energy trapped.

LABORATORY MEASUREMENTS OF REFLECTANCE

The main aim of the experiment was the determination of the hemispherical reflectance of each model as a function of the 'paint' reflectance and the urban geometry. However, the determination of the hemispherical reflectance requires the measurement and subsequent integration of light reflected from the model in all directions (over the whole hemisphere). This was approximated by light measurements taken in one plane only, as explained below (the resultant reflectance is referred to as the planar reflectance).

Three models were used, identical in plan area, 800 x 800mm., and scale, 1:500, each representing real-life ground areas of 400 x 400m. A heliodon was used to mount each model in a vertical position, so that it could be illuminated, in a darkened room, by a horizontal light beam from a slide projector, representing the sun. This light beam, centred precisely on the centre point of the model, was kept fixed and different angles of illumination (sun elevation angles) were achieved by rotating the model about the vertical axis, keeping the model baseboard in a vertical position. The light reflected back from the model was measured at a series of angles in the same horizontal plane as the light beam, using a specially constructed luminance meter. Three angles of illumination were used, corresponding to three realistic sun positions during the day (+22.5°, +45°, 67.5° from the normal) and seven angles of observation (-67.5°, -45°, -22.5°, 0°, +22.5°, +45°, +67.5° from the normal), although in practice six luminance readings were taken for each sun position due to the meter obstructing the light beam (fig. 2.10), the seventh one being extrapolated. Readings were taken for each of the three city models, and polystyrene flat reference plane, with which the city results were compared. Each of the models and the flat plane were painted at different reflectance values ranging from 89% to 14%. Some additional measurements were used to test simplifying assumptions made, namely that the texture of each form is roughly similar when rotated through 90°, and that the variation in reflected light out of the x-z plane is roughly consistent with that in the x-z plane.

The results represent the total energy reflected for each sun angle, or the average planar reflectance, for a particular urban model with a particular paint reflectance. Cosine corrections have been applied to these figures both for the observation point (to produce energy weighted results rather than luminance weighted), and the illuminating source (to refer the results to the same unit of energy in order to make them comparable). The average planar reflectance for different paint reflectances for each form are then compared with the corresponding value for the flat plane and the percentage reduction between the two are plotted (fig. 2.11).

The overall findings can be summarised as follows. In broad terms the study has shown that, for all 'paint' reflectances, urban forms absorb more sunlight energy than flat planes. This is important in understanding such issues as the urban heat island effect. Furthermore, it is apparent that the complexity, or occlusivity, of the urban texture affects the amount of light that is absorbed. Thus the reduction of light reflected from the modelled surfaces (compared with plane surfaces) is much greater for Toulouse than for London, which in turn is greater than for Berlin (fig. 2.12). In general, the results show, as one might expect, that the extra amount of light

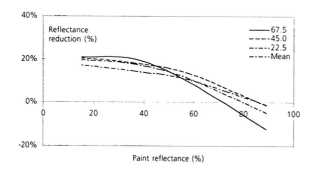

fig. 2.11 Planar reflectance for London compared to flat surface (%) — laboratory.

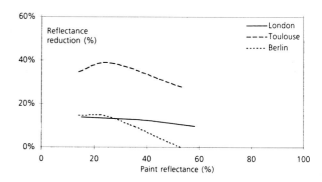

fig. 2.12 Mean planar reflectance reduction for the three cities compared to a flat plane.

absorbed by an urban form tends to increase as 'paint' reflectance decreases (fig. 2.11). A clear pattern is for more light energy to be absorbed at large incidence angles of illumination (i.e. for low angles of solar elevation) than when the angle of illumination is closer to the normal. This difference is small, becoming more pronounced at low paint reflectances. This is also the case with the flat reference planes — although at a smaller magnitude — and is due to the fact that the planes are made of polystyrene, which is not an optically flat material; it has a random texture, thus presenting a three-dimensional structure to incident light, although of different scale to the urban models. In the case of Toulouse, the curve is anomalous in terms of shape (fig. 2.12), but this may be explained by the existence of trees and how they were represented. A painted fleecy material of 30% reflectance was used throughout, and this is likely to have had the effect of decreasing the amount of light reflected at high paint reflectances, while increasing the amount reflected at high paint reflectances.

To investigate whether there are correlations between directionality and energy absorbed by the urban form, the models were rotated 90°. For Berlin and London the orientation does not have a significant effect on the results (a 7% and 8% difference respectively). For Toulouse, there is a more striking effect, the results varying by 17%, but this may be due to the single wide boulevard of trees having a large influence.

POINT MEASUREMENTS

In order to get an idea of the variation of luminance across the urban texture, a luminance meter with an angle of acceptance of 1° was used to take multiple point measurements, rather than a single integrated reading as above. In this way we identify the richness of the texture in terms of its cavities, that is to say the courtyards and narrow streets, which provide opportunities for inter-

reflection, as distinct from the roofs of buildings, which tend to reflect more of the incident light. The experimental set-up was similar to the previous experiment. However, in order to measure the effects solely due to inter-reflection and not due to existence of shadows, the observation point was directly behind the illuminating source. The experiments were carried out for the three cities and for each of the three sun angles. Readings were taken along a straight line from one side of the model to the other at 20mm. intervals measured on the model. At the higher angles of observation, this dimension was foreshortened, so that there was considerable overlap, with the model area within the 1° acceptance angle of the meter being larger than the 20mm. (representing 10m.) between measurements.

The main finding is to confirm the existence and magnitude of variations in observed luminance levels within an urban texture. These variations were least for Berlin, which the previous study found to absorb least energy, and they were highest for Toulouse and London (fig. 2.13).

COMPUTER SIMULATIONS

RADIANCE is one of the most sophisticated lighting simulation packages available, and is capable of accurately calculating direct, diffuse and inter-reflected light using its innovative algorithm based on backward ray-tracing.[3] The program was written by Greg Ward at the Lawrence Berkeley Laboratory, US, and has been comprehensively validated.[4] Although here we are primarily interested in the accurate numerical output of RADIANCE, it is also well known for its photo-realistic images. Figure 2.14 shows the three modelled areas in direct sunlight.

SIMULATIONS

Simulations were carried out with each of the three study areas. Here we are concerned mostly

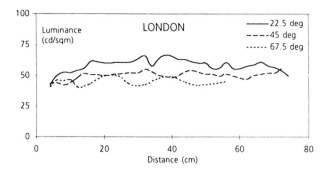

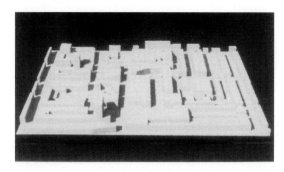

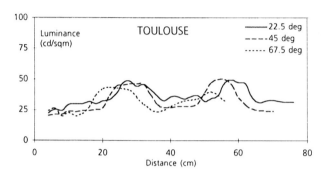

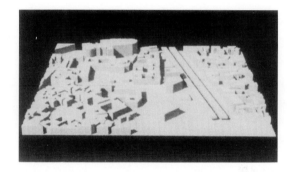

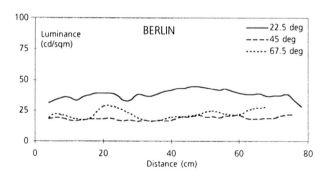

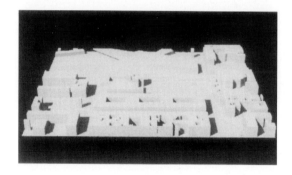

fig. 2.13 Variation of luminance across the model (laboratory measurements) for urban sites at 14% paint reflectance: London (top), Toulouse (centre) and Berlin (bottom).

fig. 2.14 Radiance images, from southerly directions, of London (top), Toulouse (middle), and Berlin (bottom).

with the effect of street canyons and courtyards, so an appropriate level of geometrical detail was used. All surfaces were defined as Lambertian diffuse reflectors, and each model was simulated as having a uniform grey colour with specified uniform 'paint' reflectance. This allowed the effects on reflectance of the geometry and urban texture to be isolated. Modelling was done under conditions of direct light, simulating the sun at different positions but without a diffuse sky component. The illumination of the model depended only on solar position, and not on the varying effect of the atmosphere for different solar altitudes. Seven inter-reflections were calculated, which is relatively high to yield accurate results.

MEASURING MODEL LUMINANCE WITH RADIANCE

To emulate the laboratory measurements, a similar series of measurements was made using computer simulations. The simulations were of the London site and flat reference planes, and used the same illumination and measurement positions as the laboratory studies. Each set of seven co-planar measurements was then integrated using the same procedure as in the laboratory experiments, to produce an estimate of the reduction in luminous energy reflected by the model in the single measurement plane (the 'planar reflectance', when compared with a uniform flat plane of the same 'paint' reflectance (fig. 2.15). The

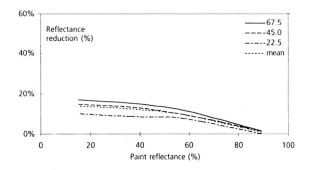

fig. 2.15 Reduction in planar reflectance for London compared with flat plane — computer simulation.

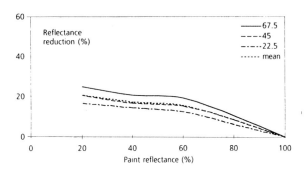

fig. 2.16 Reduction in hemispherical reflectance for London compared with flat plane — computer simulation.

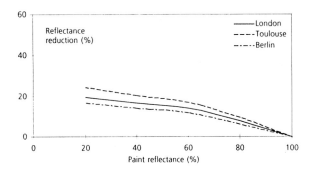

fig. 2.17 Reduction in hemispherical reflectance for London, Toulouse and Berlin compared with flat plane — computer simulation.

entire procedure was carried out for 'paint' reflectances of 15%, 36%, 58% and 89%, to match those used in the laboratory.

It can be seen that, as with the laboratory measurements, the luminous energy reflected into the measurement plane decreases with decreasing 'paint' reflectance and with decreasing angle of incidence (measured from the normal) of illumination.

MEASURING HEMISPHERICAL REFLECTANCE

Although measurement positions in one plane can give information about the relative abilities to absorb radiation of varying urban textures with varying illumination and 'paint' reflectance, to quantify the total extra luminous energy absorbed in each case we need to measure the total hemispherical reflectance under the chosen condition of illumination. This would be equivalent to using measurement positions over a whole hemisphere, then integrating the results. An alternative experimental procedure could use an integrating hemisphere. Here we use the RADIANCE software to produce equivalent results.

Using the same method of comparing urban textures to flat planes of the same 'paint' reflectance and material, total hemispherical reflectance for direct illumination was calculated for each of the three urban sites for 'paint' reflectances of 20%, 40%, 60% and 80%, with illumination incidence angles of 22.5°, 45° and 67.5°. The results presented in figure 2.16 for London are representative of results for the other locations. The comparison of the three sites is shown in figure 2.17, showing mean results for the three solar incidence angles.

It can be seen that, again, the extra captured energy increases with increasing incidence angle of illumination, and with decreasing 'paint' reflectance. The effect of the urban geometry can clearly be seen in figure 2.17. The complex mediaeval texture of Toulouse captured most extra luminous energy, with decreased reflectance of up to 24% compared with the flat plane value, at the realistic building surface reflectance of 20%. Next in magnitude is London, with figures of up to 20% decrease. Berlin was the most reflective, with up to 17% decrease.

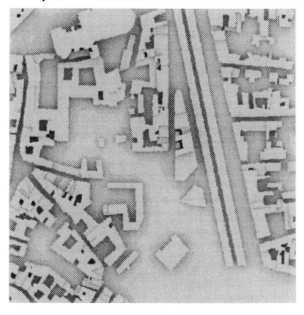

fig. 2.18 Radiance view from above Toulouse under diffuse sky conditions.

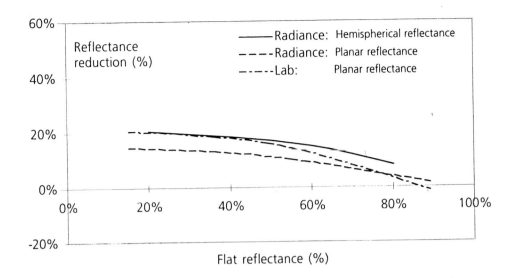

fig. 2.19 Comparison of Laboratory results with computer simulation for London — illumination incidence angle 45°.

SPOT MEASUREMENTS IN RADIANCE

Figure 2.18 shows a plan view of the Toulouse site, at 20% 'paint' reflectance with diffuse sky-light. In analogy to the spot luminance measurements carried out in the laboratory, RADIANCE can be used to measure the luminance at any visible spot. This showed that typically, the luminance of the ground within courtyards was only between 10% and 30% of the luminance of exposed streets and roofs. This is a larger differential than that found with direct light in the laboratory studies, because in addition to inter-reflection, there is an effect due to decreased sky view.

COMPARISON BETWEEN LABORATORY MEASUREMENTS AND COMPUTER SIMULATIONS

Three techniques for estimating reflectance have been described: laboratory measurements confined to one plane, RADIANCE simulations measuring in the same plane, and RADIANCE simulations to estimate hemispherical reflectance. All techniques agree in the ranking of the three urban sites, and in showing that luminous energy absorption increases with increasing incidence angle (i.e. decreasing angle of elevation) and with decreasing 'paint' reflectance. Thus we may be confident that any of the techniques may be used for this type of comparative study.

In quantifying the total luminous energy absorbed by an urban texture, RADIANCE simulations would be expected to produce the most accurate results, as they are able to consider the whole hemisphere. However, in the absence of data for the bi-directional reflectance distribution functions of typical urban surface materials,

the unrealistic Lambertian ideal diffuse surface materials used in the computer simulation will have led to inaccuracies, and the laboratory results which used more typically rough materials are valuable. It is also helpful to assess the useful-ness of the laboratory procedure, which can be carried out with relatively simple equipment. The principal inaccuracy of measuring reflected light in only one plane can be examined by considering figure 2.19. This compares the results of the three procedures for an illumination incidence angle of 45° for the London model. The results for the other incidence angles were similar. Both the sets of results measured in the E-W plane were integrated using the procedure explained above. By considering the two sets of RADIANCE results only, it can be seen that measuring only in the single plane considerably under-estimates the extra light absorbed. This can be explained by the preferential reflection of light into the plane of measurement, which may be expected for such a geometry with many planes orthogonal to the measurement plane, and a Lambertian diffuse surface. The laboratory procedure produced results with a magnitude between that of the simulation results for measurements in the plane and the simulation results for hemispherical reflectance, except at high reflectances. This can be understood when it is remembered that the surfaces used were real materials with an uneven micro-texture, which would not reflect into the measurement plane quite so much as the perfect Lambertian surfaces used in the computer simulation.

The final conclusion is that the use of a single plane for measurement under-estimates the light absorbed, as does the use of perfect Lambertian diffuse surfaces rather than realistic building surfaces. These points must both be borne in mind when making measurements of urban texture reflectance effects. These results lead us to believe that for real surfaces, at realistic reflectance values of 20%, we might expect the increase in luminous energy absorbed by the real urban texture compared with a flat plane to be significantly greater than 25%.

CONCLUSION TO REFLECTANCE STUDIES

It has been shown here that all urban textures have an increased ability to absorb solar radiation through inter-reflection, simply because of the effect of the urban geometry, and that it can be measured and predicted. All measurement methods confirm that the extra radiation absorbed increases with increasing incidence angle for direct illumination, that is, with lower sun altitude, and with decreasing 'paint' reflectance. All measurement methods show this energy-trapping ability of the urban texture is greatest for the Toulouse site, which has reflectance decreases compared with a flat plane of up to 25% for realistic building reflectances of 20%, taking the mean of the three representative solar positions. The next in magnitude is London, with the corresponding reflectance decreases being up to 20%, then Berlin with a figure of 17%. These figures are all for hemispherical reflectance for the Lambertian diffuse surfaces modelled in RADIANCE. The comparison between laboratory and computer simulations has shown that these are likely to be underestimates: figures may be higher for more realistic building surfaces which will not have such a regular reflectance distribution function. Thus the maximum value measured in the laboratory, of a 40% reflectance decrease for Toulouse, could be realistic.

To consider if this discovery is significant to urban microclimate in general, two questions arise. Firstly, which one or more urban parameters is responsible for the variation of increased absorptivity, and secondly, is the increase in absorptivity significant in terms of the heating effect of absorbed radiation, one cause of the urban heat island effect? The first question is dealt with later in the paper, where an attempt is made to correlate the urban form parameters with environmental effects. The second question is discussed below.

It is worth noting that the measured reduction in reflectance is in the visible region of the electromagnetic spectrum. Due to the predominance of non-metallic surfaces in the urban surface, we would expect that the absorptivity in the infrared region would already be close to 100% irrespective of the urban texture.

In our laboratory measurements, the maximum decrease in reflectance was found to be 40%, for Toulouse. Assuming an initial 'paint' reflectance of 20%, this would reduce the reflectance to 12% (i.e. 0.6 x 20%), an 8% absolute change. Sailor[5] has shown that an increase of optical reflectance of 8% over the whole of Los Angeles would lead to a reduction of 1.5° C in peak summer temperatures. From this we could infer that in our case the urban texture is accounting for an increment of similar magnitude. This confirms the link of this urban characteristic to the urban heat island effect.

For the other sites, the increase in absorption is less, only about 10% in the case of Berlin, and thus we would expect the temperature increment to be proportionately less. However, the reflectance measurement is averaged over the whole urban surface. As can be seen from the luminance scans of the three cities (fig. 2.13), the luminance is not uniform, indicating that the 'extra' absorption of energy is taking place in the cavities, that is, on the ground and facades of the streets and squares, and not on the roofs. This non-uniform reflectance decrease implies that the thermal impact in these spaces will be greater than the average effect. As we have shown, the decrease in urban reflectance is more marked in Toulouse with its narrow streets, than in Berlin with the wider open spaces. This may at first seem counter to the traditional view that the narrow streets of the southern European cities demonstrate an appropriate climatic response. But we must remember that, except when the street is running in a direction coinciding with the current solar azimuth, a greater height to width ratio of the street will result in very little direct radiation reaching ground level. Most will fall on building surfaces high up in the street canyon and the heating effect will be reduced by some combination of convection and wind. Since direct sunlight typically increases the effective temperature of a person by about 6° C, shading from direct sun is more important than the increase in absorbed radiation.

We conclude then that the reduced reflectance due to urban texture is more likely to affect the urban temperature at the mesoscale than at the microscale. Prediction of this effect is useful to set the mesoscale boundary conditions, but it will still need a more spatially-sensitive modelling procedure to predict conditions at street level.

ENERGY ANALYSIS

This analysis was carried out using the LT Program.[6] This method uses pre-computed data to predict the primary energy consumption for heating, lighting, ventilation and cooling, responding to a few simple inputs including: plan form, section, facade glazing ratio and orientation. It models the interaction between energy flows — for example increasing glazing area reduces lighting energy consumption and increases heating, due to increased conductive losses and reduced lighting gains. The method also takes account of the overshadowing caused by adjacent buildings, reducing the daylight availability and solar gains.

GENERIC FORMS

A number of simplifying assumptions were made in order to ensure that observed differences were the result of varying the building form and no other factor. All buildings were assumed to be for office use, located in southern UK, with 30% or 60% of the facade single glazed and a wall U-value of 0.6. A winter ventilation rate of 1 ac/h and a datum illuminance requirement of 500 lux were also assumed. Both naturally ventilated and air conditioned options were assessed.

Given the assumptions and limitations outlined above, these findings suggest that choice of urban form has far less impact on energy use, once reasonably shallow plans are adopted, than the use of air conditioning. Variations in predicted energy use were found to be small (less than 10%). This is perhaps not surprising in view of the fact that all six forms are of relatively shallow plan with the same ratio of passive to non-passive area.

The most efficient form, whether 30% or 60% glazed and whether air-conditioned or not, is the court. The highest energy user in all cases is the slab on a N-S axis. This form suffers highest obstructions to daylight with limited useful solar gains. When the glazing ratio is increased from 30% to 60%, energy use is marginally increased for courts and decreased for slabs, reducing the difference between them from 9% to 7%. When air conditioning is assumed, the difference is also reduced, from 9% to 6% with 30% glazing. It is to be expected that air conditioning irons out the differences between forms, but in doing so it increases energy use on average by 45% compared with natural ventilation. They also confirm the relevance of the degree of obstruction. What variations there were largely reflect different levels of obstruction (higher obstruction levels typically resulting in higher energy use).

LONDON STUDY SITE

For the London site the same assumptions were made as for the generic studies, with the additional assumption that buildings deeper than 12m. are fully air conditioned (corresponding to real-life likelihood). The LT Program was then applied to each of the 16 blocks within the study area. The results for total energy use per block range from 166 kWh/m^2 to 282 kWh/m^2 (a difference of 70%). This can be related to a number of urban characteristics, including plan depth (expressed either in terms of a passive to non-passive ratio or a built volume to envelope surface area ratio), level of obstruction and orientation. Thus in general the blocks with shallow plan buildings (low volume to surface ratio) are more energy efficient than those with deep plan buildings (high volume to surface ratio). However, the level of obstruction and strong orientational characteristics have an important second order influence on final energy use and can confuse the general pattern.

In defining an urban form characteristic to relate to energy use it is thus necessary to take account of these two additional factors. Further calculations were carried out assuming different building types and hours of occupancy (schools and hospitals). Although the total energy results are quite different, they show the same relative variations and lead to the same conclusions. It should be emphasised that the LT values are for potential or ideal performance where daylight and solar gains are utilised. Real buildings will fall a long way short of this performance.

URBAN FORM PARAMETERS

We have mentioned the advantages of using generalised urban form parameters characterising the urban morphology at an intermediate scale, in order to be able to predict environmental performance of complex urban textures using simplified models based on these parameters. Here we propose and discuss several such parameters. As well as being relevant to describing the physical processes of interest, it is important that any parameters can be derived easily from data which is readily available. We present simple methods of deriving the parameters and analysing aspects of urban texture relevant to microclimate, by applying image processing operations to digital representations of the urban form.

REAL URBAN MORPHOLOGICAL STRUCTURE

The urban tissue, although familiar and inhabited by over 40% of the world's population has a unique structure with no good analogues in nature. It varies from a high degree of randomness to a high degree of order, but it is never completely one or the other. For example, a mediaeval city (such as the study area in Toulouse) may be described as very random when compared with a 19th century grid-iron layout. But locally there is a high degree of order even in the mediaeval city. Right angles and straight lines prevail, while, in the third dimension, building heights tend to have quite a narrow distribution. On the other hand, an apparently regular orthogonal plan (such as the study area in London) shows considerable variation in grid size and street width. If we defined degree of order as the probability of specifying a point correctly to be street or building from a distance and direction from an origin, then we would probably be no more successful than in the mediaeval city.

The question is, how significant is the randomness? It would be very convenient if we could reduce the urban tissue to a number of equivalent simplified types. But take, for example, the availability of daylight. If we had uniform building height, the mutual overshading would be considerable, whereas if there is a wide variation of building height this will be much less. However, the impact of this difference will be dependent upon two further factors — the overall density of building and the optical reflectance of the buildings.

PROPOSED URBAN PARAMETERS

Bearing in mind the considerations above, we have investigated the following parameters:
1. Building volume to envelope surface area ratio
2. Horizontal section area and horizontal section perimeter as function of height above ground
3. Vertical section area amplitude as function of direction.

These parameters have been chosen because of their probable microclimatic significance, with the ultimate objective of using them in a simplified model. For example, considering the migration of traffic pollution (M), we could propose a generalised model of the form:

$$M = f(v),(d),(A),(B),(C)$$
where:
$$v = \text{wind speed}$$
$$d = \text{wind direction}$$
A, B, C.. are urban parameters including parameters 1 and 2 in list above, and directionality (parameter 3).

VOLUME TO SURFACE AREA RATIO

For a given building, the building volume to surface area ratio relates well to the mean distance from an occupant to the envelope. It has the dimensions of metres and can be considered to be the average depth of the building from the envelope and thus indicates the potential for daylighting and natural ventilation. It will also in-fluence the heating costs in cool climates (in a negative direction), although this will be modified by the insulation value of the envelope. These effects can be evaluated using the LT model. The temperature-moderating effects of buildings in the urban climate will also be dependent upon the surface admittance of buildings which itself is area-density dependent. The average volume to surface area ratios for the three study areas, Berlin, London and Toulouse have been determined using image processing techniques described below. Their values are 5.9, 4.6, and 4.0 respectively, and can easily be associated with the diminishing grain size of the three cities.

HORIZONTAL SECTIONS
AND PERIMETER WITH HEIGHT

These parameters are concerned with the openness of the city to the sky, the so-called occlusivity of the urban surface. This is likely to relate to both the capture of incoming radiant energy and the loss of longwave energy to night sky. It would be important in describing the dilution of pollutants by interaction with the free-flowing wind.

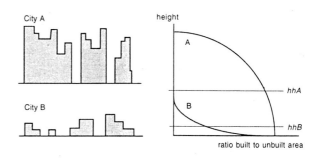

fig. 2.20 Horizontal section built area/height curves for two hypothetical urban forms.

Figure 2.20 shows two hypothetical urban sections and how the horizontal section area varies with height. Curve A shows a high density city with a relatively uniform building height. Curve B describes a lower overall density with

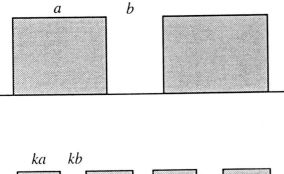

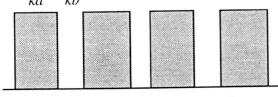

fig. 2.21 Hypothetical simplified cases where the urban fabric has the same area/height curve but clearly has different occlusivities if defined in terms of integrated sky view.

proportionately a much greater variation in building height. Note that the total built volume is the area under the curve. The definition of the upper limit of the urban surface is not obvious; clearly it is not set by the tallest building but rather the 'average tall building'. But how tall is tall? It may be useful to define the half area height. This is defined by the line *hh* such that the areas under *a* and *b* under the curve are the same. This allows us to define a mean built density in three dimensions, although the upper boundary of the built layer is not defined. An alternative would be, say, a 10% area height. The choice of defining parameter will be informed by the nature of the climatic phenomenon being considered such as wind effects or solar radiation.

The spaces between the buildings in type A on average have a much smaller view of the sky than in type B. Radiation entering this cavity is inter-reflected over a much larger surface and is therefore more likely to be absorbed than in case B. Long-wave radiation, which will not be reflected from most building materials, will tend to be retained. We can describe this as having a high occlusivity.

However, the comparison only works for buildings of similar ground floor area. To illustrate this, in figure 2.21 we show two simplified cases where the urban fabric has the same area/height curve but clearly has different occlusivities if defined in terms of integrated sky view. Taking the perimeter of the intersected building as a function of height (instead of the area) removes this problem. The area under the curve now indicates the total vertical surface area of the buildings, and a half-area height can

be defined as before.

The envelope surface area, together with its optical properties, clearly will have some relevance to radiation absorption and inter-reflection. However, the area/height parameter can be considered to indicate a 'blockage fraction' and may be of greater relevance to urban ventilation. We have not defined occlusivity in terms of the parameters of these curves, but it is likely to involve both the absolute value of area or perimeter density and the slope of the curve at the half-area or half-perimeter height. The built area/height curves for the Berlin, London and Toulouse study areas are shown in figure 2.22.

VERTICAL SECTIONS AND DIRECTIONALITY

The main directional climatic factors are solar radiation and wind direction. We could expect both of these to interact with both the direction and width of streets. The blocking effect of buildings (in a given direction) can be assessed by taking a vertical section or a mean height. The anisotropy of the urban tissue can then be indicated by plotting the mean height whilst moving the section plane in a direction normal to the plane, producing a mean height profile. The normal to the plane is then rotated (in azimuth) and successive plots are made. For an isotropic urban tissue we would expect little variation in the profile amplitude whereas tissues with strong direction elements such as grid-iron plans and major boulevards, will result in a profile with much greater amplitude.

Using the NIH image processing package described above, pixel array maps containing height data (Digital Elevation Models) were scanned. The average height profile for four orientations is shown in figure 2.23 for the London site. The variation in amplitude between the E and S group and the SW and SE group is readily visible. The direction (azimuth) at which the maximum amplitude occurs will define one (or more) axes of directionality (it will be at right angles to it). Figure 2.24 shows polar diagrams of the mean square deviation plotted against azimuth angle. By taking the mean square rather than just the amplitude a strongly geo-metric plan of very small streets, and a less perfectly regular plan which has very wide streets can be distinguished, the latter showing stronger directionality. We have termed the mean square deviation the 'permeability parameter' because we expect it to relate to the permeability of the urban fabric, for the reasons already described. The polar diagram of permeability against azimuth has been termed

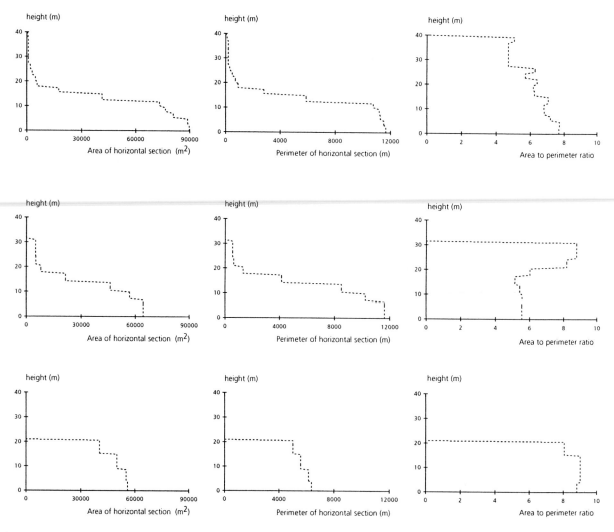

fig. 2.22 Parameters of the horizontal cross-section as a function of height for London (top), Toulouse (middle), and Berlin (bottom). Area of horizontal section as a function of height (left). Perimeter of horizontal section as a function of height (middle). Ratio of area to perimeter of horizontal section, as a function of height (right).

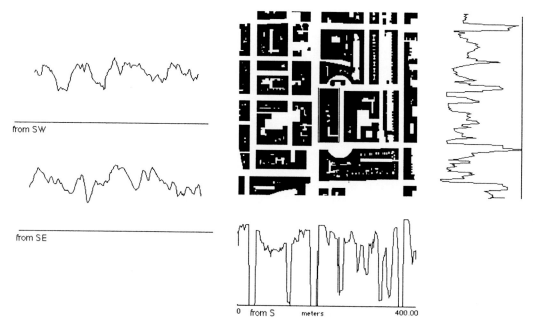

fig. 2.23 Average height (vertical section area) profiles for London study area showing effect of orientation.

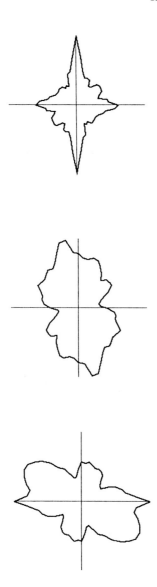

fig. 2.24 Permeability rose diagrams (Mean square deviation of the mean height profile perpendicular to a certain direction plotted against that direction for London (top), Toulouse (middle) and Berlin (bottom).

the 'permeability rose'. Evidence for the significance of these diagrams in terms of wind climate is discussed in our conclusion below.

IMAGE PROCESSING TECHNIQUES
APPLIED TO URBAN TEXTURE STUDIES

The computation of the urban form parameters which have been defined above can be done using image processing techniques. The input format should be urban Digital Elevation Models (DEMs), where the urban ground area is represented as an array of pixels, and a numerical value is associated to each pixel according to the building's height on it. This array can be viewed as a grey-scale image: a level of grey between 0 and 255 is assigned to every pixel, according to its height (level 0 street level, level 255 top roof

fig. 2.25 Digital elevation models (DEMs) of London (top), Toulouse (middle) and Berlin (bottom). A level of grey between 0 and 255 is assigned to every pixel, according to its height (level 0 street level, level 255 top roof level).

level). Figure 2.25 represents DEM images of the study sites in Berlin, London and Toulouse: the three 400 x 400m. areas are represented on 600 x 600 pixel grey-scale images.

Currently, the production of such DEM images requires a considerable inputting effort, which is based on the volumetric definition of a whole portion of city. However, it is likely that in a few years' time urban DEMs will be available at low cost. The investigation of digital photogrammetry techniques for automatic 3-D rendering in urban zones is an area of active research, and great progress has been made in recent years. The aim is to process stereoscopic images for the automatic production of DEMs. This is already possible in rural areas with smooth topography, but poses a number of problems in the case of cities, where vertical walls create important surface discontinuities. When simple procedures for the construction of urban DEMs become available, image processing techniques to evaluate the environmental performance of urban texture would have great potential for applications in urban studies.

NIH IMAGE PROGRAM

The software which has been used for processing DEM images in this study is NIH-Image 1.60 (simply called NIH below). This is a public domain image processing program for the Macintosh. Originally developed for analysis of medical images, it has a range of conventional image processing operations, but the most useful feature is its ability to be customised by writing user defined macros in a Pascal-based language, to combine the image processing operations with arithmetic and logic functions. Such macros were written for this study to automate the analysis of urban textures.

All of the parameters already discussed were calculated using this method. In addition, the following paragraphs discuss some other quantities of relevance to urban texture and microclimate, which can easily be obtained by image processing from a DEM of the site.

SIMPLE NUMERICAL DATA

Information concerning areas, volumes and perimeters can be extracted from DEMs. Built areas can be measured just by counting the number of pixels of a certain value (i.e. with a certain height) on the image. Built volumes can be computed by adding together all the pixels with a weight proportional to their height. Perimeter lengths can be with edge detection operations, but they require a higher computational effort. Perimeter is a measurement of length, while digital images only provide measurements of areas (or pixels). The conversion between these two measurement modes is not straightforward: objects with different perimeter (and even infinite, as shown by fractal theory) can be contained within the same area. The assumption that every pixel on the edges of a building represent the same perimetral length is not safe. Therefore, a procedure has been developed to detect the slope of the perimetral outline of a building on DEM images, in order to obtain a corrected perimeter measurement. As in the case of volume, the computation of vertical surfaces can be computed by adding together all the perimeter pixels with a weight proportional to their height. The above techniques were used to calculate ground floor area, unbuilt area, built volume, vertical surface area, and built volume to envelope surface area ratio for Berlin, London and Toulouse (Table 2.5).

The above Macros can be adapted to compute area and perimeter at different heights. The subtraction of a grey level from a DEM image will produce another DEM image which represents the original urban portion horizontally cut at a certain level. By iterative cutting of a DEM and by subsequent application of the above macros, it is possible to compute the variation of the urban built area and perimeter with height. The evolution of those parameters and also of the ratio of area to perimeter with height is presented in figure 2.22 for Berlin, London and Toulouse.

PASSIVE AND NON-PASSIVE AREAS

Passive areas are defined as those situated within 6m. of the building envelope, while non-passive areas are those beyond this distance, unable to benefit from direct daylight and natural ventilation and needing much more energy.[7] Non-passive areas can be identified on DEMs by appropriately defined 'image-erode' commands. The computation of non-passive areas at different levels and their addition gives the total non-passive volume of the city. Proportions of the total volume which is non-passive for each of the study sites are: London 23.24%, Toulouse 16.37% and Berlin 38.78%.

SHADOW CASTING

A very efficient shadow casting macro to work with DEM images has been written by P. N. Richens. Given a certain solar angle (azimuth, altitude), the algorithm assigns to each pixel of the DEM image a value corresponding to the height of the shadow on it, by doing iterative translations of the whole DEM in the altitude direction, together with the reduction of the value of each pixel of a quantity proportional to the tangent of the altitude. Areas in shadow will be

fig. 2.26 Shadowing in Toulouse on 21st December at 9.00a.m., 10.00 a.m. and 11.00a.m. local time.

	LONDON	TOULOUSE	BERLIN
Ground floor area per unit site area [-]	0.56	0.40	0.35
Unbuilt ground area per unit site area [-]	0.44	0.60	0.65
Built urban volume per unit site area [m]	7.63	6.04	6.51
Built volume to surface ratio [m]	4.62	4.04	5.93
Total vertical urban surface (facades) per unit site area [-]	1.09	1.09	0.75
Ratio of non-passive volume (< 6m from facade) to total built volume [-]	0.23	0.16	0.39
Average view factor from city to sky, computed on all horizontal surfaces (roof and ground) [-]	0.81	0.83	0.86
Average number of hours of sun on 21 December, computed on all horizontal surfaces (roof and ground) [h]	3.5	3.9	3.4
Average number of hours of sun on 21 June, computed on all horizontal surfaces (roof and ground) [h]	10.8	10.4	12.6
Maximum reduction in planar reflectance found in laboratory study	14%	39%	15%
Reduction in hemispherical reflectance caused by urban texture at 20% 'paint' reflectance (computer simulation)	20%	25%	17%
Smoke clearing efficiency	Intermediate	Worst	Best

	LONDON	TOULOUSE	BERLIN
Digital elevation model			
Permeability rose			
Fouriergram			
Built area as a function of height			
Built perimeter as a function of height			

Table 2.5 Three city comparison of key urban form parameters and environmental characteristics

detected by the condition $h_{\text{shadow}} > h_{\text{model}}$, other areas being directly illuminated by the sun (fig. 2.26).

The total number of hours of sun on a certain pixel for a certain day can be computed easily by adding all the corresponding images together. An average value over all pixels for each study site is shown in Table 2.5. It should be noted that this result is not solely determined by the city geo-metry, because daylight hours are different at the three different locations.

THE VIEW FACTOR FROM THE CITY TO THE SKY

The view factor is a physical parameter which is related to many urban environmental processes. Also called shape factor, form factor or config-uration factor, it was originally introduced in heat transfer theory to model radiant exchange between diffuse surfaces. Given two diffuse surfaces A1 and A2, the view factor from A1 to A2 is defined as the fraction of the total radiation leaving A1 which reaches A2. The urban view factor from the city to the sky is an important parameter in urban climatology. It represents in general the openness of the city to the sky and takes part in three major environmental processes: the loss of long wave radiation from city to sky, responsible for the cooling down of the urban surface during the night, the absorption of sol ar short wave radiation within the urban texture; the illumination received by the urban surface from a uniform horizontal plane, which may approximate overcast sky conditions.

An interesting algorithm for the computation of sky view factors was obtained by adapting the above shadow-casting procedure. Shadow views are produced from solar positions generated to sample from the desired sky distribution, then view factors are calculated from the addition of the shadow views resulting from these sun positions. Results for Berlin, London and Toulouse are presented in figure 2.27. The main contrast is between roofs, which have an unobstructed view of the sky and look bright, and deep courtyards, which look very dark. Streets are characterised by average values darkening progressively toward the edges. Junctions have values which are on average twice as high as streets, which is reasonable according to the additive property of view factors. Average view factors for all horizontal surfaces for each of the three city sites are: London 0.814, Toulouse 0.827 and Berlin 0.861.

FOURIER TRANSFORMS

Fourier analysis of the section area spectra will identify regular structures showing fundamental frequencies and their amplitude. If this transform is carried out for all azimuth angles the result can be displayed also as a polar diagram where the direction of the normal is represented directly by angle, the frequency is represented by the radius, and the amplitude is represented the pixel value on a grey or colour scale.

Using the image processing software described, we have produced Fouriergrams for the three sites in London, Toulouse and Berlin (fig. 2.28). Interpretation of these Fouriergrams requires a little effort. It is a way of observing the distribution of varying degrees of order, smeared over the whole sample area. This meets our objective of finding a generalised parameter. The most striking feature of the images is the in-

dication of directionality. Major and secondary axes are very clearly shown. Note that the strong lines occur at right angles to the streets to which they relate — on these axes Fourier components have high amplitudes. However the irregular periodicity results in almost a continuum of frequencies. The frequency (or strictly wave number — i.e. number of cycles per metre) varies from zero at the centre to 0.3/m at the edge. The high frequencies are of little importance since they describe small scale detail. At the scale of these urban samples the outside of the diagram represents information on a scale of about 3 meters. It is reasonable to propose that the scale in which we are interested is of the order of 10m corresponding to a frequency for the sample area of 0.1. We can eliminate the higher frequencies and restore the image by an inverse transform, to see what level of detail we have left. Thus we can concentrate on extracting information from the central third of the Fouriergram.

Comparing London with Toulouse, apart from the strong bi-axial symmetry of London, we note that the central spot decays more slowly in the case of Toulouse. This is indicative of a richness in low frequencies suggesting large periodic objects — the river, squares and public spaces. This is found also in Berlin, but in this case it is superimposed by a much stronger biaxial directionality.

CONCLUSIONS

The main objectives of the theoretical research reported were firstly to characterise the optical and ventilation characteristics of generic urban fabric types and of the three study areas, and secondly to identify and derive morphological parameters to which the physical phenomena could be related. The main conclusions concerning the key relationships follow. Then we present key environmental and urban form parameters for the three cities, in chart format. Finally we make a summary conclusion to the whole theoretical study.

GRAIN SIZE AND COMPLEXITY OF THE URBAN FABRIC IN RELATION TO SOLAR RADIATION ABSORPTION

It is obvious when looking at images of the study areas of London, Toulouse and Berlin that the urban texture is quite different. Berlin has the largest grain size, followed by London, then Toulouse. Berlin also has the least convoluted or

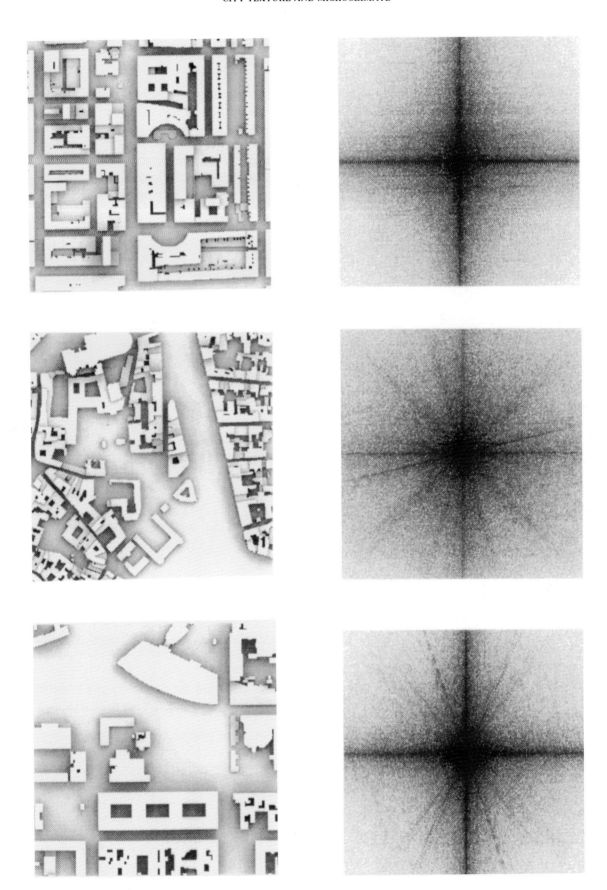

fig. 2.27 View factors of London (top), Toulouse (middle) and Berlin (bottom). The grey value of each pixel is proportional to the sky view factor. White = view factor 1, black = view factor 0).

fig. 2.28 Fourier transforms of London (top), Toulouse (middle) and Berlin (bottom).

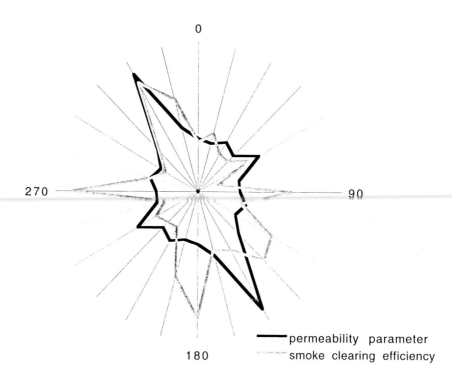

0

270

90

180

permeability parameter

smoke clearing efficiency

fig. 2.29 Combining the urban form parameter for permeability with the modelled smoke clearing efficiencies for the London site shows some significant correlations.

complex building outlines. Both of these characteristics may be seen by visual inspection, but as a more quantitative measure we can use either of two parameters: the non-passive volume, or the ratio of built volume to building envelope surface area. Each of these parameters would be expected to reflect both grain size and complexity. In the studies, both parameters are found to follow the same pattern, with the values for Berlin being the highest, followed by London then Toulouse (Table 2.5). Interestingly, the value of the built area does not follow this pattern, with London having the largest built area.

To relate these urban form parameters to radiation absorption, we may use the results of the reflectance studies. These concluded that Berlin has the lowest value for reflectance decrease compared with a flat plane, followed by London followed by Toulouse with the largest decreases. Therefore, at least for the three very contrasting sites chosen, low values of non-passive volume, or low ratios of built volume to surface area, result in large optical reflectivity decreases compared with a flat plane, indicating increased solar absorption with its associated environmental effects.

GRAIN SIZE AND COMPLEXITY OF THE URBAN FABRIC IN RELATION TO POLLUTANT DISPERSAL

The smoke dispersal test results comparing the clearing efficiencies of London, Berlin and Toul

ouse show an interesting correlation with the urban form parameters. As explained above in the discussion on smoke analysis, the most clear-cut results from these tests are found after most of the smoke has dispersed but some remains in the least easily cleared areas. At this point, Berlin has the least smoke remaining, followed by London then Toulouse. This follows the same pattern as the radiation absorption and the two urban form parameters discussed above in the context of grain size. Thus, the textures with lowest values of non-passive volume and lowest ratios of built volume to surface area have the most smoke trapped, indicating poor pollutant dispersal.

DIRECTIONALITY OF PERMEABILITY PARAMETER IN RELATION TO POLLUTANT DISPERSAL

The directional permeability parameter described above in the discussion of vertical sections and directionality was developed to characterise the permeability of the urban fabric to airborne pollutants, and it is interesting to compare the values of this parameter for the London site with the results obtained in the smoke dispersal tests. The two quantities are plotted on the same polar diagram in figure 2.29, for the same compass directions at intervals of 15°. A good correlation between the two can be seen in the values relating to northerly directions (correlation coefficient = 0.88 for 11 values), but the southerly half of the diagram is not correlated (correlation coefficient = -0.01). The correlation coefficient for all 24 values is 0.27. It is interesting to speculate on why the two halves show such different correlations, and this could be due to the results of the wind tunnel experiments being influenced disproportionately by the different geometries on the upwind and downwind faces of the scale model. In spite of this, and other limitations of the wind tunnel method discussed earlier, it is felt that the strong correlation shown in part of this data shows promise for the permeability parameter as a predictor of pollutant dispersal, and further development and validation work is worthwhile.

CITY COMPARISON

Table 2.5 gives a comparative overview of the characteristics of the three study cities. It highlights the conclusions made above and provides an impression of the differences and similarities in terms of form and environmental parameters at a glance. It becomes clear that it is possible to analyse and compare any urban texture, or different areas of one city, in this way in order to inform decisions about, for example, effective urban locations for PV arrays; the most promising positions for urban wind generators; urban areas with poor or high energy use potential for refurbishment or new-build and implications for the positioning of atmospheric pollution sources (such as major traffic routes or industrial activities) as well as indicators for the design of comfortable urban spaces in terms of wind and sun.

To summarise, the studies of the environmental processes of radiation exchange and the ventilation of urban interstices indicate that both of these are influenced by the urban form. These two process are crucial in determining microclimate and its impact on buildings, relating to heating and cooling of urban space; availability of daylight to building and ground surfaces; air movement to influence outdoor comfort; effectiveness of natural ventilation of buildings; and dispersal of pollutants.

Physical measurements (optical absorptance and wind tunnel) on models, and computer calculations (SHADOWPACK RADIANCE and LT) have shown that these environmental effects show good correlation to a small number of morphological parameters, which have been defined and derived for the three urban study sites. For example the increase in absorption due to the urban roughness correlates well with the volume to surface area ratio. And the street ventilation (implied by the smoke clearing efficiency) as a function of wind direction relates reasonably well to the directionality of the permeability parameter, as described by the 'permeability rose'.

It is encouraging that these correlations are demonstrated, although not strong in every case due to the relatively low precision of some of the experimental technique. It is also encouraging that the urban parameters upon which these processes depend can be readily extracted by processing urban images in the form of digital elevation maps DEMs. Developments in this area make it hopeful that soon these will be available from aerial photography.

The image processing approach to the derivation of the urban parameters also allows us to address the problem of scale of microclimate effects, i.e. over what distance should we take account of the morphology. Although the question is not answered in this work, the use of the decay function, i.e. where the impact of the urban form diminishes as we move away from the point of interest, offers a method for future study.

We see this work as the first step in establishing a simplified urban microclimatic model, describing the key environmental processes influential in building energy use and environmental quality. The urban parameters enable the intermediate scale to be modelled — more local than existing urban-scale models using concepts such as urban roughness and urban canopy, yet not requiring precise descriptions of local geometry, and providing synoptic results rather than single time frame 'snapshots'. With suitable interfaces, perhaps involving 'expert system' support and interpretation, this model could form the core of an urban environmental planning tool.

Koen Steemers, Nick Baker, David Crowther, Jo Dubiel, Maria-Heleni Nikolopoulou, Carlo Ratti
The Martin Centre for Architectural and Urban Studies, University of Cambridge

ACKNOWLEDGEMENTS

This research was funded by the European Union DG XII under the Actions de préperation, d'accompagnment et de support (APAS) program (contract number RENA-CT94-0016). It was carried out at the Martin Centre, Department of Architecture, University of Cambridge, under the direction of Dr Steemers and Dr Baker with Dr Crowther as Senior Research Associate and Ms Dubiel, Ms Nikolopoulou and Mr Ratti as research staff.

NOTES

1 L. Martin & L. March (eds), *Urban Space and Structures*, (Cambridge University Press) Cambridge, 1975.

2 Developed at the US National Institutes of Health and available on the Internet at http://rsb.info.nih.gov/nih-image/.

3 G. Ward, 'The RADIANCE lighting simulation and rendering system', *Computer Graphics Proceedings, Annual Conference Series*, 1994, 459-72.

4 A. Grynberg, 'Validation of RADIANCE', LBID 1575 LBL Technical Information Department, Lawrence Berkeley Laboratory, Berkeley California, July 1989; J. Mardaljevic, 'Validation of a lighting simulation program under real sky conditions', *Lighting Research and Technology*, vol. 27, no. 4, 1995, 181-188.

5 D. J. Sailor, 'Simulated urban climate response to modifications in surface albedo and vegetative cover', *Journal Of Applied Meteorology*, vol. 34, 1995, .1694-1704.

6 K. Steemers & N. Baker, 'Informing Strategic Design — the LT method', *Proceedings of North Sun 94 International*, Glasgow, 1994, 191-6.

7 Ibid.

Urban Design Studies, Volume 3, 1997

SOCIAL EFFECTS OF LAND USE CHANGES IN KIRTIPUR, NEPAL

UTTAM SAGAR SHRESTHA NATALIE H. SHOKOOHY AND MEHRDAD SHOKOOHY

In developing countries nothing has, perhaps, been more destructive to the traditional culture and social structure of small local communities than the population movements of the last few decades. In most Asian countries, the economic forces governing local communities were in an equilibrium for many centuries, providing a stable way of life for the people, little effected by population movements, and as a result people were able to develop a strong sense of belonging to the area they lived in. This played an important role in their cultural identity, and is also expressed though arts and folklore.

In recent decades the political and economic forces of modern times — often imposed from outside the community — have provided grounds for massive population movements in these countries. It is well known that the concentration of wealth, along with government ministries, departments and agencies, and also semi-government agencies in the capitals and principal cities, in contrast with the lack of basic facilities elsewhere has forced people to abandon their towns and villages and move to these centres, and as a result the cities are growing without any control or appropriate planning. There is hardly any major city in the developing world which is not surrounded by miles of recently constructed and often substandard housing of the newly arrived population. These areas were once occupied by farmlands, villages and small towns, each with its own community, the culture of which has often been drowned in the wave of newcomers, many of them poor and culturally disorientated. Many such communities have now lost their identity, and it is too late to study the forces which changed them, let alone find a way to reinforce what might remain of their cultural identity.

In Nepal, however, the population was relatively small in the first place, and the county's isolation resulted in modern global economic forces arriving there relatively later than to most other Asian countries, so many small towns and communities are only now undergoing these changes. Kirtipur, in close proximity to the capital, Kathmandu, and with a strong community with a rich culture, is undergoing such changes, and a close study of the underlying currents governing the process is needed urgently, not only to understand it more clearly, but also to find a realistic method of preventing further erosion of the town's cultural heritage. There is no doubt that similar studies are needed for many other towns in a similar situation elsewhere in the developing world, before a wider and more profound knowledge of this international problem can be reached.

Kirtipur[1] has undergone unprecedented social upheavals linked to changes in land use in the Kathmandu Valley in the 1990s. A relatively static medieval type of society existed in Nepal until as late as the 1950s, when a motorable road link to India made modern facilities available to the country, and over the years gradual changes in the organisation of local government, as well as the development of the capital and the nearby University in the late 1970s, had their effects on the balance between farm land and built up areas of this small agricultural town.

The town, once a capital of the Kathmandu Valley, and strategically located on a trade route, had retained, in spite of invasion, earthquakes, and neglect, much of its mediaeval layout and its traditional way of life. The temples, houses and kitchen gardens were clustered mainly on an outcrop of rock and within the fortification walls, further protected by a band of woodland, maximising the defensive potential of the site, and leaving the fertile land around for agriculture. A study of the land use[2] between 1954 and 1989 had revealed a gradual densification and expansion of the historic core, a reduction in the area of kitchen gardens and woodland, and some new housing along roads and tracks to the town. The main reduction in the agricultural area had come with the acquisition of about 40% of the farmland to the east by the Tribhuvan University and the Horticultural Research station in 1957, and the increase in fallow and bad lands as a result of land speculation and development of brick kilns to the north from the 1980s.

RECENT DRAMATIC SOCIAL CHANGE

Many factors have caused the recent changes in Nepalese society, but perhaps the most noticeable acceleration in these changes came about following the restoration of multi-party democracy in 1990. Since 1951, apart from a brief period of parliamentary democracy in 1959, power had mainly been wielded by the Shah kings, and in 1962 King Mahendra had introduced a partyless system of Panchāyat democracy: local councils with representation at village and town level. The effects of the adoption of a multi-party system in 1990 — while not as harsh as, or on the scale of the experience in post-Soviet Russia — was nevertheless characterised by a period of uncertainty in government, and a free-for-all atmosphere in which building and planning controls were flouted, land changed hands, and, in the case of Kirtipur, a large proportion of the remaining agricultural land became building plots.

CENTRALISATION

The impact of improved transportation links and the concentration of resources in the capital and Kathmandu Valley in recent years has led to a general increase in migration to the cities from the countryside and small towns where conditions are harsh, and making a living through agriculture a struggle. Nevertheless, the new migrants still retain their links with their native villages, while seeking a cash income in the centre. In the Kathmandu Valley towns, people have also become more prepared to move to where opportunities are to be found, with the result that in Kirtipur, with its proximity to the capital, there is now a demand for housing by people who are from outside the town — a new phenomena in a traditional town where in previous decades the main need for additional accommodation had been for growing families already living there for generations.

The inhabitants of Kirtipur are Newars, one of the oldest population groups in Nepal. The Newars were originally Buddhist, but with the introduction of Hinduism to Nepal by the ruling classes in the middle ages, many became Hindu. In Nepal the proportion of Newars who practice Hinduism or Buddhism in different communities is not the same, and in the case of Kirtipur, the Hindus are in a majority, but, as with the rest of the country, the two religions co-exist side by side. Although the caste system under which a person's ritual status, as well as social position and occupation was rigidly fixed, has been officially abolished in modern Nepal, religion and caste still play an important role in religious ritual, social organisation, marriage, personal relations, occupation, and the areas in which people live. Traditional Newar village settlements focus on a particular place of worship, and where a settlement is more complex a number of neighbourhoods known as *tols* each comprise people of particular castes (fig. 3.1). In Kirtipur the main Buddhist population is settled around the Chilāncho stupa (figs. 3.2, 3.3) in the southern sector of the historic town, and the Hindus occupy the north, with the higher castes (formerly priests, administrators, scribes) near the old palace area and the main temples, dedicated to Bāgh Bhairav and Umā Maheśvara, but many Hindus, particularly of the dominant farming caste, now live in former Buddhist areas. At the lower level, castes whose traditional occupations involved contact with ritually polluting materials lived in discrete areas, sometimes outside the walls of the town.

As far as housing density was concerned, the cultural traditions of living in areas determined by one's caste, (fig. 3.1) and more to the point, living in the ancestral home, meant that on the whole a family would divide a house and add extensions rather than break up the family by moving to a new plot (fig. 3.4). Accommodation for outsiders in the town was limited, until a new area, known as Naya Bāzār (new market), began to develop in the south-east of the town (fig. 3.5). This came as a result of redistribution of land to landless people by the local authorities in the 1960s. Small plots were sold for a nominal amount, but soon changed hands and were mostly bought by better-off people from the town or outsiders. Large numbers of tenements with shops at ground level were built and let, almost entirely to outsiders — leading to an intermingling of people of various castes. The newcomers were however, mostly of lower income brackets than those who would be able to afford to live in Kathmandu. Other social factors which have had their effects on land use in Kirtipur have been improvements in education and the gradual erosion of the caste system, permitting the realisation of aspirations

fig. 3.1 Kirtipur, map showing the traditional division of the town into neighbourhoods or *tols* comprising people of the same trade or rank in society (M. Shokoohy, B. Leissi).

Key:

1 Samal	8 Kochhen	15 Chaphal	22 De Pukhū	29 Chilañcho
2 Nagacho	9 Sāyami	16 Satako	23 Gutapau	30 Mārakhyo
3 Deu Ḍhokā	10 Sāgāl	17 Salichhen	24 Kuṭujhol	31 Tuñjho
4 Gachhen	11 Khasi Bāzār	18 Bāgh Bhairav	25 Bahirīgāoṅ	32 Gāyine
5 Jochhe	12 Hitigaḥ	19 Iṭāchhen	26 Mvana	33 Poṛe,
6 Kvācho	13 Pāliphal	20 Loṅ Degaḥ	27 Chīthuṅ	34 Amalshi
7 Lāyaku	14 Dopacha	21 Hva Kuncha	28 Tananī	35 Naya Bāzār

fig. 3.2 The great Buddhist stupa of Chilañcho surrounded by subsidiary stupas. The Buddhist area at the south of the town centres on this stupa, which incorporates centuries of artistic and cultural tradition (photo: M. Shokoohy, 1986).

fig. 3.3 New water tank under construction in 1996 and encroaching into the platform of the Chilañcho Stupa (photo: M. Shokoohy).

for a more modern lifestyle to groups for which this had in the past been out of the question.

DEMOCRACY

With the recent 'democratisation' of the government, a large number of the older administrators of high and medium rank, who were felt to be affiliated to the former system of rule by the monarch, were made to retire. On the other hand, the new generation of politicians, who had to rely on the electorate for their position, proved initially to be ineffective at making decisions which might perhaps be unpopular. The new political atmosphere created a sense of insecurity among the remaining administrators, many of whom were perhaps also confused as to where their loyalty lay, and accounted for a change in the attitude of the authorities to enforcement of regulations.

Officers who had previously been responsible to the crown to implement regulations and programmes found themselves for the first few years of the 1990s in an ambiguous situation in which any form of control was resented by the public, but no consensual system had taken its place. Unsure of their own position, the same officials were reluctant to spark opposition or protest by the 'people' by enforcing regulations, and the public, aware that the situation would not last, hurried to build, sell or in some cases appropriate

property in a caricature of the 'will of the people'.

Appropriation of land in Kirtipur at the time included the historic defensive land near the fortification walls, and even an unsuccessful attempt to divide an old pond, Pale Pukhū, to the north of the town, into three plots. Some land has been appropriated without certification. In Amalshi, for example, according to the Chairman of the Chī-thuñ Vihār Village Development Committee,[3] if all the present certificate holders were to build, the footprint of the buildings would cover the area completely.

RESULTS — SALES OF LAND AND PLOTS

Until the 1950s the people of Kirtipur had control of the agricultural land within, and even beyond the four kilometre area surrounding the town, and expansion of buildings in the settlement was confined within the perimeter of the historic walls, although by this time the walls themselves had been removed. The only built up area outside the walls was a linear settlement of 23 houses in Khasi Bāzār, to the west of the town (fig. 3.6). The distribution of grazing land at a nominal price to landless people in Pīgoñ to the north-east and Amalshi to the south-west in 1969 brought significant changes to these areas of the town, and a government 'Back to Village'

fig. 3.4 Satako, a traditional neighbourhood near the main Hindu temple in the heart of the town. The square and open areas are used as extensions to the houses for drying grain and numerous domestic and social activities, unencumbered by motor vehicles because of the stepped access lanes (photo: M. Shokoohy, 1986).

fig. 3.5 A metalled road from the nearby University campus now gives motor access to the modern development of Naya Bāzār to the south-east of the town. The lack of access until a couple of decades ago meant that building operations by the townspeople were limited by what materials could be carried by porters up the stepped tracks to the town (photo: M. Shokoohy, 1986).

fig. 3.6 Plan of Kirtipur showing the newly developed areas, and housing on former agricultural land in 1996 (M. Shokoohy, B. Leissi).

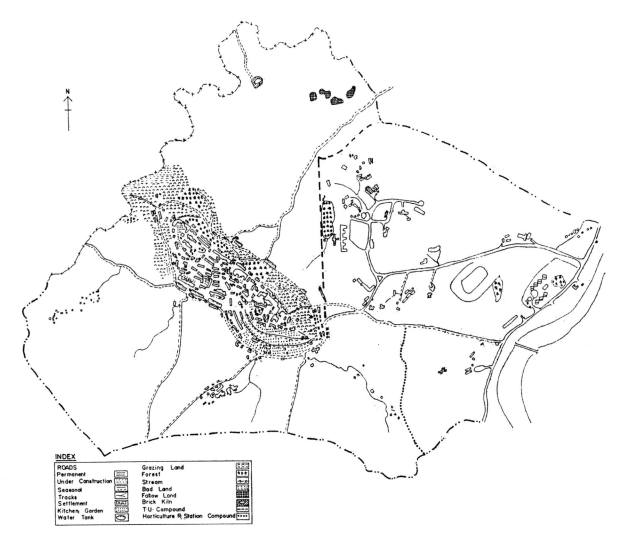

INDEX

ROADS		Grazing Land	
Permanent		Forest	
Under Construction		Stream	
Seasonal		Bad Land	
Tracks		Fallow Land	
Settlement		Brick Kiln	
Kitchen Garden		T·U· Compound	
Water Tank		Horticulture R; Station Compound	

fig. 3.7 Land use map 1981 showing the compact medieval settlement with the new addition of Naya Bāzār at the southeast on the side of the University Campus, and the location of a brick kiln to the north (U. S. Shrestha).

programme in 1967, involved the demolition of one of the last remaining parts of the old fortification wall, to let motor vehicles into the town, which until then could be accessed only on foot. This vehicular route facilitated the transport of construction materials to the town, and as a result the use of the space in the town changed and the density of housing increased. The improved access and facilities such as water supply and electricity in the Amalshi area resulted in further expansion in this area.

The land use changes since 1989 are closely related to government decisions made prior to that period. The land acquired for establishing Tribhuvan University in 1957 and the additional acquisition of 600 Ropanis[4] of land in 1972 had drastically reduced the cultivated land from 89% in 1954 to 55% in 1972 (fig. 3.7). Between 1972 and 1989 brick kilns were established in the irrigated land at the northern edge of Kirtipur, and land sales continued unabated. Areas on the northern and southern sides were also sold (fig.

3.8), as a reaction to rumours in 1987 and 1989 that there were government plans for new land acquisitions.

REASONS FOR SELLING LAND

Many factors or combinations of factors are involved in the changes of ownership of land, including Government acquisition; a shift from farming to off-farm activities; the availability of cash in the form of bank interest; increased land values; the need for housing; the purchase of consumer goods and social factors. In a recent survey of 32 households (Appendix), it was found that an important motivation for land sales comes from rumours propagated by land brokers of plans for government acquisition. Past history has shown that compensation is minimal, and may not be forthcoming if there is insufficient documentation of ownership. Some 15% of the people whose land was acquired by the University are still awaiting compensation due to administrative

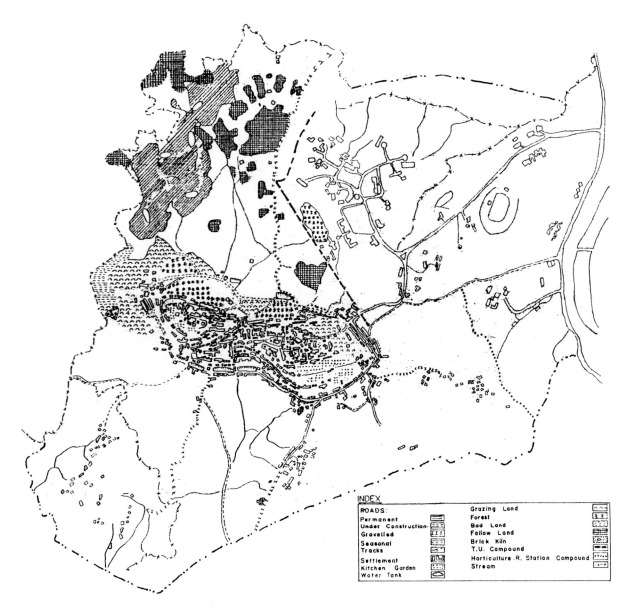

INDEX			
ROADS:		Grazing Land	
Permanent		Forest	
Under Construction		Bad Land	
Gravelled		Fallow Land	
Seasonal		Brick Kiln	
Tracks		T.U. Compound	
Settlement		Horticulture .R. Station Compound	
Kitchen Garden		Stream	
Water Tank			

fig. 3.8 Land use map 1989, showing the rising density of housing in the built up area of the town, and the increasing areas of farmland land left fallow or used for brick production (U. S. Shrestha).

problems, and inadequate records in the field books in Government offices. It is felt that neither the University or the Government have taken adequate steps to rectify the situation, and the people have been left with nothing. Owners of land do not have confidence in being able to get reliable information from the authorities on such plans, and the apparently large sums offered by brokers make them feel it would be safer to sell.

In the early 1990s there was some active local opposition to government acquisition associated with planned urban development in the northern part of the town, as it was felt that it would involve restrictions and interference, so the opportunity for properly planned development was missed. However, the positive effects of the acquisition of the Tribhuvan University land on the infrastructure are now gradually being felt, and it

is possible that people would welcome a development plan if it were presented in the future.

The increase in off-farm activities is a further reason for land sales, though the desired result is not always achieved by the family in question. Many of the townspeople have found that as their land has decreased and family size increased there are insufficient job opportunities on the farm, and members of the family are likely to be employed in other sectors, making investing in business or joining the general labour force a logical step to take. In the survey of 32 households, in nine cases the reasons for land sales were connected with a shift away from agriculture to off-farm and business activities.

The move from agriculture to other trades has not always proved a good option, as the townspeople may not have appropriate skills, and in

fig. 3.9 Paper workshop in Thatujhol to the south of the town, an example of the family run cottage industries of the town (photo: M. Shokoohy, 1986).

fig. 3.10 Carpet weaving, a newly introduced trade in the town. The cottage industry of the town is now often owned and staffed by outsiders (photo: M. Shokoohy 1996).

trades traditionally associated with the town such as carpentry and masonry there may be unwelcome competition for work, including with migrant workers from India who are said to be prepared to work for less. The local cottage industries were formerly family run, (fig. 3.9) and included weaving, but the handloom and recently introduced carpet industry are both showing a decline at present, and in many cases outsiders rather than people from Kirtipur are employed in the carpet workshops (fig. 3.10). As a result it has been seen that after five or six years the money from the land sales may all be spent, and the formerly self-sufficient land holders have become both landless and unemployed.

Based on rough calculations, many land holders may consider that bank interest will produce more cash than sales of grain from a given piece of land. This was given as a reason for land sales in two cases out of the sample of 32. Labour and other costs make it difficult to make a profit growing wheat on unirrigated land, but the return on rice paddy continues to be favourable. The

calculations made by the sellers again tend to be seen more in terms of the temptingly large lump sums, and ignore inflationary factors, and inevitable rises in food prices to consumers as land in general goes out of production.

The recent dramatic increases in land prices would have been unimaginable to the farmers, who hastily sold land ten or fifteen years ago. For example, land in Narwocha and Ikha Bahal which sold at Rs.50,000 - 60,000 per Ropani[5] would now be worth about Rs.100,000 deposited in the bank, whereas the value of the same land would be as much as Rs.3,000,000. On the whole the money from sales was not invested in other cheaper land at the time, so the seller, as well as regretting the bargain, is also faced with the impossibility of acquiring more land in the future. While there are capital gains for speculators and brokers from investment in land, it is not usually let for farming activities because of laws giving the tiller rights to acquire the land after a certain time. Land bought on speculation is therefore usually left fallow, increasing scarcity of arable land, and a general decline in food production.

Historically, poor living conditions and primitive health care resulted in only small increases in the population, with disease and conflict sometimes leading to decreases. The existing acreage and housing was therefore adequate. Now, with a rapidly growing population, if farming is to support a family, larger acreage is required, and there is a need for accommodation outside the traditional family home. In the absence of effective controls or sanctions, houses are being built on public land on the eastern and western side of the town. Land encroachment is considered a serious offence, but in some cases the encroachers themselves may be in positions of authority locally.

OCCUPATION	1974/5	1980	1989
Masons	35.51	23.00	20.27
Carpenters	6.59	16.00	11.38
Farmers	24.89	15.00	12.52
Weavers	26.10	12.00	12.07
Office workers	0.86	8.00	21.18
Traders	3.04	5.00	8.66
Tailors	0.16	7.00	3.64
Blacksmiths	0.42	3.00	0.69
Barbers	0.16	1.00	0.69
Sweepers	0.50	2.00	2.97
Other services	1.77	6.00	5.93
Unemployed	....	2.00	....
TOTALS	100.00	100.00	100.00

Table 1 Changes in Subsidiary Occupation (%).

According to the proverb, selling land in exchange for goods made of iron is a mistake, as iron rusts away, but mud lasts for ever. However, cars and motorcycles, along with televisions and satellite dishes are important status symbols. From the 10 motorcycles and 11 privately owned cars in 1989, the number had risen in 1997 to as many as 85 motorcycles and 42 other vehicles including cars, mini-buses, taxis and mini-trucks. If these vehicles are not for business use to generate income, such as by taxi driving, or delivery of goods and services, the running and repair costs soon make them a burden.

Social factors and economic aspirations as people become more involved in off-farm activities also play an important role in making landholding a lower priority for families. The percentage of people who gave their subsidiary occupation as farming dropped from 24.89% in 1974 to 12.52% in 1989, while the rise in the percentage working in offices was from 0.86% to 21.18% in the same period (Table 1). Although the work may be at the lowest grades, it is regularly paid, and far lighter than the heavy physical work of farming operations. People working in a white collar environment may also feel that activities such as guarding crops are beneath them, when previously they were part of the routine of any farming family. In the case of extremely steep terrain typical of the Nepalese landscape, where the fields are terraced into tiny plots of paddy, the owner may feel it is no longer worth the trouble of cultivating it (see Appendix, reasons for sales). Lack of appreciation for the quality of farming life, compounded with family divisions, unfriendly relationships within families and with tenants, as well as problems associated with shared ownership, registration of land, and land held under religious endowments (gūṭhī lands), as well as difficulties in receipt of land ownership certification from the government (lāl pūrja) and shares of the crop due to the owner at harvest time (bālī), all variously contribute to the general shift away from farming and landholding, although as noted above, without a long term alternative. Another investment option for a family with cash from the sale of land may be for members to seek employment as guest workers abroad. This involves considerable expense, and inexperienced applicants run the risk of loosing their money to unscrupulous brokers, as happened in the case of one of the households surveyed. Some 72 people have gone as guest workers to the Middle East and other areas (Table 2).

PERCEPTION OF POSITION
AND REALITY OF POSITION

On the whole it can be seen that the perception of the results of land use changes and the reality of the position differ, both from the point of view of the authorities, and of the townspeople.

Category	1952/4-61	1961-71	1971-81	1981-89
Outside Kathmandu Valley	249	10	5	20
Within Kathmandu Valley	132	6	3	56
Outside Country	21			
Unknown	36			
TOTALS	438	16	8	76

Table 2 Migration from Kirtipur (source Field Survey 1989).

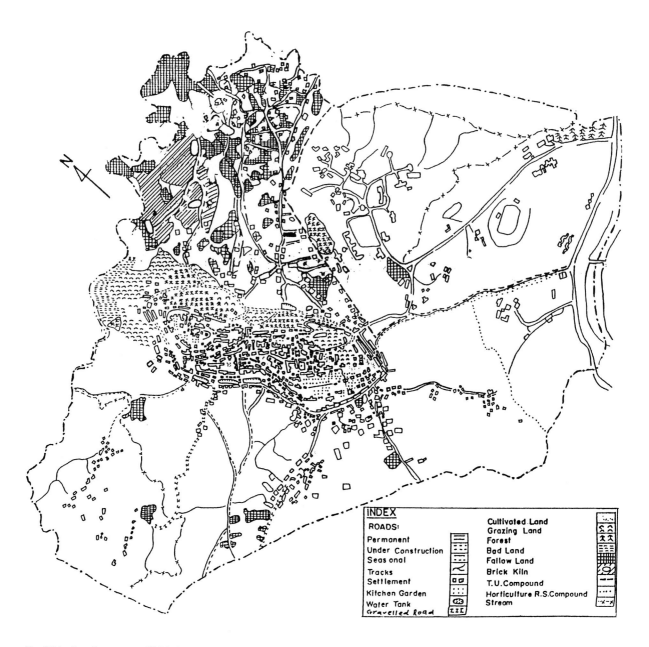

fig. 3.11 Land use map 1996 showing the recent expansion of the town, the ribbon development in the vicinity, new buildings scattered over the former agricultural land, and the land left fallow or used for brick kilns (U. S. Shrestha).

The scenario envisaged in the Kathmandu Valley Development Plan in 1969 was that the building and establishment of the University would provide the villagers with opportunities for wage earning.[6] While the proximity of the University and some associated improvements in Kirtipur's infrastructure have had a gradual effect on commerce and service provision in Kirtipur, particularly in Amalshi in the recently developed area called Naya Bāzār close to the road to the campus (fig. 3.5), there was no dramatic rise in the number of townspeople directly employed by the University, who at present number about 47, including cleaners and sweepers. Similarly, the increased amount of disposable cash in the town

has not circulated in such a way as to make either individual families or the town as a whole more prosperous.

It should be born in mind that many people in Kirtipur, and the rest of the country, are of the opinion that changing land use from agricultural use to non-agricultural use is essential for speedy growth, urbanisation and progress. Kirtipur is felt to be lagging behind in terms of opportunities and modernisation. The situation is constantly evolving with positive and negative effects long and short term. How much planned urban development in the future could play a positive role needs to be considered, but first some details of what has actually happened should be given.

CHANGES IN URBAN AREA 1989-97

Between 1987 and 1996 (fig. 3.11) there has been continuous development of the built up area on either side of the road to the south-east of the town between Amalshi and Khasi Bāzār. Facilities such as piped drinking water, transport and other amenities not available in the core of the town have begun to attract people from the older parts of Kirtipur, as well as outsiders, making the area far denser than before. On the line of the fortified wall some 24 houses have been built, with another 13 on the opposite side, leaving little of the historic wall standing. Within the southern area (fig. 3.14) formerly enclosed by the fortification wall near Majā Degaḥ, as well as in Dhokasi, Amalshi and the Poṛe Ṭol to the south (fig. 3.19), both situated outside the walls, 42 houses have been constructed in former kitchen gardens. In the area east of Amalshi fallow ground has also now been densely built up with 28 houses. The expansion of Gorakhnath School occupied another 2.8 Ropanis of land, and the Mangal Secondary School (Madhyamik Vidyala-ya) added a building in front taking up 6 Ropanis in 1990. In addition along the metalled access route from Amalshi east to Chīthuṅ Dhokā 13 new tenement houses (small blocks of flats rather than single family homes) have been built, some without permit, or on appropriated land.

The area near Kirtipur Secondary School now has densely constructed houses on the southern

Ṭol	No. of households	New households
Lāyaku	42	12
Bahirīgāoṅ	34	10
Gachhen	32	13
Bāgh Bhairav	65	21
Luppau	59	13
Tungha	10	3
Tanani	53	8
Loṅ Degaḥ	24	7
Khasi	42	7
Totals	361	94

Table 3 New houses built in the old *tols* of the town between 1989 and 1997.

side. Within the core of the town, money from land sales has been used for building houses on the kitchen gardens, leaving hardly four such gardens in the town, when traditionally most houses had one (Tables 3-4). On the western side buildings have also been constructed on the route towards Machhegāoṅ from Bahirīgāoṅ, and the route to Salyanthān from Khasi Bāzār. Further to the north-west there are now 13 new houses on the western side of Samal Dhokā, and the lanes to the Pīgoṅ (Pīgāṅ) area. There is a dramatic change in Pīgoṅ itself, where 42 houses have been built encroaching on public land.

From Tables 4 and 5 it will be seen that there has been an overall increase in the built up area of 77 Ropanis, and a decrease in kitchen gardens of 42, and of grazing land of 51 Ropanis. Part of

CATEGORY	1989	%	1996	%
Built up area	436	31.99	513	38.20
Kitchen garden	255	18.71	213	15.86
Grazing	457	33.53	406	30.24
Woodland	201	14.75	201	14.96
Quarries	12	0.88	10	0.60
Bad land	2	0.14	2	0.14
Totals	1363	100.00	1345	100.00

Table 4 Change in Urban Area (in Ropanis, 1 Ropani equals approx 74′sq. or 509.4sq m.).

CATEGORY	1989	%	1996	%
Cultivated land	5978	48.00	5818	46.72
Urban area	1363	10.95	1440	11.56
Tribhuvan University	4012	32.22	4012	32.23
Horticulture Research Station	900	7.23	900	7.23
Brick Kiln	45	0.36	32	0.25
Roads	33	0.26	49	0.39
Fallow land	122	0.98	202	1.62
Totals	12453	100.00	12453	100.00

Table 5 Change in Agricultural Area (in Ropanis, 1 Ropani equals approx 74′sq. or 509.4 sq m.).

fig. 3.12 Chobar, a village on a hill to the south of Kirtipur with an old settlement around its temple at the top of the hill. As with Kirtipur there are new developments on the outskirts near the motorable roads (photo: M. Shokoohy, 1996).

the quarries at Amalshi have also been built up. Institutional use by the Kirtipur, Bāgh Bhairav, and Mangal Secondary Schools account for 10 and 16 Ropanis respectively, and 3.5 Ropanis at Nikhash Pukhū have been occupied by Shahīd Smarak College. Near the northern side of the Indrāyaṇī Temple (Pīgoṅ Degah) 52 Ropanis have also been allocated for the construction of the Kathmandu Model Hospital.

Altogether it is estimated that since 1989 about 148 households or 8% have been involved in residential relocation from the core of the town to mainly the eastern and western fringes, a significant change from the old practice of remaining in the ancestral home. In the new built up areas on the northern side with access to the ring road to Kathmandu, people from Kirtipur are outnumbered by people from outside the Valley. The changes are still in the initial stages of infrastructure development, and mostly take the form of ribbon development along existing tracks and roads. Although there is no plan behind the development, the major changes seem to be taking part in the northern and southern areas. The tendency is for people to build first, and then, on the basis that the houses need services, apply to the authorities. The services are then provided ad-hoc rather than to a laid out plan. The same pattern can be seen in other small towns and villages, for example Chobhār, a village with an important Hindu temple on a hill to the west of Kirtipur, where buildings within

reach of the road have been constructed at the base of the hill (fig. 3.12).

CHANGES IN AGRICULTURAL LAND USE 1989-1996

In the period between 1989 and 1996 there has been an increasing trend of keeping land fallow to the north of Kirtipur (Table 5). In Naravocha 42 Ropanis of fallow land have now been built up (fig. 3.13). More patches of fallow land can now be seen in the Khoyanala and Dhalpāh areas, as well as some patches near Salyanthān at the south-west. To the south the proximity of the road and other facilities available at the junction of the road between Panga, Bhajangal and Kirtipur at Salyancha Chikhu have led to the construction of 56 houses (fig. 3.14) by people from Kirtipur and also from outside the Valley.

Along the road to Machhegāoṅ and Dhalpāh there has been an increase from two Ropanis of fallow land in 1989 to 29 in 1996. Because of high land prices on the north (Kathmandu) side of the town the southern area has become attractive to people from Kirtipur. Land to the north may fetch 2.5 to 3 million rupees while similar land to the south may be bought for 800,000 to 1,000,000. So far only 13 houses have been built in the middle part of the paddy fields in Dhalpāh, but development along the road from Salyanthān to Dhalpāh has become denser. There are about 15 Ropanis of land kept fallow along the road from Salanthān to Sāgāl Ṭol in the south-west of the

fig. 3.13 New buildings in the fields to the north-east of Kirtipur in 1996, with Kathmandu in the background (photo: M. Shokoohy).

fig. 3.14 View from the south of Kirtipur in 1996, showing the new tenement-type buildings and, in the background, the ribbon development on the road to the nearby village of Panga (photo: M. Shokoohy).

fig. 3.15 De Pukhū, the central town square in 1986, with its traditional pond and range of four-storeyed family houses. The ground floors are shops, while the upper floors become progressively more private (photo M. Shokoohy).

town, and a total of 44 Ropanis in the area. Some houses have been built here, and in the area called Khonacha, below Ta Dhān Gā seven houses have been built by outsiders. In Khoyanala there are also many patches of fallow land. The number of brick kilns has been reduced from six to three, now that the clay is exhausted. The land is sold to outsiders for building plots as it is no longer usable for farming.

ROADS AND TRACKS

Some of the trails have now been widened into motorable roads by the Village Development Committees, and the irrigation channel of Khoyanala known as Jan Dha has also been made into a motorable road. The trails from Khasi to Dhalpāḥ and Chhugāoṅ, and the route from Nagāoṅ to Dhalpāḥ on the west have also been widened for vehicles, but without making a substantial change in the value of the land. The land kept fallow in Norwocha and Tyangla has become residential, and is accessible from the Ring Road.

The University Boundary runs to the east of the road from Kirtipur to Kalimati, on the south-western outskirts of Kathmandu. Because of fears

that the University boundary might be expanded up to the road no houses were built on the eastern side of the road up to 1989, and land values were lower than on the western side. In addition the farmers had frequently been harassed by staff, even at lower levels, in the University administration. In one case an ex-British Gurkha who had bought 27 Ropanis of land and was refused permission to construct houses in the area appealed against the government's decision in court. The court decided that if there were special restrictions on the use of the land, government should have prevented the transfer. Building was therefore permitted, in spite of the University authorities' objections. There was a subsequent rapid change from agricultural to residential use on the site, and the road was widened to give access to the plots. Altogether in the period 160 Ropanis of cultivated land was built up, or its use changed, and there was a considerable increase in fallow land.

SCHOOLS AND INSTITUTIONAL BUILDINGS

The River Valley School has now built its own building at the eastern side of Nagāoṅ, and the

fig. 3.16 De Pukhū in 1996 showing modern concrete houses on the north-west side. The large flat roof terraces and horizontal division of the buildings have produced changes in traditional social patterns to do with how homes are used (photo M. Shokoohy).

Puspa Sadan Secondary School in Lāyaku, the former palace area, has added classrooms on 3 Ropanis to the south of the present road between Khasi and Bahirīgāoṅ. In addition the Kirtipur Secondary School has expanded taking up one Ropani of land. As well as this, the newly established Nepal Telecommunication office had a plot of 3.5 Ropanis to allow for further expansion of its present building.

BUILDING REGULATIONS

Under the Kathmandu Valley Land Use Plan adopted by the government in 1976 Kirtipur is regarded as a Rural Settlement area lying next to an Educational Zone. Under the Kathmandu Valley Town Development Board Land Use And Building Regulations[7] of the same year the regulations for rural areas are less detailed than those for the main towns, and those applicable to Kirtipur are broadly concerned with the buildings retaining the look and character of the adjacent houses, but allow improvement in the facilities, as well as plastering and pointing of the exterior. Ground coverage ratio of the buildings is restricted to not more than 50% of the plot with buildings set back five metres from motorable roads, and the height to four storeys. New buildings within or adjacent to a designated Monument Zone are however to be constructed according to guide-lines and directions of the concerned Town Plan Implementation Committee (TPIC). The regulations also discourage new building on good agricultural land, and permit only small scale cottage and agriculture based industries, subject to permission from the concerned TPIC. The concerned village authorities are responsible for issuing building permits according to land use and building regulations prescribed by the TPIC.

On the whole these regulations do not appear to have been used even as guide-lines for recent building activity in Kirtipur or the establishment of industry nearby. For example, the Himal cement works at Jala Vinayak three miles away is close enough for its smoke to cover the town frequently. The result of the lack of concern with the traditional methods of space allocation and building has been a marked change in the character of the town, and the individual *tols* or neighbourhoods.

fig. 3.17 Deu Ḍhokā, the neighbourhood near the old northern gate of the town in 1986 (photo M. Shokoohy).

fig. 3.18 Deu Ḍhokā in 1996, reconstructed houses. Modern plans and features replace the traditional arrangements (photo M. Shokoohy).

fig. 3.19 The Poṛe Ṭol, an area to the south, outside the old settlement, for members of the sweeper caste. The ancient stone path has been repaved with brick in 1996, and some old two and three storey houses have been replaced with larger buildings, reflecting the improved condition of members of 'untouchable' castes (photo M. Shokoohy).

STREET LIFE

As mentioned above, the *ṭols* consist of clusters of houses along a street or round a square or open area (fig. 3.1), often associated with a temple or other religious building, and traditionally inhabited by families of similar caste. Until recently, the complete lack of access for motor vehicles into the town because of the stepped lanes allowed the open spaces in the *ṭols* to be multifunctional semi-public spaces used as an extension of the houses for every kind of domestic and social activity, as well as for activities connected with agriculture such as drying grain (fig. 3.4). As the facilities in the houses in the core of the town are mostly limited to an electricity supply for light, and the water supply is via shared taps in the open areas, as well as wells, springs, ponds and tanks, socially the *ṭols* provided a semi-private setting, especially for women, for daily activities and chores such as washing dishes, laundry and bathing (figs. 3.15, 3.17). One hardly needs mention the huge contrast between the social interaction which prevails in such a setting with that in a 'neighbourhood' in

the western urban context, where the residents may not know the people in the next door houses even by sight, would be unlikely to have ever been in each other's homes, and have no need for any contact with each other to do with practical matters, but feel satisfied that they live in a 'nice', even 'friendly' area, although they would never consider leaving the front door unlocked, or open it to an unknown person.

With money from land sales, modernisation and improvements to the facilities of the houses (figs. 3.14, 3.16, 3.18) mean that the need to be outside and interacting with neighbours all the time diminishes. With houses divided horizontally into apartments, with bigger windows, lighter rooms and larger terraces on the roofs the use of internal and external space changes, and more activities can go on inside in a family centred, rather than neighbourhood centred environment. The isolated setting of sitting watching satellite TV has already become normal for children whose parents and elder siblings worked and played in the streets, fields and streams, and were constantly in contact with other members of the community. This does not of course mean that

69

fig. 3.20 An old brick pavement in the centre of the town at Chafala which has recently been cleaned by residents. Before the improvements in sanitation a number of ancient back alleys like this one were used as open latrines, and had gone out of use as thoroughfares (photo: M. Shokoohy, 1996).

everyone lived in an arcadian setting of trust and mutual respect, and in fact the pressures of dealing with difficult relationships may make the prospect of a more enclosed and private life appealing. However, the security and safety that comes as a matter of course with an environment such as a *ṭol*, and which has evolved as a side effect of broader concerns for safety from external enemies and raiders, is likely be diminished as the street life becomes less personal and intermeshed.

As well as families loosing their source of grain by selling farm land, building over vegetable gardens means that households need cash income for purchasing their daily food, a very different situation from the past, where a household would be self sufficient as regards feeding itself. Socially this means that the townspeople as a whole consider and take up a broader range of employment opportunities for both men and women than they would have done in the past.

In spite of cars being an important status symbol, there are still relatively few private cars in the town. Because of the relatively enormous cost of a motor vehicle, ramps have been made to allow them to negotiate the stepped changes of level in the streets so that they can be kept under the owner's eye. As the core of the town is unlikely to develop the kind of markets and bazaars found in Kathmandu itself, the suffocating pollution that exists there is not so much of a threat, and the main effects motor vehicles are likely to have on the street life if they are allowed to penetrate the core of the town, are to initially make less space available for the domestic and agricultural activities mentioned above, and in the long term to gradually reduce the function of the narrow lanes to access routes. This would gradually deprive the residents of the neutral space in which much social intercourse takes place, as caste rules among the Newars restrict who can enter the private living space of a house.

The impact of changes in land use on the town, and the shift from agriculture to wage earning can be seen to have had both positive and negative social results. There has, for example, been a marked improvement in the quality of life of some groups, such as the *poṛe* or sweeper caste whose unenviable traditional occupation was to remove night soil and ordure, and other unhygienic tasks, and who lived in an area outside the town walls because of their ritually unclean status. Gradual improvements in their opportunities for education and employment, including working as cleaners in institutions such as the University and schools as well as in hotels in Kathmandu, have resulted in a considerable improvement in the environment of the Poṛe area (fig. 3.19). Houses have been improved and simple sanitation installed (this group had declined to participate in a programme to install latrines which was carried out in the 1970s and '80s as they felt they would loose their source of income), and with the help of international funding in 1996 from Plan International, the lanes and steps repaved. Some houses now have shops in the ground floor rooms, which are patronised by other castes, and people in general now walk through the area, while they would have avoided it in the past. The main complaint about the *poṛe* now is more likely to be that they charge too much for emptying the pits of the self composting latrines, and householders decide they may as well defy convention and do it themselves.

There has also been a change in attitude to dirt in other parts of the town, and some ancient

fig. 3.21 Small shrine at Dabuche to the south-east of the town, housing the elephant headed god Gaṇeś in 1986. Gaṇeś shrines mark important ritual points of transition in the town (photo M. Shokoohy).

fig. 3.22 Concrete shrine replacing the old Gaṇeś shrine in Dabuche (photo: M. Shokoohy, 1996).

lanes which had for many years been used as public latrines, and had gone out of use as circulation areas have now been cleaned and reinstated by the efforts of residents (fig.3.20). This can be seen as part of a general feeling that people do not have to accept things the way they are, and can take action to change the way they live. This sense of empowerment is not to do with any particular programmes, or encouragement from the authorities, but stems more from a general rise in expectations, and a sense that the householders domain extends past the immediate area of the house. In Kathmandu itself this sense of responsibility has been eroded to a large extent, and prosperous citizens put up with broken paving and rubbish piled up outside the walls of their property.

One unfortunate effect of individuals having lump sums of cash available has been that as a demonstration of wealth and public spirit, a number of historic structures for public use in Nepal have been demolished and replaced by modern concrete substitutes. In Kirtipur these include some of the shrines in the streets (figs 3.21, 3.22, 3.24), as well as the covered public platforms, which serve as seats and meeting places (figs. 3.23, 3.24). In some cases the rebuilt version retains its original social function, but in others may be enclosed or allocated for some precise use, or even appropriated as part of a neighbouring house, leading to the loss of a traditional feature of the neighbourhood.

NEGATIVE EFFECTS ON COMMUNITY RELATIONS

Although Kirtipur is a city with firm roots in history, the town and its community were left to decline for some two centuries because of the townspeople's fierce resistance to the Gurkha conquest, which culminated in the devastation of the city in 1767. While services and infrastructure were developed for Kathmandu, Patan and Bhaktapur, Kirtipur, though only six miles distant from the capital remained as undeveloped as any distant inaccessible village. In modern times it was reduced for administrative purposes in 1980

fig. 3.23 Deu Ḍhokā in 1988, an old *sattal* or public roofed platform with a rest-house above before demolition and reconstruction as a concrete platform. These buildings are a feature of Newar towns and provide shelter for travellers and a communal meeting place for the neighbourhood (photo: M. Shokoohy, 1988).

fig. 3.24 Reconstructed *sattal* and shrine in Dabujho to the north-east of the town (photo: M. Shokoohy, 1996).

to the status of four villages. Although these divisions are somewhat artificial, they sometimes result in conflicting ideas about what is best for the communities of each of these four divisions, and reduce the opportunities for discussion or planning for the city as a whole by the townspeople. Attempts by a particular Village Development Committee to enforce building controls in its own area may be met with strong opposition, on the grounds that similar construction has been carried out without hindrance by neighbours and relatives in the other sectors. These kind of obstacles make it difficult to establish an impartial forum where such difficulties can be aired and resolved, and concerted plans made. The negative effects of the changes are however being felt, but it is the outsiders who are blamed.

Lack of effective local organisation has led to a lack of means of liaison with government or non-government agencies who may be waiting for an opportunity to assist in implementing proposals coming from the town. It is generally accep-

ted, however, that without such consensus, and also active support from the community, including investment of money and time by the eventual beneficiaries, there is no point in trying to force planning proposals on an area. The government is aware that it neither has the means or the power to enforce controls in an impartial way on an unwilling population.

THE WAY FORWARD

The townspeople themselves therefore need to take a broad view of the existing situation, and establish what is feasible to consolidate what remains of the cultural heritage and living environment of the town, and improve the infrastructure and services to the core of the town as well as the outskirts to prevent a doughnut effect. As land prices and the proximity to Kathmandu mean that further development is inevitable, strategic planning confining developments to pockets where infrastructure can be provided, producing green belts to prevent agricultural land and woodland disintegrating further, restricting transport within the town, and providing good motorable access around it so that all parts can be easily reached, as well as improving transport services, all need to be addressed.

Without the consensus of the population and the motivation to push for what is needed, it is accepted there is no point in attempting to implement or where needed enforce these kind of programs, as experience in Nepal and many other countries has shown that without commitment from within, the effects of the grandest and best planned projects fizzle away shortly after the project is completed or the funding bodies leave the scene. An essential part of the process would therefore be to establish an educational programme, using people from the community as far as possible, to set out and explain the issues to all levels and ages of people, and to organise effective long term arrangements for maintenance.

Here is a town, a community, a culture, with every possibility of moving into the 21st century and incorporating what is valuable from its past into modern life. There is no question of trying to preserve it as an intriguing survival of an ancient way of life to be protected by a metaphorical glass cage as an anthropological curiosity in a museum in the open. It is therefore to be hoped that the people of Kirtipur will sink their differences and find a way of looking at their town as a whole, or as mutually supportive parts, and establishing a consensual framework for what needs to be done, and then demand action. Otherwise these few acres of built up area are destined to fall into the vortex of typical third world decline seen in the past three decades in many other parts of the world, under the pressure of similar political and social changes.

Uttam Sagar Shrestha
IUCN, The World Conservation Union, Nepal
Natalie H. Shokoohy
Royal Asiatic Society
Mehrdad Shokoohy
University of Greenwich

ACKNOWLEDGMENT

The field work of the present study has been carried out with the assistance of the Frederick Williamson Memorial Fund, University of Cambridge. The aim was to monitor and record urban change — both morphological and social — in Kirtipur since the conclusion in 1990 of a study of the town (for publication see note 1 below). The work is part of an ongoing research project on the town, based at the University of Greenwich.

NOTES

1 For a full report the town see M. & N. H. Shokoohy (eds), *Kirtipur: an Urban Community in Nepal — its people, town planning, architecture and arts*, Araxus, London, 1994.

2 U. S. Shrestha, 'Land use changes in Kirtipur', Kirtipur, 155-176.

3 Kirtipur has four Village Development Committees corresponding to the Town's division for administrative purposes into four villages. Lāyaku: the north-west area including the two main Hindu Temples; Chīthuṅ Bihār: the north-east including the main Buddhist stupa and the new developments at Naya Bāzār; Pāliphal to the south-east and Bahirīgāoṅ to the south-west.

4 1 Ropani equals approx 74'sq. or 509.4sq m.

5 1 $ = 88 Nepalese Rupees, £1 = Rs. 55 approx. in 1996

6 HMG Nepal, Physical Development Plan for the Kathmandu Valley, Kathmandu, 1969, 150.

7 Padam B. Chetri, 'Kathmandu Valley Land Use Plan and Kirtipur', *Kirtipur*, 147.

APPENDIX

USE OF MONEY FROM LAND SALES

HOUSEHOLD	TOL	LOCATION OF LAND	REASONS FOR SALE	USE OF PROCEEDS
1	Chīthuṅ Ichhen	Nr. Narwa	Terraced (poor) land	House built
2	Chīthuṅ Ichhen	Khoyanala	Scarcity of money	Taxi purchased
3	Chīthuṅ Ichhen	Nr. University	Scarcity of money	Shop opened
4	Dhokasi	Nr. Jawa Hiti	Bank deposit interest	Given as loan to a 3rd party
5	Bāgh Bhairav	Nr. Jawa Hiti	Work in Saudi Arabia	Lost (appropriated by manpower company)
6	Chaphal	Tyangla	Invest/off-farm activities	TV shop opened, motorcycle purchased
7	Gutapau	Chakhe	To open a shop	Shop opened
8	Naya Bāzār	Chakhe	To open a shop	House constructed
9	Bahirīgāoṅ	Pankgakwa	Off-farm activities	Purchase and maintenance of motorcycle
10	Deu Ḍhokā	Khoyanala	Invest in other activities	Shop opened
11	Dearkha	Balkhu and Ikhābāhā	Construction of a house	House built in Tekusi
12	Jhochhe	Naravocha	High value of land	House built in Tyangla
13	Kuṭujhol	Tyangla	High value of land	House built in Tyangla
14	Kuṭujhol	Tyangla	Employment for son	Invested in carpet industry
15	Hva Kuncha	Gasi	Marriage of son	Spent on wedding celebrations
16	Lāyaku	Khoyanala	Bank deposit interest	Deposited in the bank
17	Tyangla	Tyangla	Construction of a house	House built, motorcycle purchased
18	Paudhu	Nagāoṅcho	Construction of a house	House built, motorcycle purchased
19	Paudhu	Nagāoṅcho	Construction of a house	House built, motorcycle purchased
20	Paudhu	Khosi	Construction of a house	House built, motorcycle purchased
21	Dearkha	Naravocha	Building house and shop	Opened a cotton shop
22	Gutapau	Balkhu, Naravocha etc.	Off-farm opportunities	Opened a restaurant
23	Samal	Naravocha	Building house extension	House extension built
24	Kuṭujhol	Khonacha	No longer farming	Opened a shop
25	Jhochhe	Naravocha	House extension	House extension built
26	Jhochhe	Norwocha	Investing in construction	Motorcycle and TV purchased
27	Dopacha	Dhalpāḥ	Accommodation needed	House constructed
28	Dopacha	Dhalpāḥ	Accommodation needed	House constructed
29	Dopacha	Dhalpāḥ	Accommodation needed	House constructed
30	Deu Ḍhokā	Khoyanala	Tenant's rights	House erected on public land
31	Baryan Pukhū	Khoyanala	Tenant's rights	Deposited in bank
32	Chapa	Gasi	Cultivation problems	Invested in carpet factory

Urban Design Studies, Volume 3, 1997

RE-LEARNING FROM LAS VEGAS:
THE BIRTH OF THE PARADOXICAL MONUMENT

PAUL GROVER

A studio introduction at Yale School of Art in 1968[1] suggested that the physical form of a commercial strip such as route 91 passing through Las Vegas should be seen as an archetype as important to architects and urbanists today as were studies of medieval Europe and ancient Rome and Greece to earlier generations. It was argued that there was a need for a definition of this new type of urban form emerging in America and Europe, radically different from any previously known; one that we had been ill-equipped to deal with and that, from ignorance, had been defined as urban sprawl; and that therefore open minded and non-judgemental investigation would be needed to arrive at a definition and an understanding of this new form, so that techniques for its handling could be evolved.

These ideas were persued, and *Learning From Las Vegas*, published in 1972, has since become the seminal text dealing with the extraordinary phenomenon that is Las Vegas. The book has also by extension become one of the defining mantras of Post-Modernism. Its publication coincided with a definite movement away from orthodox Modernism which, because it 'is progressive — if not revolutionary, utopian, and puristic; it is dissatisfied with *existing* conditions'.[2] By contrast Venturi and Scott-Brown advocated learning from the existing conditions, regarding popular culture as a guiding principle rather than as a *bête noire*: 'There is a perversity in the learning process: we look backward at history and tradition to go forward; we can also look downward to go upward'.[3] A quarter of a century on the text is still of importance to the study of architecture and urbanism. In fact it is perhaps only now, as popular culture becomes increasingly reconciled into the mainstream of cultural theory, that its full effect is being felt. Revolutionary and iconoclastic in 1971, it is now part of most theory of architecture courses both in America and Europe. Little more than a hundred years after its foundation as a small town on the San Pedro, Los Angeles and Salt Lake Railroad, Las Vegas has continued its earlier prolific development, and today Venturi

and Scott-Brown's text stands in an uneasy relationship to the city. In the late 1960s they discovered what they regarded as a new Rome. The Rome of car-oriented, pleasure-driven, consumer-powered America; a city where architecture had humbly taken a secondary place behind the symbolism of massive neon signs. Las Vegas seemed an antidote to the mega-structural and deterministic pretensions of Modernism; to the Modernist concept of architecture as pure forms in space.

Today the architecture of Las Vegas is increasingly less humble. Symbolic megastructures are fashionable, with whole buildings acting as signs in themselves. The scale of the railway gave way to the scale of the car earlier in this century; now, in its turn, the scale of the car has given way to the global scale of transatlantic air travel and tourism. Paradoxically this seems to have led to a 'pedestrianising' of Las Vegas with an accompanying rise in spectacle, street theatre, public shuttle systems and most recently to a strange kind of planning strategy which is turning the city into nothing less than a gigantic model village (fig. 4.1). Much of the research undertaken in Las Vegas by Venturi and Scott-Brown remains valid today, nevertheless it seems necessary to take a fresh look at the city in order to account for the dramatic effects of tourism, popular culture and information technology which are defining characteristics of the late twentieth century. Las Vegas, unlike the forum in Rome or the palace at Versailles, is not a monument to a past age, it is a rapidly growing city; one which can shed much light on the status and trajectory of architecture and urbanism in our own times. Here we will discuss the resort aspect of the city, which in spite of the recent development of industry, the university and other features of a 'real' city, still has a pivotal role.

SIGNS, SYMBOLS AND THE
DEVELOPMENT OF THE 'DUCK'

Arriving in 1968 by car on Route 91, the first thing that would have struck the visitor to Las

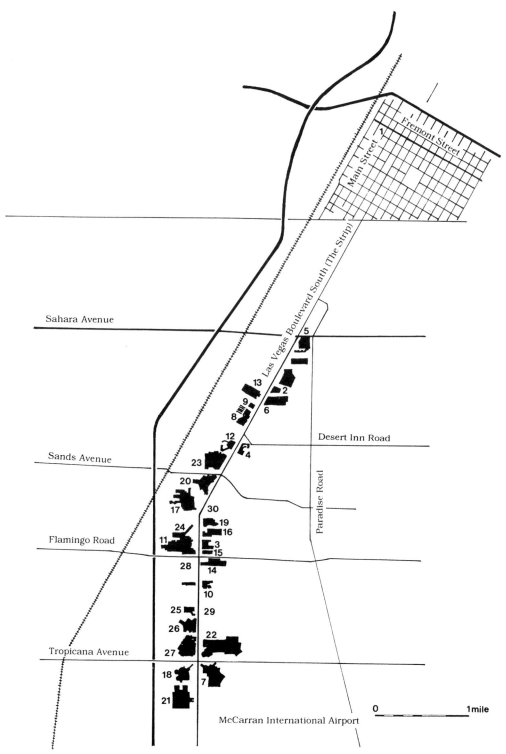

fig 4.1 Map of the resort area of Las Vegas.

Key:

1 Fremont St. (c. 1905)
2 El Rancho (1940)
3 Flamingo (1946)
4 Desert Inn (1950)
5 The Sahara (1952)
6 Riviera (1955)
7 Tropicana (1957)
8 Stardust (1958)
9 Westward Ho (1961)
10 Aladdin (1966)

11 Cesar's Palace (1966)
12 Frontier (1967)
13 Circus Circus (1968)
14 Bally's (1973)
15 Barbary Coast (1979)
16 Imperial Palace (1980)
17 Mirage (1989)
18 Excalibur, 1990
19 Harrahs (1990)
20 Treasure Island (1993)

21 The Luxor (1993)
22 MGM Grand (1993)
23 Fashion Show Mall (1995)
24 Forum Shops (1995)
25 Holiday Inn (1995)
26 Monte Carlo (1996)
27 New York New York (1997)
28 Bellagio (to open 1998)
29 Paris (to open 2000)
30 Venice (Sands) (to open 2000).

Vegas would have been the signs. Everywhere signs and billboards of the casinos, hotels, gas stations and wedding chapels, were witness not only to the persuasive power of advertising in consumer America but also to the fact that commercial art had replaced representational architecture as the primary language of its civic symbolism. This, of course, was in stark contrast to the canon of the Modernist orthodoxy which, reacting against nineteenth-century eclecticism, had rejected 'symbolism of form as an expression or reinforcement of content: meaning was to be communicated, not through allusion to previously known forms, but through the inherent, physiognomic characteristics of form'.[4] In Las Vegas one was confronted not by connotational architecture, heroically determined by program and structure alone, but by vast, 'debased' denotational signs attached to what were little more than 'decorated sheds'. This was not the habitat of the traditional monument, of the megastructure or the landmark edifice. Rather, just as the nearby Nellis Air Force base was the testing ground for the aircraft and continental nuclear weapons of the Cold War, Las Vegas itself was the testing ground for the hyper-modern art of the Young Electric Sign Company. As Tom Wolfe put it:

'Las Vegas takes what in other American towns is but a quixotic inflammation of the senses for some poor salary mule in the brief interval between the flagstone rambler and the automatic elevator downtown and magnifies it, foliates it, embellishes it into an institution.

For example, Las Vegas is the only town in the world whose skyline is made up neither of buildings, like New York, nor of trees, like Wilbraham, Massachusetts, but signs. One can look at Las Vegas from a mile away on route 91 and see no buildings, no trees, only signs. But such signs! They tower. They revolve, they oscillate, they soar in shapes before which the existing vocabulary of art history is helpless. I can only attempt to supply names — Boomerang Modern, Palette Curvilinear, Flash Gordon Ming-Alert Spiral, McDonald's Hamburger Parabola, Mint Casino Elliptical, Miami Beach Kidney'.[5]

In language that is demonstrative of the age of the car, the space race and of the unashamed belief in the 'white heat of the technological revolution',[6] Venturi and Scott-Brown explain this aspect of Las Vegas as the logical communication system of a new landscape; a landscape which is anti-spatial. As speed increases so space collapses. Orientation which was easy for a driver in the past was now made almost impossible due to the increased speed of the automobiles they were driving. The driver of the 1960s had no time to 'ponder paradoxical subtleties... he or she relies on signs for guidance — enormous signs in vast spaces at high speeds'.[7] The diagrams and photographs of the Strip produced by the Yale students were used to examine this phenomenon, and to demonstrate the layered stratification of a new typology that was its result: the building was set back from the road, obscured by the parked cars in the car park which was placed in front as:

'It is a symbol as well as a convenience. The building is low because air conditioning requires low spaces, and merchandising techniques discourage second floors; its architecture is neutral because it can hardly be seen from the road. Both merchandise and architecture are disconnected from the road. The big sign leaps to connect the driver to the store'.[8]

The modern equivalent of Versailles, it was argued that the asphalted car parks substituted for the herbaceous parterre, lamp posts for the garden statuary, and parked cars for the directional order of paving and manicured hedges.

'Symbol dominates space. Architecture is not enough. Because the spatial relationships are made by symbols more than by forms, architecture in this landscape becomes symbol in space rather than form in space. Architecture defines very little: the big sign and the little building is the rule of Route 66 ... Sometimes the building is the sign: the duck store in the shape of a duck, called "The Long Island Duckling" is sculptural symbol and architectural shelter'.[9]

Just as the pop artists of the time were taking the forms of consumer art as the cue for their work, in defiance of the orthodox Modernism of Clement Greenburg, so Venturi and Scott-Brown were instrumental in the process of dismantling the Modernist project in architecture which had, by starting from dissatisfaction with existing conditions often sought to dominate them. By taking popular culture as the site of their investigations in Las Vegas, the 'ugly and ordinary' was held above the 'heroic and original' as a new model for architects. Nevertheless, it is hardly surprising that after some twenty-five years it now fails to fully account for a city which has undergone many changes, both symbolic and superstructural. The 1970s saw the legalising of gambling in New Jersey, and Atlantic City became the centre of the industry there. Thousands on the east coast, who became familiarised with gambling, helped to make it seem a legitimate

fig. 4.2 Tourists visiting a 'Wild West' old town (photo: P. Davies).

recreation not unlike any other. This is a feature of Post-modernism, which dissolves cultural boundaries and acts to de-differentiate between them.

Not only does popular culture begin to inhabit high culture but the boundaries between once differentiated cultural activities become blurred: art, education, tourism, television, architecture, sport, and even gambling develop soft edges and merge into one another.[10] Once openly seen and represented as the home of organised crime and of dubious morality, the majority of large casino operations in Las Vegas are now run by 'cosy' multinational corporations like MGM and Holiday Inn, which may each own several different establishments. However, even today, as witnessed by the latest glut of movie releases, Hollywood remains reliant on shadier representations of Las Vegas like those portrayed in *Bugsy* (1991), *Honeymoon in Vegas* (1992), and in 1996 *Casino*, *Leaving Las Vegas*, and *Showgirls*. *Mars Attacks* (1997) has Las Vegas saving the world from marauding aliens! Since the late 1980s especially, Las Vegas has accommodated the changing tastes and requirements of its prospective visitors; the growth in tourism and air travel have made the city a respectable destination for a clientele drawn not only from the United States but from all parts of the world, and this has had a major influence on the forms and symbols that are put to the service of the hotel and casino owners in the city.

THE BIRTH OF THE 'OXYMONUMENT'

The construction boom apparent in Las Vegas since the late 1980s can be seen merely as the continuance of long line of similar flourishes that the city has undergone throughout this century. In its early days casinos and hotels were centred around Union Station, on Fremont Street in downtown Las Vegas. The symbolism of the architecture, reflecting expansion west of the Rocky Mountains and the localism of the station, was of the Wild West (fig. 4.2), the frontier and the cowboy, with resorts appearing with names like El Rancho, Last Frontier, and El Cortez. When the Strip, to the south of the city, came to be developed, the automobile dominated planning decisions, and as Venturi and Scott-Brown showed, the typology of the architecture accommodated this. Themes expanded, aided by films like *Casablanca*[11] coming out of Hollywood, and the romance of the desert location; with help from the advertising men Las Vegas lost its dependence on Western themes, and hotels began to use the symbolism of the Moorish desert (Desert Inn, Sahara, Sands, Dunes, Aladdin), glamourous Monte Carlo (The Riviera), the Caribbean (Tropicana) and even the Roman Villa (Caesar's Palace).

Typological change

What marks the new resort developments as different, however, is the scale of the operations involved and the typological change that has been caused by the need to reflect global tourism and its attendant growth in the number of visitors with diverse tastes. In the late 1960s massive spectacular signs stood in front of the resorts which were little more than humble 'sheds' accommodating casinos, showrooms and hotels. It was the sign that denoted the casino-ness of the buildings and attracted the car-driven visitor, not the buildings themselves. The majority of the new casinos on, or presently being built on, the Strip are vast megastructures which act as signs in themselves. Furthermore, being less dependant on the Strip as a feeder artery for the automobile and ever more on the shuttle buses and courtesy cars coming from McCarran airport, development has extended further south along Los Angeles Boulevard, and the typology of the buildings has changed again. They have become spectacular 'Magic Lands'[12] which rely on theme park attractions and their status as giant symbols in space to entice visitors into the casinos, which in themselves have changed little. Arriving at the airport one is struck by the Luxor pyramid (fig. 4.3) or the Manhattan skyline of New York New York, whereas one cannot see even the biggest signs that stand before the older casinos which remain locked into communication with the older technology of the automobile; given the momentum of change is not surprising that many of these have expansion plans of their own. Places with expansion programmes already underway are Cesar's Palace, the Sahara, Aladdin, Hilton, Bally's and Harrahs. At the beginning of 1997 the Sands was blown up to make way for a new resort complex that is to be themed as 'Venice'. 800,000 square feet of shopping (twice that of Cesar's Forum shops) will be negotiated using gondolas. As tourism becomes ever more global the developers in Las Vegas seem to be realising that shopping is a more sustainable activity than gambling. As with the Medici and their palaces, the power and omnipotence of the new Las Vegas moguls resides not only in the ponderous weight of marble but also in the ephemeral quality of the spectacle.

As Tom Wolfe had to resort to neologism to adequately describe the signs of Las Vegas in 1965, finding the vocabulary of art history helpless, so today, architectural terms like 'monument' and 'megastructure' are similarly unable to fully describe the new buildings that are appearing on the Strip. In order to deal with this problem of nomenclature I have developed the mnemonic 'oxymonument', from oxymoronic-monument, that attempts to define buildings which are paradoxically monumental, simultaneously massive and ephemeral.

Theming

The characteristics of the 'oxymonument' include the management of intimate experiences within vast environments, and the choice of finish and material related to speed of construction and phenomenal effect within a rubric of total theming: theming being the architectural response to consumer choice within the wide field of informational (as opposed to mechanical) technology. Conventional architectural criticism retreats into invective railing against the debasement of authentic symbolism in these new buildings, describing Luxor as 'a saggy prop possessing none of the terrifying mystery of the original',[13] and remains nostalgically ignorant of the fact that the anti-spatial 'placelessness' and themed literalism is reflective of the shift from 'hot' mechanical technology to 'cool' information. Whilst Venturi and Scott-Brown are equally bemused by the new Las Vegas, preferring to revisit Caesar's Palace for a BBC documentary in February 1995,[14] the theorists of the 'oxymonument' would include Umberto Eco, Guy Debord, Jean Baudrillard and Marshall McLuhan.

LUXOR: AN EPHEMERAL PLEASURE DOME

The Luxor (fig. 4. 3), when built in 1993, contained 2,500 rooms within a glass-clad pyramid of almost the same dimensions as its model: the Great Pyramid in Giza. Arrival is under a huge porte cochère in the shape of a sphinx, whose eyes light up at night and stare hypnotically towards visitors disembarking from their charter flights at McCarran airport. Valet parking and baggage handling is undertaken by staff dressed in Egyptian costume, their Nevada-tanned skin adding a flourish to one's entry into King Tut's casino empire. Inside, a 29 million square foot atrium in which nine Jumbo jets could stack (to continue the global theme), contains a hotel, casino, simulated village-scape (European in style) and a 'Back to the Future' theme park. The

fig. 4.3 The Luxor pyramid (1993), whose sphinx stares our towards the airport (photo: P. Grover).

diversions change from time to time: round the lower level on a simulated River Nile (with real water) *dhows* may float silently by, powered not by the wind, but by state-of-the-art hydraulics. During the trip one is given an introduction to the myriad attractions currently available within the kingdom, whilst jobbing musicians play on synthesizers. Two stuffed camels, which would not look out of place in a museum of natural history, graze in the foyer and engage in conversation with voices reminiscent of well known 'Loony Toon's characters. Above this, rising terraces of hotel rooms hang from all four sides of the pyramid and climb vertiginously towards its apex (fig. 4.4), a feat of audacious engineering in itself. Painted hieroglyphics, which remain untranslated, are 'carved' into hollow, replica sandstone lotus columns and temple walls of synthetic material. The casino itself is traditional: low-ceilinged like all casinos in Las Vegas, not primarily for air-conditioning but for security purposes, with the same generic slot machines and tables as everywhere else.

The only things which change between establishments are the ephemera: the patterns on the carpets, the Dixie buckets (for collecting dimes), the coloured baize and casino's logo on the gaming tables, and the generally minute costumes of the drinks hostesses. If the functional *raison d'être* remains constant, the method for attracting customers is increasingly frenetic. Above the gaming floor escalators rise to a higher level under the atrium, which is bisected through the centre by a seventy-five foot tall obelisk. Here shopping, eating and entertainment attractions abound. There are two themed rides 'In Search for the Mystery of the Pharaoh', variously priced restaurants, a virtual reality arcade, holographic displays and a museum containing the treasure of King Tutenkhamen's tomb. Whilst the exhibits here are replicas, on the basement level there is a merchandise store called 'The Source' where one can purchase, among other things, authentic ancient sarcophagi for around $40,000 a piece. In a bizarre inversion of London's British Museum, instead of viewing authentic artefacts, and buying plastic replica Rosetta Stone paperweights or gold-plated King Tut letter openers, in the shop here one views the simulated and buys the real thing. Or one did. The speed of change on the strip of Las Vegas affects not only the creation of new resorts, but also the rate of change to the interiors of existing ones. Returning in February 1997 one finds an almost complete overhaul has taken place on the inside of the Luxor. Gone is the replica Nile with its boats, the Source with its real artefacts, and the camels (although they were to be seen under wraps, perhaps awaiting

80

fig. 4.4 The Luxor interior in 1997, with dramatic Egyptian theming, the ubiquitous slot machines, and hotel rooms above (photo: P. Grover).

fig. 4.5 The MGM Grand with company logo as entrance foyer (photo: P. Grover).

installation at the entrance to the new pedestrian link to the resort's sister casino Excalibur. The changes put in place are very instructive. Entering into the foyer of the Luxor one is now faced with a more traditional entrance to a casino — the section of the building has been altered ensuing no troublesome changes in level from outside to inside. The upper level with the attractions is reached via the casino itself, which is a more traditional Las Vegan Architectural gesture. What seems to have happened at the Luxor is that it has come of age; it has matured. It also betrays a certain nervous conservatism. This is certainly no more apparent than in the design of the new extension to the north side of the pyramid. Gone is the pedantic application of fake authenticity of the original, it has been replaced by two rectilinear hotel blocks (albeit with a ground level themed after the temple of Karnak) that would not look out of place in any other metropolitan area of any other American city. Inside one notices that the carpet patterns have become more sober, and the hostesses uniform is below the knee. If fashion historians are right and lower hem-lines are associated with austerity, this may be one of the indications of what is being called a 'slumpette', but which more exactly is a 16% decrease in gaming revenues in 1996-97. Given this it is no wonder that one is led directly into the Casino.

fig. 4.6 Excalibur (1990), Disney inspired, hyperreal Arthurian castle (photo: P. Grover).

THE HYPER-REALITY OF SYMBOLISM IN A SPECTACULAR SOCIETY

Across the road, Excalibur (fig. 4.6), a Disney ins-pired version of an Arthurian castle, with gaudily coloured pinnacles, pearly-white escarpments and a laser-eyed Merlin above the portcullis, is no less of a spectacle. Its financial success, like that of its neighbours (Luxor paid for itself within three months of being opened), proves it to be no quixotic enterprise. In the basement two sittings of King Arthur's Banquet are held each evening with the added entertainment of knights fighting jousting tournaments (on real live chargers). In the castle's Winchester Chapel, couples can get married in chivalric surroundings to the accom-paniment of sedentary minstrels. Further along, the MGM Grand (fig. 4.5), whose three storey high trademark lion guards the entrance, used to house themes and attractions based on the Emer-ald City, now replaced by a more homogenised Hollywood theme; checking-in desk after the 1932 blockbuster Grand Hotel (Greta Garbo: 'I want to be alone'),[15] and an 'over the rainbow' styled casino.

Symbolism and meaning

Whilst obviously monumental in size these devel-opments call to be understood through different terms. Luxor is of a different order than its coun-terpart in Egypt; Excalibur is symbolic, but at the same time evasive of, those ancient buildings that form a resonant part of an American understand-ing of 'Olde Worlde England' (fig. 4.6). Prior to qualification the two evade direct comparison. 'Oxymonuments' are paradoxical in that their symbolism derives not from some authentic his-torical datum but from spectacular scenographic equivalents and theatrical techniques, Cinderella's castle at Disneyland or Disney's cartoon version of Robin Hood, for example. The referents for the MGM Grand occur historically only on cel-luloid. On the other hand, whilst New York New York's edifice is comprised of well known build-ings which actually exist in Manhattan, they are no less dependant for their symbolism on cinem-atic sources, from Woody Allen to *West Side Story*. Furthermore, the artifice of the concept designer is heroically employed to create a composite that is at once possible to read as how Manhattan should look but which refuses any dir-ect comparison to the real thing. This phenomena is what Umberto Eco described in *Travels in Hyper-Reality*:[16] the 'oxymonument' must seem completely real and authentic, whilst at the same time actually be more real than the original.

These environments approximate more closely to our imaginative expectations than those which they simulate; and in a world that is ever more

fig. 4.7 Tintagel Castle, Cornwall (13th cent.) according to Goeffrey of Monmouth the birth-place of King Arthur (photo: P. Grover).

dependant on the tourist's gaze it has been realised that it is economically unwise to ignore these expectations. Unlike Tintagel Castle in Cornwall (fig. 4.7), for example, presented (spuriously) to tourists as the home of King Arthur, and little more than a pile of crumbling stone and earth mounds, Excalibur is how the majority imagine it would have been. New York New York (fig. 4.8), built in only eighteen months at a cost of $270 million, utilises an 'external installation and finish system' that effortlessly replicates, at surface level, the Seagram Building, Lever House, the Whitney Museum, Grand Central Station, the Empire State and Chrysler Buildings, not to mention City Hall, Brooklyn Bridge and a half-scale Statue of Liberty. What you don't get here are the original's social problems and rampant crime. Disneyland shows that dreams can be made real, 'Disneyland tells us that faked nature corresponds much more to our daydream demands ... Disneyland tells us that technology can give us more reality than nature can'.[17] Here you get your money's worth; in real life, which is more and more difficult to disentangle from the touristic, traditional monuments and sites have become commonplace — and are less and less likely to excite the passion experienced by past

travellers. Bombarded by televisual, photographic and other media representations of the 'Wonders of the World' we are no longer innocents abroad, and are perhaps more likely to be found in the queue at Luxor to 'snap disposable cameras at ghostly holograms of Pharaohs',[18] than we are to be boarding a plane to Cairo. We seem to have become accustomed to consuming 'representations of representations of representations'. In these buildings one finds a most developed and complex example of Venturi and Scott-Brown's concept of the symbol in space: their paradoxical monumentality leads a shadowy existence behind the more 'concrete' structures of mythology, symbolism and spectacle; and they are definitely resistant to the Modernist ideal of form in space. Twenty-five years on and it is possible to see that Vegas has transformed from the 'American Dream' to the 'American Daydream'. This is the site of Debord's 'society of the spectacle' and of Baudrillard's 'simulacrum' par excellence. For, in Debord's terms, this is a looking glass world where a simulacrum (the spectacle) of real life is offered up in an effort to conceal the absence of real, authentic life:

'One cannot abstractly contrast the spectacle to actual social activity: such a division is

fig. 4.8 New York New York (1997) Nevada style, so good they built it twice (photo: P. Grover).

itself divided. The spectacle which inverts the real is in fact produced. Lived reality is materially invaded by the contemplation of the spectacle while simultaneously absorbing the spectacular order, giving it positive cohesiveness. Objective reality is present on both sides. Every notion fixed this way has no other basis than its passage into the opposite: reality rises up within the spectacle, and the spectacle is real. ... In a world which *really is topsy turvy*, the true is a moment of the false'.[19]

'ALL THAT IS SOLID MELTS INTO AIR'[20]

Styling, atmosphere and material finishing of the intimate experiences within the new 'oxymonuments' are no less affected by what has been described above. When Jay Sarno envisaged Caesar's Palace in 1965 he longed to build something grand and distinctive. Since Wild Western, African, Caribbean and European styles had already occupied the Strip, Sarno sought something unique: a Graeco-Roman Palace in the desert. To achieve a realistic look he imported tons of Italian marble and stone. Obsessed with the notion that oval design promoted relaxation, Sarno not only ordered an egg-shaped casino, but also repeated the elliptical theme throughout the resort's buildings and grounds. Roman fountains and statuary were lavished on the resort. It was an immediate sensation with its crescent-shaped fourteen storey tower of sumptuous rooms, 800 seat Circus Maximus Theatre (made to resemble the Coliseum) and 18 huge fountains which bordered the 135 foot driveway. The imported Italian Cypresses, the Florentine statuary and extravagant banquets in the Bacchineal Room all contributed to the scene. Whilst Caesar's Palace, set a new standard in Las Vegas for glamour and self-conscious styling, the buildings of the latest construction boom continue to reflect the shift away from mechanical to informational technology, from the architectural to the spectacular. Marshall McLuhan described this shift as being one which 'is more involving. It obliterates the distance between people. It is literally more "intimate" ... We are moving out of the age of the visual into the age of the aural and tactile'.[21]

Put into architectural terms, whereas Caesar's Palace spared no expense with the importing of authentic marble from Italy to achieve the right look, the massive weight of stone and marble have ephemeralised at Luxor into the lightness of tinted glass and plastic. Not only that but the moguls have realised that physical environment:

sound, smell, temperature, humidity and spectacle, are of equal importance, if not more important than the architecture. This is no more obvious than at the Mirage (fig. 4.9) built in 1989 by one of Las Vegas's latest success stories, Steve Wynn. It is may be relevant to note here that Wynn suffers from a debilitating condition of the eyes which renders him almost clinically blind. Visualisation for him must surely take on a different meaning than in a normally sighted person, and is perhaps why his resorts prioritise other senses that the visual. In the Mirage various things are at work to create a totally themed terrain of tactile imminency. The first is spectacular. In front of the entrance, in the place that was reserved in older times for the symbolically convenient car park, stands a large conical fake volcano overlooking a floodlit lake of azure blue (and chlorinated) water. Myriad natural sounds, bird and animal calls, emit from speakers cunningly hidden within unnatural rocks. Every twenty minutes, after dark, an initially gentle subterranean rumbling is followed soon after by dramatic explosions and gaseous flames that lick at the night air as the volcano comes to life. Lava begins to 'flow' down the mountain side and enters the lake with hissing steam and boiling water. It is a spectacle which never fails to draw the crowds who stand, faces warmed by the heat, handy-cams rolling, caught in the flickering light like so many bonfire night revellers. Owners of the older establishments across the road can only look on enviously as people make their way obliviously past the gently turning wheels of their once state-of-the-art Mississippi paddle-steamer (now dismantled), or the polite lines of their Imperial Japanese Palace.

The second distinguishing characteristic is atmospheric. Inside, the designers have created a rain forest world where it is possible both to learn, taking the nature trail past plastic and real exotic tropical plants and trees (with their botanic names), or to relax, sipping equally exotic cocktails in humid, tropical bars. The greenery, and moisture which are in abundance, just like the flames, heat and steam outside, serve to evaporate and dissolve the architecture: this is not so much a visual feast, a place to look at, but rather a tactile experience to enter and wallow in. As such, the Mirage seems to be an inspired choice of name.

Finishing everywhere is high quality, as it is almost everywhere in the new resorts; the attention paid to details such as the coiled rope-effect steel balustrades reveals the fact that this is no tacky 'end of the pier' establishment, as certain

fig. 4.9 The Mirage (1989) a terrain of totally themed tactile imminency (photo: P. Grover)

fig. 4.10 Treasure Island (1993) $70 million public street theatre and window dressing (photo: P. Grover).

critics would still have one believe. In fact the detailing reveals something further. In Las Vegas, glamour is democratic and involving; one can, indeed one is implored, to play and take on roles; the distance between the architecture and the person is obliterated and he or she takes centre stage in their very own theatrical performance. In this mode of thinking the placement of the Snow Tigers of Siegfried and Roy, conjuring entertainers of the casino's showroom, seems no less choreographed. The tigers are encountered (when they are not working) in a glass fronted enclosure directly outside the casino proper. Passing by these noble beasts or for that matter visiting the dolphins that perform in their humanely large pool, presumably has the desired effect of creating empathy in the hearts of customers, an eminently sensible aim for the casino owners.

It should, however, be well understood that this 'involvement' by the holiday makers, that is the customers, is clearly circumscribed and on the casino owners' terms: a customer wearing a costume or entering too enthusiastically into the spirit of the theme would be politely cautioned by security staff. This control is so global, that far from being obtrusive, it apparently makes the customer feel comfortable and secure: nothing challenging or untoward will mar his enjoyment,

or by extension the commercial success of the enterprise.

It may be argued that the all-encompassing pleasure palace is nothing new, but with Las Vegas, what is relatively new, at least on this scale is the democratisation (linked to commercialisation) on such a scale. All who wish to play by the rules are free to participate, an elderly widow in curlers is as welcome to put coins in a machine as a high-stake player to take his or her place at the table. Beggars or homeless people can not, however, slip in through the ever open doors. Psychological, social and physical barriers are as far as possible eliminated: the machines are immediately accessible, dress is run-of-the-mill casual (with 'exclusive' enclaves with dress codes), food and accommodation is plentiful and subsidised. Any negative reinforcement (losing money) is tempered by positive reinforcement, proportional to the sums dispensed by the customer, and palliatives such as luxurious suites and even free air flights for regular visitors and high rollers.

TREASURE ISLAND

Next door to the Mirage, Treasure Island (fig. 4.10), again by Wynne, operates in a similar manner to its neighbour. Built at a cost of over $300 million, it held a world record for occupancy, being sold out for 112 consecutive days when it opened. All the techniques of his earlier resorts are incorporated in the composition: spectacle, atmosphere, quality of detailing, and customer participation. 'Hoards of pirate treasure' from emporia in Morocco and similar places decorate the interior of the casino; caskets and chests spilling over with trinkets, jewels, chalices and the like cram the niches over the 'rafters'. Carved doors are placed blindly into walls, leading nowhere, but suggestive of state rooms and harems. The hotel rooms above are more restrained, but artifice is continued in the balcony balustrades made of plastic foam. At the foot of the bed stands a distressed wooden chest surmounted by brass maritime navigational equipment. It comes as only the briefest of surprises that, on touching a switch, a television rises out of it. The hotel's information booklet expounds on the twelve themed restaurants and bars from the 'sumptuous' Buccaneer Bay Club, or The Plank — an intimate 'pirate's library featuring seafood and mesquite grilled specialities, to the more utilitarian Swashbucklers bar in the casino'. At the front desk in the foyer, guests check into the hotel in an atmosphere air conditioned with coconut scent. Once again all the elements of the 'oxymonument' are present, creating a primarily phenomenal, rather than architectural magic-land.

The car park again makes way for spectacle as the front elevation takes the form of a pirate village overlooking 'Buccaneer Bay'. This can be seen merely as an enlargement of a grand mechanical Christmas display in a shop window, but it has another function in the context of Las Vegas; it makes the street part of the attraction, rather than only a means of access and circulation. Furthermore Treasure Island acquired the rights to the sidewalk outside the hotel from Clark County. This was a shrewd, and until then, unheard of arrangement, for it not only allows the presentation of street theatre, but also gives the owners the right to prevent employee's unions from picketing the entrance during any dispute with the management. Just north of Treasure Island, the Frontier has been picketed by the Teamsters for over two years with as yet no sign of there being a resolution.

With elaborate scenographic detail the Treasure Island display presents roughly plastered and weathered houses, with figurehead balconies and cargo-laden wooden quays, jostling together with live palm trees on a cliff, below which a 'full-size' pirate ship, the Hispaneola, lies at its moorings. The pavement on Los Angeles Boulevard is

in the form of a boardwalk auditorium from where, every hour and a half, the public are treated to a live sea battle. HMS Britannia sails into the bay where the pirates are busy unloading their lately won booty and after a mutual haranguing the English man-of-war opens fire. The result of the battle which ensues is never in doubt: playing to an audience predominantly comprised of members of a sympathetic host nation, the English, obviously representative of order, conservatism and blind colonialism are endlessly defeated by the lawless, freedom-loving pirates. The myth of the frontiersman is the same as it was in the early days of the century, only the costumes have changed; horses give way to men-of-war and stetsons to powdered periwigs.

FROM 'AUTOPIA' TO TRIBAL SHOPPING MALL

The fronts of these new resorts are as instructive as they are spectacular. They form a new order of architectural communication. In 1968, as Scott-Brown and Venturi explained[22], the automobile enjoyed predominant status: the Strip accommodated the U-turns necessary to a vehicular promenade for casino crawlers, and transitions from highway to parking. The Casino lights, through consistency of form and position and their arching shapes identified the continuous space of the highway. Immediate proximity of related uses, as on a street where you walk from one store to another, was not required along the Strip, and interaction by car and highway, even with adjacent establishments, was not considered disagreeable.

Today's Las Vegas, in an attempt to expand the base of its market, uses tourism as both cause and effect in its development. This is nowhere more apparent than on the Strip which represents what John Urry has described as the 'changing nature of public space in contemporary societies. An increasingly central role is being played by privately owned and controlled consumption spaces'.[23] The attractions which line the Strip, and which, aside from those mentioned include the new shopping malls and the themed Forum Shops at Caesar's Palace (fig. 4.11), have displaced the vehicular promenade with one that is by necessity pedestrian. The customer wanders between spectacles which prioritise and involve the pedestrian tourist in a modern form of street theatre, or strolls down a meandering ancient street, the sky-painted ceiling above lit variously as sunset, twilight or storm, between boutiques housed in copies of antique temples. In a manner well understood by McLuhan, the experience is intended to re-tribalise the visitor and transform the most

fig. 4.11 Entrance to the Forum shops at Cesar's Palace, hypereal basaar of the 1990s (photo: P. Grover).

modern of shopping malls into a hyper-real bazaar. People become flâneurs, gazing at myriad attractions and in turn being gazed upon. 'Their wandering footsteps, the modes of their crowd practice constitute that certain urban ambience: a continuous re-assertion of the rights and freedoms of the marketplace, the *communitas* of the carnival.[24] One feature of street furniture is, however, conspicuous by its absence in Las Vegas: seats. Those who wish to sit down may do so at the gaming machines inside.

People processing

For longer distances it is easier to take the various, and mostly free, forms of public transport that have recently been developed. Trams, streetcars and even monorail 'bullet trains'[25] are being experimented with all along the Strip, in an obvious attempt to fill even the void moments between casinos with spectacle and engaging exper-

iences. Cars parks are increasingly consigned out of sight to the rear of the buildings, because apart from being an uneconomic use of land if placed at the front, they have become symbolic merely of a mechanical culture rendered obsolete by the informational and touristic age. In addition, the infrastructure and services of the casinos and the expanding city are rigourously excluded from areas used by customers in the resort area, unifying the whole environment, and making it specialised, socially and economically.

RE-LEARNING FROM LAS VEGAS

Revisiting Las Vegas in the 1990s it is possible, as I have shown, to discern a new typology of building that is supplanting that which was identified by Venturi and Scott-Brown in 1968. This typology is typified by the 'oxymonument', which accommodates most, if not all of the following features. The 'oxymonument' is a vast, themed and symbolic development which constitutes a complete 'Magic Land' of itself and contains a variety of amenities not solely determined by its function. It will be spectacular, either of itself (Luxor) or via attractions that occur about it (Mirage, Treasure Island). The symbolism that is evoked will be hyper-real: through the use of technology and scenography the copy is made to seem more real than its referent (Excalibur). Architectural physicality will dissolve with what Marshall McLuhan saw as the shift from the visual age to the tactile age, into an environment that is intensely intimate and ephemeral: places to wallow in rather than look at (Mirage). Finally, the 'oxymonument' will tend to reflect changes to the nature of public space brought about by tourism, leading to a return to street life and theatre together with the pedestrian, rather than vehicular, promenade.

THE GLOBAL MODEL VILLAGE

The current building boom in Las Vegas seems destined to continue. Not only is New York New York complete, but it is soon to be joined by resorts that will add a further 8,000 hotel rooms in the city. Las Vegas seems to be undergoing a further transformation. This time turning into nothing less than a model village of gigantic proportions. People stroll, 'gazing at the signs of different cultures. People can do in an afternoon what otherwise takes a lifetime: gaze upon and collect signs of dozens of different cultures — the built environment, cultural artefacts, meals, and live, ethnic entertainment'.[26] Already one can

fig. 4.12 Paris — Nevada (photo: P. Grover).

visit England (albeit King Arthur's England), Egypt (albeit the Pharaoh's Egypt), Monte Carlo, Ancient Rome, New York, 1920's Louisiana, an 18th century desert island, a tropical Caribbean resort, a Japanese palace, and a handful of Moorish paradises. There are even plans ahead for a casino with a Parisian theme (fig. 4.12), presumably with scaled-down Arc de Triomphe and Eiffel Tower white-knuckle ride. The promotional billboard seems to prophesy, perhaps rightly, that when it's finished there will be no need to visit the original, 'until then take Concord'.

The ephemerality of the effects produced has been mentioned; the actual structures are, it seems, of similarly limited consideration to the owners. Their function is to produce the required spectacular effect, but like a light-show they can go out — sometimes with a bang, like the Hacienda and the Sands, dynamited for New Year, 1997 — when another setting is favoured.

Whilst Las Vegas may seem distant from Europe, the dramatic changes that are brought about by Post-modernism, and information technology the world over, serve to dissolve the borders between once distinct cultural activities: between work and recreation, education and entertainment, high and low culture. Tourist sites around the world, are self-consciously reflexive of the demands of consumer choice. The sites themselves are not enough. Most these days are likely to have visitor centres, souvenir shops and a whole range of auxiliary amenities. Furthermore, as witnessed by the changes to museums and other once purely educational institutions, this occurs not only at sites of traditional tourist activity. Architects have tended to ignore Las Vegas and tourism alike, regarding them both with a pious form of conservatism that chooses not to analyse them on the basis of their architectural communication, but on the basis of their morality. And yet, the same people would be happy to analyse the structure of a Gothic cathedral without getting involved in the moral issues of mediaeval religion and Church patronage. This seems to be a short-sighted approach given that the near endemic nature of tourism will almost certainly require architects and urbanists to gain new skills and understanding to be able to handle it satisfactorily in the future. The incandescent volcano at the Mirage may seem to be a world away, but its seismic convulsions are sending ever larger ripples across the Atlantic.

Paul Grover
South Bank University

NOTES

1 Studio Introduction at Yale School of Art and Architecture; Robert Venturi & Denise Scott-Brown, 1968.

2 Robert Venturi, Denise Scott-Brown and Steven Izenour, *Learning From Las Vegas*, (MIT Press) Cambridge Mass., 1972, 3.

3 Ibid.

4 Ibid., 7.

5 Tom Wolfe, 'Las Vegas (What?) Las Vegas (Can't Hear You! Too Noisy) Las Vegas!!!!', *The Kandy-Koloured Tangerine-Flake Streamline Baby*, (Picador) London, 1981, 20.

6 A phrase used by the Prime Minister of Britain, Harold Wilson, in a speech given at the 1963 Labour Party Conference.

7 Venturi, Scott-Brown and Izenour, *Learning From Las Vegas*, 1972, 9.

8 Ibid., 9.

9 Ibid., 13.

10 For further reference see John Urry, *The Tourist Gaze*, (Sage Publications) London, 1990, chapter 5.

11 *Casablanca* won three Oscars in 1943, and was an obvious choice for romantic resort theming.

12 See: John Findlay, *Magic Lands*, (University of California Press), 1992.

13 M. Newman, 'The Strip Meets Flaming Volcano', in *Progressive Architecture*, February 1995.

14 *Viva Las Vegas*, BBC2, February 1995.

15 MGM shrewdly marketed this film by withholding its general release for many months after its Hollywood premiere, and allowing a tremendous word-of-mouth campaign to heighten expectation from viewers and critics alike. Made at a cost of $695,341.20, *Grand Hotel* took in $2,594,000 in its first year of release and won the Oscar for Best Picture, 1931-32.

16 Umberto Eco, *Travels in Hyper-Reality*, (Picador) London, 1986.

17 Ibid., 44.

18 M. Newman, *Progressive Architecture*, February 1995.

19 Guy Debord, *Society of the Spectacle*, (Rebel Press) London, citations 8 & 9.

20 Taken from Karl Marx and Friedrich Engels, *Communist Manifesto*, 1848 and the title of a book by Marshall Berman, London: Verso, 1982.

21 Marshall McLuhan, quoted by Tom Wolfe, 'What If He Is Right?', *The Pump House Gang*, (Black Swan) London, 1989, 136.

22 Venturi, Scott-Brown and Izenour, *Learning From Las Vegas*, 1972, 20

23 Urry, *The Tourist Gaze*, 1990, 149

24 R. Shields, 'Social Spatialization and the Built Environment: the West Edmonton Mall', *Environment and Planning Design: Society and Space*, 7, 1989, 161.

25 These trains, which travel for example between Ballys and the MGM Grand, have plastic body shells and travel at speeds approaching twenty miles per hour.

26 Urry, *The Tourist Gaze*, 1990, 153.

Urban Design Studies, Volume 3, 1997

THE NATURE AND ROLE OF NEIGHBOURHOODS

AMOS RAPOPORT

With the approach of the new millenium the continuing discussion and research regarding the survival, nature and importance of neighbourhoods in contemporary and future urban areas is intensifying, and the future of cities, among other topics such as housing, technology and lifestyle, is increasingly under scrutiny. In such discussions the future of neighbourhoods plays an important (if sometimes implicit) role. It thus seems an opportune time to carry out a further review and synthesis of this topic in the light of work carried out in the last twenty years since the present author's earlier assessment in *Human Aspects of Urban Form,*[1] taking as a starting point the hypothesis that neighbourhoods no longer matter.

THE VIEW THAT NEIGHBOURHOODS NO LONGER MATTER

Suggestions that the role, importance and the very existence of neighbourhoods in modern cities needs to be questioned appear as early as the work of the Chicago School of Urban Ecology in the 1920's and 1930's,[2] and more specifically to the early 1960's when two influential papers of Webber's appeared[3] questioning the continuing relevance of neighbourhoods as spatial units whereby their inhabitants establish social links on the basis of propinquity. It was argued that in modern cities such links are being replaced by extensive networks based on common interests, the so called 'non-place realm' leading to 'community without propinquity'.

This line of argument emphasises the impact on social space of increased physical mobility and greater, improved, and ever more accessible communication technologies and has been taken up by a number of researchers,[4] the underlying theme being that communities based on locality, propinquity and geography become unimportant, and are being replaced by interest-based communities which are not defined territorially. Location matters little and neighbourhood less.

Contacts are non-localised, resembling networks linking people of like interests wherever they live.

These phenomena are also related to the decline of public space and 'the fall of public man'.[5] It could, alternatively, be argued that the privatisation of life may represent *choices* people are now able to make[6] rather than the results of technology which do not, in fact, determine urban form. In Gottmann's 'transactional city'[7] new technologies and the service function of cities do not lead inevitably to the disappearance of compact cities, nor make them obsolete. It depends on choice — and this also applies to neighbourhoods.

This is a result of the importance of latent functions which cities, neighbourhoods and housing fulfil, functions which also depend on restaurants, golf clubs, theaters, and which Gottmann[8] has pointed out, are not only important for transactional business, but are locality-specific. This has implications for the 'non-place realm' generally, and indirectly for the neighbourhood. Also important is the environmental quality of the 'hosting environment' of such quaternary services.

Even more striking is another effect of the new communication technologies. While making it easier to work at home and leading to the growth of such work, it has had effects opposite to those predicted in that the immediate community environment becomes more important,[9] with home workers using neighbourhood services more (increasing the 'neighbourhood quotient' as will be discussed below)[10] and requiring that the nature and environmental quality of the surroundings communicate meanings (another latent function) to clients, customers and others.

The argument about the disappearance of neighbourhoods was never fully convincing. Firstly, people whose links are to a world-wide community of interest rather than to neighbours, those living nearby, seemed to be a rather small minority, characterised perhaps by academics and intellectuals generalizing from their own, possibly limited and atypical way of life, which seemed different to that of many, or most, people whose lives continued to be much more localised and spatially circumscribed. Secondly, these analysts themselves seemed acutely concerned with where they lived — both at the large and small scale, being found in high concentrations in certain urban areas around the world and hardly at all in others. Their networks thus can be seen to coincide with circumscribed geographical areas, in clusters within certain limited and defined localities. While explicit studies of the location of such commentators are lacking, other than some of the marketing analyses of lifestyle clusters to be discussed later and one student paper,[11] informal observations of the place of residence of academics in urban areas in a variety of countries suggests that the areas they inhabit have certain clear locational, physical and social attributes: they are neighbourhoods, in the sense of being areas of specific ambience, and represent choices based on values and ideals.

Thirdly, these very people tend to be active in defending *their* neighbourhoods against demolition, development, freeways, tree-cutting and the like. This type of political and physical defense — for example lying down in front of bulldozers, indicates strong attachments to specific localities, and is also demonstrated by less mobile people, whose movements may be more circumscribed and who depend on locality, family, friends, near neighbours, and local institutions and services, and who are, in a word, highly dependent on social networks,[12] which in turn, are influenced by the nature and forms of neighbourhoods.[13] As has been observed by Olson,[14] neighbourhoods continue to persist in spite of changes in social, economic, ecological, technological, and one might add, lifestyle conditions and circumstances. Local communities selectively incorporate and adapt these new conditions and contexts,[15] thus making the survival of neighbourhoods possible.

The concept of the importance of neighbourhoods thus seems likely to persist, and it has continued to be a subject of discussion in the popular media, and of study and scholarly research, as is indicated by the sheer amount of literature, a sample of which is noted or reviewed here. The discussion can be explicitly about neighbourhoods,[16] or implicit, as in the case of work which implies clustering and enclaves.[17] Before dealing with this further, however, we need to define the nature of 'neighbourhood.'

THE NATURE OF NEIGHBOURHOOD

What actually constitutes a neighbourhood is frequently taken for granted or is implicit, at best being defined arbitrarily and normatively, as in planners' 'Neighbourhood Units of the Modern Movement'.[18] These units, as adopted for some English and other New Towns, were defined in terms of population (between 6,000 and 10,000 people) and centred on a school, but never seemed to work. They were rarely accepted by residents, tended to be vague, and were later transformed in various ways and only then popularly recognised.[19] Why these units did not work became gradually clear in the 1970's.

Systems of settings

Primarily people live in what may be called *systems of settings* in which their activity systems occur. These link the dwelling with many other settings in the urban, and even larger, milieu. Certain critical activity systems may take place in different parts of the system of settings, at distinct times, be linked or separated in particular ways, and include or exclude various people. These systems cannot be assumed *a priori*, are not at all self-evident or obvious, and may be counter-intuitive. They need to be discovered in any given case. Also, what happens in one part of the system influences what does or does not happen, in others. People thus use many settings in houses, other buildings, streets, parks and so on, the question being who does what, where, when, including or excluding whom — and why. The answers vary for given groups in terms of their lifestyles, and hence, culture.[20]

Sub-systems

One sub-system is the neighbourhood, intermediate in scale between the individual and his dwelling on one hand, and the city, metropolis or megalopolis on the other. The neighbourhood is similar in that sense to other intermediate social units which mediate between the individual and the state — family, kinship groups, interest groups of all sorts, parties, ethnic groups, unions, clubs, and religions, which have been called variously 'intermediate organizations', 'mediating structures' or 'mediating institutions'. American sociologists such as Peter Berger and Robert Nisbet have emphasised the social aspects, at best implicitly including social aspects of neighbourhood, but these concepts also apply spatially, as those units intermediate in scale between the individual and the larger urban realm, and may play an important, indeed critical, role in supporting the relevant intermediate social units.[21]

An important change in the understanding of neighbourhood, and why neighbourhood units had not worked, began in the late 1960's with T. R. Lee's paper,[22] which emphasised the importance of the subjective, cognitive definition of neighbourhood, the neighbourhood that exists in people's minds and with which they identify. This effectively revolutionised the definition of neighbourhood and led to a significant body of findings which are still not given the attention they deserve. In a review of findings then available[23] it was shown that the urban units called 'neighbourhoods' tend to be defined in terms of area, not population; are significantly smaller than the traditional planners' neighbourhood unit; that the definition of boundaries plays a major role and is influenced by social and physical aspects.

Size of neighbourhoods and micro-neighbourhoods

The variation in neighbourhoods appeared to depend on these subjective definitions. Thus, in general, it appeared that such neighbourhoods in the USA were larger than in the UK, due, in part, to lower densities, greater mobility and use of cars leading to more extensive networks. Since these, and other cultural attributes characterise groups as much as, or more than, countries and regions, one finds that in each place different groups define neighbourhoods of very different sizes, from a few blocks to many hundreds of acres, from one street to 25 or more. This depends on the type of population, the density or intensity of social networks, and how local facilities are used (what Lee called 'the neighbourhood quotient'), factors which still apply 15 years later. Given such cognitive, subjective definition, 'neighbourhood' remains an elastic concept that can range from being a small section of a subdivision to a whole subdivision (or even more than one).[24] However, it was striking then, and remains so, that a size of between 100-200 acres is commonly found. Moreover, part of the size difference is also due to the distinction between a neighbourhood and a micro-neighbourhood, which is typically very small in the US, often just one block, or what one can see from one's front door.

Home ground

In addition to micro-neighbourhoods within the neighbourhood, Stanton proposed the concept of home ground,[25] the area which evokes a feeling of being near one's dwelling. Home grounds can take on eight different forms related to 'experiential networks'. These tend to be linear rather than spatial, and are related to streets, routes and the like. Stanton does not, however, suggest that home grounds supersede neighbourhoods. In fact, the majority of residents thought even of experiential networks as having continuous boundaries. Thus, home grounds are a useful addition to the subjectively defined neighbourhood rather than a replacement.

If this concept is valid, then it is possible that what we are seeing as being perpetuated and reinforced are, in many cases, home grounds — at least for significant portions of the population. In other words, 'neighbourhood' is a familiar area which makes one feel close to one's dwelling, without necessarily involving social variables and only partly affective ones. Should that be the case, it might help resolve many of the arguments about 'neighbourhood' which implicitly assume the importance of neighbouring and other social links in defining that concept, and hence assume that as these weaken or even disappear,[26] so does the need for neighbourhoods as areas intermediate in scale.

On the other hand, the nature of the population and the many variables subsumed by its lifestyles, and also social homogeneity, remain important. Thus Varady[27] argues that both neighbourhood decline and upgrading depend on changes in social variables, such as race and class, and on shifts in such populations and their lifestyles — perhaps the best predictor.[28] This further confirms Lee's[29] initial insight on the centrality of the socio-spatial schema. This involves not only 'experiential networks', but social and cultural aspects, together with activity systems and physical aspects such as house forms and styles, vegetation, and levels of maintenance.[30] The unit of analysis for these studies, however, remains the 'neighbourhood.' Thus, for example, Haney and Knowles[31] emphasise that urban areas are made up of a mosaic of neighbourhoods (local communities) with clear boundaries and high levels of identity. These are defined subjectively by residents, with considerable degrees of agreement, usually showing a variation according whether located in an inner city, outer city or suburb, tending to be larger in the suburbs.[32]

Baltimore

In the case of Baltimore, Sauer[33] points out that the city has many distinct neighbourhoods.[34] He had been asked by the city for a design to 'create a neighbourhood', and used that concept for analysis and also design. He shows an implicit agreement with Lee that neighbourhood is a social as well as a spatial reality, an area with limits clearly recognised by its inhabitants, and with which they identify. Within such areas the various formal and informal interactions which take place, and the residents' regular use of neighbourhood services reinforce residents' awareness of the neighbourhood image as part of their identity, leading to a complex interaction between social and physical variables which could be described as a 'socio-spatial schema'.[35] Sauer also describes the design decisions taken to achieve the goal of 'creating a new neighbourhood.' No specific evaluation to determine the success or otherwise of the scheme has yet been carried out, but would be likely to furnish useful guide lines for future projects.

From the designers' point of view, the 'creation' or reinforcement of neighbourhood involves not only understanding the sizes of such units, their functions, and the types of social homogeneity necessary, but also knowing which physical cues, elements, attributes, and which levels of redundancy of these clues are most effective to produce agreed upon and clear boundaries.[36]

THE MEANING OF NEIGHBOURHOOD

The emphasis on the subjective definition of neighbourhood does not mean that this definition is purely mental, although Rich's title *Neighbourhood — a State of Mind* puts forward this proposition.[37] Wohlwill,[38] on the other hand argues that 'the environment is not in the head'. As a compromise one might suggest that the environment is not only in the head, as what is there depends also on the various social, cultural and physical attributes of the environment 'out there.'

The meanings behind the subjectively defined neighbourhood could be categorised as follows:
1. Just the dwelling, the area around it being merely a matter of convenience (this might be the case with people without children, or with extensive networks based on community of interest); it may also be an area with which one is most familiar, which evokes a feeling of being near one's dwelling.
2. An area immediately around the dwelling, communicating identity and hence symbolizing status.
3. A set of people, either liked or disliked, but forming the immediate social environment.
4. Some ideal, such as a village-like or small town community with face-to-face associations and intimate relationships, or related to ideal central city area, such as Bloomsbury or Chelsea in London, or Greenwich Village or SoHo in New York.[39]
5. A named area, widely known and accepted.
6. An area based on services and the people who run and provide them.
7. A distinctive physical area, separated from other areas by clear physical and conceptual boundaries, which depend on differences in block layout, street type, greenery or location, creating a specific cultural landscape and ambience.[40]
8. An area of people subjectively homogeneous by some particular attributes, such as ethnicity, religion, lifestyle, or ideology, and reinforced by activity patterns and social networks. This homogeneity may become perceptible not only through the population, but through a variety of consistent cues creating a specific ambience.[41]

In all these cases, however, neighbourhoods are what Lee called socio-spatial schemata, and can acquire particular positive or negative reputations, and specific names which have an important role in establishing neighbourhood identity, and also serve as marketing tools.[42] Blake and Arreola[43] define 'identity' as a subjective meaning projected by a distinctive combination of name themes or landscape characteristics, or both. Identity also implies belonging to a particular group and includes feelings of attachment — all attributes of 'neighbourhood' as socio-spatial schema. It is also the case that names trickle down from upper to middle-class areas and vary with time, as do other elements that help to establish identity, such as landscape features. In lower priced areas personal features were seen to be more important in establishing identity whereas institutional features apparently play a larger role in higher-priced areas.[44] Finally, neighbourhoods also vary by location, income, race, ethnicity and other such variables which are all reflected in *lifestyle*.

A recent example in Milwaukee,[45] highlights the relationship between names and status. According to the system widely used in the US of naming downtown streets by number, (with intersecting streets designated A Street, B Street etc) the name North 26th Street implied that the inhabitants lived in the inner city, rather than the suburb of Glendale, Wisconsin. Residents had the name of the street changed to Braeburn Lane. Names were also found to convey status in London and Sydney[46] and also in Rome, where the knowledge of names was much more precise than that of boundaries (reflecting their neglect), and it was found that these names did not correspond to the official ones,[47] that is they were subjectively defined.

Physical and social definitions

The eight possible meanings of 'neighbourhood' discussed above fall into two major classes — physical and social — and neighbourhoods are most clearly defined when social and physical space coincide, such as when physical boundaries, social networks, homogeneity, local services and facilities, and symbolic as well as emotional connotations overlap and are congruent. Thus all of these, and many other 'meanings of neighbourhood', have some 'truth' to them. Given that the subjective definition is crucial, it is clearest and strongest when all variables coincide, providing maximum redundancy. It can further be suggested that, the subjective definition of neighbourhood depends on three types of variables: **social**, comprising a variety of more specific social aspects such as levels of interaction and support, control, networks and lifestyle; **affective**, involving a variety of affective reactions and relations with both an area and a group of people; **cognitive**, involving mental mapping, perceptible environmental cues of sufficient redundancy, image, meanings, and name.[48]

In general, then, neighbourhood as subjectively defined is a cognitive construct, a **sociospatial schema**, altogether a combination of social and spatial factors, reinforced by name, symbolic elements and so on. Thus an agreed upon, clearly defined distinctive area needs at least three elements: distinct boundaries and physical character, comprehensible cues and symbols; some form of subjectively defined homogeneity with agreed upon use of streets and other settings; together with some name, image and/or identity which people can accept and with which they can identify.[49]

The role of social interaction

It is traditionally assumed that neighbourhood involves neighbouring which, in turn, involves social interaction and attachment (affective interaction) with people and area. What is added is the cognitive component involving redundant physical cues which help define neighbourhood subjectively. There is an additional complicating factor: the subjective definition of neighbourhood probably varies for insiders (residents) and outsiders (other urban residents, visitors, tourists). Evaluations of environmental quality also vary,

and may even be more variable.[50] Since ideally one needs agreement about social (and physical) boundaries between insiders and outsiders[51] this raises a new set of issues. The appropriate response for reinforcing the separateness of the neighbourhood would seem to be to pin-point these differences and what causes them, use the strongest, clearest cues from the repertoire available, and apply the highest possible levels of redundancy.

The greater the congruence among the various attributes that enter into the schema the more is agreement likely about the existence of a neighbourhood, its extent or its boundaries. These aspects have perhaps not been given the necessary weight by Lee[52] or much subsequent research. The strength, clarity and sharpness (or fuzziness) of boundaries vary depending on a large set of attributes, as can be seen in the case of Mexico City, New York, Sydney (Australia) and other places.[53] These arguments, based on general considerations, have since received at least some empirical support. For example, Sims[54] examines the case of Columbus, Ohio, and provides much data on which of the boundary cues are important in themselves (depending on how strong and clear they are), and also emphasises the importance of redundancy. He found that residents used a number of physical edge and path features cognitively to differentiate their neighbourhood from other areas. Elements most frequently noted were streets, express-ways, railway lines and streams, but other attributes also came within that framework, such as noticeable differences like the quality and style of houses, levels of maintenance, changes in land use and use patterns, types of people, vegetation, street layout and activities.[55] Redundancy among these cues is also very important.

Given that the repertoire of potential cues is large[56] it follows that designers can look to environment behaviour research to make the subjective definition of neighbourhood among residents both easier and more consistent. Congruence among natural, physical and social characteristics can be expected to give boundaries that will tend to be clear rather than fuzzy, or gradients. Maximum redundancy among the full repertoire of potential cues will mean that the maximum number of people will agree, so that individual definitions will aggregate into group definitions. While such definition will be probabilistic rather than absolute, the higher the level of agreement the clearer the definition of neighbourhood will be. Sims notes that the results of subjective neighbourhood definition (although in

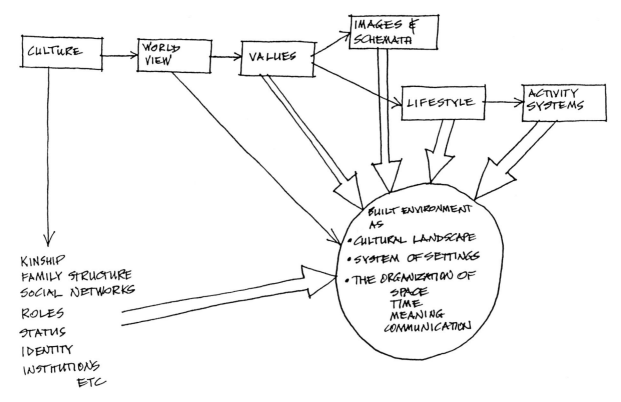

fig. 5.1 Relating expressions of culture to the built environment (width of arrows approximates feasibility and ease of relating the various elements).

an aggregated form) were used in the case of a detailed report by the Department of City Development of Columbus, Ohio in 1973.[57]

Further empirical support comes from a study by Frick[58] of the St. Martin *quartier* of Paris. The study not only finds that the boundaries and extent of this neighbourhood are subjectively defined, but also that the attributes used in this subjective definition are very similar to those suggested on general grounds, and found elsewhere.[59] Moreover, Frick, also emphasises the importance of the neighbourhood to the quality of life (based on an environmental quality profile).[60] In fact, it becomes clear from the recent literature that housing satisfaction depends not only on the dwelling itself, but on the adjoining open spaces (the lot, garden, the nature of common open spaces and the neighbourhood). This is found in many different cultures, an example being low-income public housing in Yemen.[61]

In Belize City[62] it was also found that neighbourhoods are subjectively defined. Upper income areas had the most clearly defined boundaries, reinforced by private security guards or spatial separation.[63] Unlike in other cities, in Belize ethnic minorities do not cluster, demonstrating the cultural specificity of such phenomena. The study also points out the clarity of 'the figure' of one's own neighbourhood as against the

vagueness or lack of knowledge of 'the ground' of the remainder of the city. In Belize, the social geography is based on a combination of age, gender, ethnicity, class and occupation which can described by *lifestyle*.[64] In fact, lifestyle, and its resultant activity systems, and other social variables provide essential data for relating built environments to 'culture' (fig. 5.1).

Ethnic enclaves

In other places lifestyle does correlate with ethnicity, and ethnic enclaves are common. For example, in U.S. cities names like Little Italy, Little Havana, Chinatown and, more recently, Koreatown, Little Taipei and Little Saigon, clearly indicate their distinct identity.[65] Although such enclaves are rarely 100% homogeneous, the dominant groups, through changes, personalisation, use of space and colour, as well as activities, give these areas a noticeable ambience,[66] especially along arterials with specific shops and institutions.[67] This involves the visibility of those attributes, and the frequency with which they are seen: thus the extent of activity systems and home ranges, routes, and modes of transport have an impact and also help explain differences between insiders' and outsiders' definitions, which typically vary, the former being more influenced by social networks, local service activity and usage. However, housing areas also play a role.[68] This ambience varies in different cultures and locales[69] changing as one group replaces another, such as Chinese replacing Italians in Lower Manhattan.[70] These specific ambiences in turn help in the subjective definition of areas through differences in the hundreds of attributes in different sensory modalities.[71] They add to the redundancy that makes neighbourhood definition easier and more consistent — in effect neighbourhoods become small urban regions[72] The more these attributes coincide, the clearer the character or ambience becomes and the clearer the changes where one area ends and another begins — and hence the boundaries.

The number and range of possible attributes is immense: this makes planners' and designers' tasks easier in the creation of neighbourhoods, since they can use various components and combinations of this large repertoire to produce varied ambiences or clear boundaries, and use names (especially traditional, well-known ones) effectively, tying them in with administrative boundaries, school and service districts.

Once again, with greater congruence and redundancy, greater agreement is possible. Although insiders' definitions are primary, there also needs to be agreement with outsiders that a neighbourhood exists, that it is acceptable, on the extent of 'ownership' and the rules that apply, as well as about its borders by analogy with ethnic groups and boundaries.[73] While the general characteristics provides a palette, or repertoire, the specifics will vary for different places, times and groups.

Change in environmental quality

The above discussion reinforces the point made elsewhere that neighbourhoods need to be studied cross-culturally and over time.[74] The nature of neighbourhoods, their significance and importance, their relationship to various groups, and evaluations of their environmental quality have all varied cross-culturally (over space) and over time (even in the same place), occasionally even experiencing reversals. One recent study[75] points out that in Kyoto during the classical period (ancient Heiankyo), the many quarters into which the city was divided were enclosed, and shunned exterior space. Streets were seen as ambiguous and often dangerous space, evaluated negatively and avoided. During the medieval period, on the contrary, these quarters opened up to the streets which were evaluated positively and became the

settings for daily and social life, with many activities taking place in them, including festivals and parades which were popular among all social groups. The life of the quarters was organised around the streets.

This can be interpreted in two ways. The enclosed quarters had become less the setting for daily life, and, through the use of streets life became more widespread, using more of the city. This leads to the second interpretation — that systems of activities and the systems of settings within which they occurred also changed.[76]

The role of advertising

Location is of course crucial in real estate marketing,[77] and advertisements, as well as novels, films, and TV are useful background sources for environmental design research.[78] The detective novel *Flesh Wounds*,[79] for example, reflects the concerns under discussion when the author writes 'Seattle is divided into neighbourhoods, I discovered, each with its own name, boundary, commercial core and socio-economic stamp. Fremont was hippies....' While this kind of division may apply to many cities, in the case of Seattle the increasing importance of neighbourhood has been confirmed by Guest's study[80] which analysed real-estate advertisements. It confirmed the importance of community names and showed that such areas and their identity were not in decline but were increasing — especially in high-status areas,[81] and reiterated that such neighbourhoods tend to be *small*, so that there is a need for subdividing census tracts to reflect this characteristic.

THE CONTINUING AND GROWING IMPORTANCE OF NEIGHBOURHOOD

While one cannot generalise for 'people' as a whole, neighbourhood as a concept appears to be group-specific, depending on the values, preferences, resources, ways of life, and culture expressed through lifestyle of a particular group. People's needs and wants generally, and certainly regarding their dwelling places and their environmental quality, are diverse.[82] In studies dealing with housing, location in rural areas, small towns, suburbs or large cities, migration, consumption patterns, marketing and advertising, the populations are commonly segmented in increasingly numerous and diverse ways. Extensive ranges of alternatives may be available to groups of migrants to given countries, people in countries, regions and urban areas, and consumers, but the

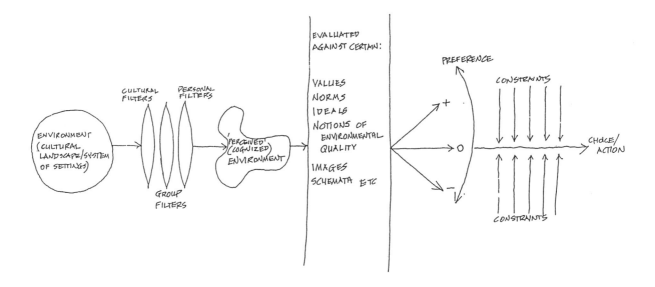

fig. 5.2 Environment and choice.

basis for the choices they make is different.[83]

Choice, in the form of *habitat selection*, plays a primary role. People match desired attributes of dwelling, external spaces, locations, neighbourhoods, cities, regions and social aspects against values and norms as incorporated in ideal images of people, the life they lead, and their settings (fig. 5.2).

These ideals can be expressed as environmental quality profiles comprising physical, social and other variables,[84] which may be not only of specific neighbourhoods or cities, but of settlement types, such as large cities, suburbs or small towns[85] or of neighbourhood types.[86]

New technologies and job diversification have made possible a search for safety, combined with certain physical and social aspects of environmental quality leading to a trend (at least in the U.S.) towards a return to small towns, especially those reasonably accessible to larger centres.[87] In many ways a small town is similar to a 'traditional' neighbourhood, and is one of the ideal neighbourhood types described by Brower.[88] The relationship between such clusters of habitation can be diagramed (fig. 5.3) as follows.[89]

Continuity

A result of this matching and choice is that different groups finish up living in areas with particular characteristics. Even under conditions of high mobility, such areas often remain stable — those leaving and entering were very similar in background. People thus tend to continue to cluster with others like themselves, so that the existence of areas of different character con-

tinues, and there are even suggestions, to be discussed below, that such clustering is becoming more important. Such areas develop not only in new towns,[90] but also in suburbs. Thus, Abrahamson[91] examines a number of socio-economic, ethnic, racial and religious groups: elites in Beacon Hill, Boston; 'Back of the yards' and other working-class areas in Chicago; African-American enclaves in Detroit; Little Taipei in Monterey Park (near Los Angeles); Chinatown in San Francisco; male homosexuals in the Castro district of San Francisco and female homosexuals in the Mission area of San Francisco; Little Havana in Miami; and Hasidim in Brooklyn, N.Y. The present author has also considered some of these groups[92] and one could add to the list.[93] The residents of these enclaves are united by ethnic, lifestyle and/or economic attributes and come to be associated with a specific locale, which in turn acquires a certain ambience and character, continuing to attract similar people.[94]

Abrahamson[95] further points out that such enclaves then become distinguished through both commercial and institutional development which is also culture-specific,[96] for example the differential use of child care facilities, which require characteristics such as extended family proximity.[97] Other cultural needs may also play a role, such as the increasing use of Feng Shuei, and hence specific layouts in California encouraging the clustering of Chinese in suburbs,[98] or the very different types of layout preferred by Hispanics and Anglos in Tucson.[99]

Such enclaves often started as magnets for particular types of immigrants, a continuing world-wide phenomenon. These then become sub-

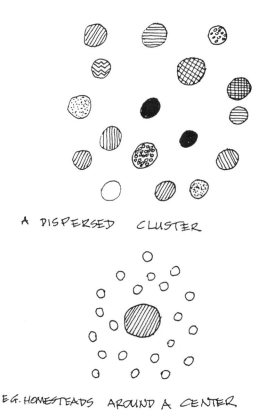

A DISPERSED CLUSTER

AN AGGLOMERATED CLUSTER

E.G. HOMESTEADS AROUND A CENTER

AS DWELLINGS 'MOVE CLOSER' THE RESULT IS A VILLAGE.

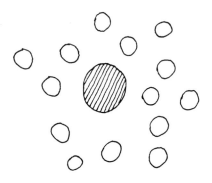

E.G. VILLAGES AROUND A CENTER

AS VILLAGES 'MOVE CLOSER' THE RESULT IS A TOWN OR CITY (THE CONSTITUENTS OF WHICH OFTEN ARE 'NEIGHBORHOODS')

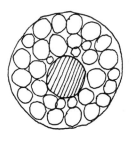

fig. 5.3 Dispersed and agglomerated units of a settlement.

cultures clearly identified with a specific area, such as the Turkish neighbourhood developing in the Sunnyside section of Queens, N.Y.[100] 'Asian villages' such as Little Taipei and Chinatown mentioned above fit this pattern, as do Korea Town in Los Angeles, as well as Vietnamese and Hmong areas. However, attempts to deliberately create such areas[101] may fail because of political

and legal obstacles, which make the procedure 'unconstitutional'.

The term 'Asian villages', of course, implies ethnic neighbourhoods, and is a specific subset of 'ethnic villages.' Margulis[102] identifies three functions for such enclaves. Firstly, as immigrant reception areas providing needed and strong social network links, based on sentiment and attachment. They also provide links to secondary ethnic neighbourhoods, resulting from dispersal, in more peripheral urban locations or suburbs. Secondly, they provide sanctuaries, social support, and specialised services for elderly non-English speaking Asians, or new immigrants.[103] Thirdly, they function as tourist attractions due to their specific ambience resulting from the use of space and streets, types of culturally specific shops and restaurants, sounds and smells.[104] Some such areas have also proved to be extremely open-ended and 'resilient', allowing for changing populations in the same physical locale, and this suggests areas for research in the context of open endedness and urban frameworks.[105] Margulis[106] concludes that such Asian villages are being revitalised, and that they are not only surviving, but thriving.

Heterogeneity

Although the above references are mainly to the United States, the continued survival of neighbourhoods, particularly in the case of populations with high perceived homogeneity,[107] is found elsewhere, even after major transformations in the physical environment, as in Thessaloniki, Greece[108] or the case of the new town of Marne-la-Valleé in France.[109] The reasons for the continued, and possibly growing, importance of neighbourhood hinge on the greater diversity of populations in most countries and urban areas, that is their growing heterogeneity, which tends to encourage like people to cluster more, given the desire and the need for such clustering. The increase in individual choice, and greater freedom from traditional group constraints, paradoxically leads to the clustering of people who make similar choices; more choice means more such groups. The rise in crime leads to mutual cooperation which becomes easier, as do other forms of joint action, in a relatively homogeneous area with a 'sense of community'. Local political action in the U.S., and the growth of decentralization and rise in local political action even in more centralised countries, again makes it important to have some commonalty among people in given areas — it makes cooperation easier. The growing information overload generally, and in large urban areas particularly, means that being able to feel secure in an area which becomes a 'backstage region' (or 'home ground') is helpful, partly because it becomes easier to understand cues, non-verbal communication, unwritten rules and so on.[110] With educational standards (at least in the U.S.) becoming highly variable, location with regard to schools also becomes increasingly im-

portant.

Since neighbourhood, at the very least, implies or involves social clustering in space, neighbourhoods, understood as areas where people tend to congregate among others like themselves, remain important. Thus Halle[111] emphasises the role of neighbourhood among blue-collar Americans, using the term throughout the book unselfconsciously, as a self-evident and relevant unit of analysis. He also emphasises the importance of stability of residence within an area.[112] This stability, as well as the homogeneity of the population and shared standards lead to dense kin and friendship networks, which become more important to certain groups with 'reduced competence'.[113] In addition, ethnicity is sometimes used to differentiate one blue-collar neighbourhood from another,[114] a form of cross-cutting of group membership common in the United States,[115] and seen increasingly elsewhere.

One example is a study by Taylor and Covington,[116] who identify three major dimensions of community structure in U.S. cities — status; racial (or ethnic) composition; and lifestyle and family status. They point out that these are widely used to differentiate communities and neighbourhoods (e.g. in factorial ecology). They also emphasise the role of stability and the effects of change.[117] Ethnicity figures in the subjective definition of neighbourhood in many cases, but not all,[118] and is frequently found in both research and the media.[119] This in turn, supports both the continuing importance of neighbourhood and the role of perceived homogeneity.[120] The role of physical elements is also important,[121] not least because they communicate the social identity of areas.[122] Neighbourhood may thus be understood as that place where social networks tend to be most concentrated. As clustering continues and grows we need to discuss the reasons for this in some detail.

THE CONTINUED IMPORTANCE
OF NEIGHBOURHOOD

Biologically, humans are a single species. However, considered over the full time-span of history, and cross-culturally,[123] one finds that it typically divides into mutually exclusive groups, differentiated by language, religion, food habits and way of life,[124] that is by culture. One of the many roles of culture is precisely to distinguish among groups;[125] it has even been suggested that such groups are almost like species in other organisms — to the extent that they have been called 'pseudo-species.'

Clustering

Although this is not universal, most commonly such groups also have geographical, spatial equivalents, as a result of the tendency to cluster just discussed. This creates a mosaic of groups, a social geography whether of the earth, of continents, countries, regions — and urban areas, where the elements of the mosaic are neighbourhoods. Historical and archaeological data, travel accounts, novels, songs, myths, and popular media[126] all reflect the phenomenon of diverse groups clustered in space. Tribal societies, for example, commonly refer to themselves as 'the People', implying that others are not quite human, and this is also inferred by the term barbarian used for outsiders by the ancient Chinese and Greeks. Human groups have thus always tended to cluster with like, and social homogeneity has often led to geographic and spatial homogeneity. In the case of urban areas, it has been more formalised in some places than in others (for example, India and the Middle East,[127] and at certain times — for example during periods of massive migration (and hence increasing heterogeneity), rapid culture change and so on. Also, it is more important, hence more prevalent, for some groups such as those under stress and with particular lifestyles, those handicapped in some way, or of reduced competence, because such clustering provides mutual support.

Subjective definitions

The specific criteria for homogeneity used for clustering have varied, and have included: religion, class, race or ethnicity, tribe, place of origin, kinship, caste, language, stage in life cycle, education, community of interests, occupation and age. This results in areas homogeneous on the basis of the particular variables relevant in any given case. One is therefore dealing with perceived homogeneity, a subjective definition by the people concerned, rather than any *a priori* set of variables, which helps explain the success of areas which seem to be extremely heterogeneous on the basis of standard measures of race, income and the like. One such area, La Clede Town, in St. Louis, Missouri (USA) which has been studied, can be understood to consist of people who have chosen to live there. They share an ideology, in that case of wanting to live in the central city in a heterogeneous area. Paradoxically, and possibly counter-intuitively, the heterogeneity based on ideology leads to an unusually high degree of perceived homogeneity.[128]

Today, increasingly, lifestyle is becoming the major variable defining perceived homogeneity, and helping to explain clustering in neighbourhoods. Lifestyle is best understood as the outcome of decisions about how to allocate or use resources of money, effort and time.[129] These depend on choices based on certain values, and lead to a set of attitudes to child rearing, food and shopping habits, time patterns, leisure activities, meanings, non-verbal communication, and degrees of tidiness and maintenance. Since lifestyle expresses choice, in a society where such choices are possible where one lives may also represent a choice regarding location, environmental quality and social attributes of areas, so that the two sets of choices match — or can be matched.[130] In this view, income is an enabling rather than a determining variable.

Lifestyle thus explains preferences and choice, while income and monetary resources act as facilitators or constraints, making certain choices possible or impossible. Within a broadly defined lifestyle allocation of personal income for dwelling, food, transport, or perhaps the choice of a better house in a less desirable neighbourhood or the opposite, can all vary greatly.

If the lifestyle attributes that underlie clustering vary among different groups it follows, as already suggested, that one cannot generalise about neighbourhood, its nature, importance, future, specifies of location, ambience or environmental quality without specifying the group, and its cultural or sub-cultural context. The underlying processes, however, seem to apply broadly.

Perceived homogeneity

The reasons behind the prevalence of neighbourhoods based on perceived homogeneity may be outlined as follows.
1. Homogeneity increases predictability, or reduces unpredictability, thus reducing stress. It also reduces the need to process information, reducing information overload.
2. Homogeneity allows meanings to be taken for granted, leading to much clearer and more effective non-verbal communication. It becomes much easier to understand body language, clothing, behaviour, tone of voice, and cues in the physical environment, and to relate them to rules, to appropriate situations and contexts, and thus to behave appropriately. This, once again, reduces the amount of information to be processed, and hence information overload.
3. In these, and other ways, homogeneity helps reduce the perceived density of areas, again

reducing information levels.

4. Homogeneity allows for a large number of psychological, cultural and other 'defenses' to operate more effectively and is, in itself, a major defense, tending to reduce conflict;[131] fear of crime[132] as well as crime itself.[133]

5. Homogeneity leads to agreement about notions of environmental quality, reducing conflicts about various standards regarding maintenance, front lawns, colours, children's behaviour, time use, rhythms and tempos, periods of quiet or noise, acceptable noise levels and so on. This makes self-governance much easier and makes possible the use of informal rather than formal rules and controls. This, in turn, makes working together, cooperation, involvement and participation much easier and more likely. All this becomes possible due to agreement on goals based on shared values and meanings.[134]

6. This has implications for the design quality of areas. As a result of homogeneity, personalisation (colours, planting, additions, decorations and so on and on) are not random, but take on a coherent character as they 'add up'.[135] This, in turn, results in greater clarity of character and cues, because of greater redundancy. Another result is increased complexity at the urban scale, as the consistent character within areas creates noticeable differences, and clear transitions, among them. Also, by resulting in areas with distinctly different and comprehensible character it helps groups, and individuals in these groups, more easily and clearly to communicate various forms of identity.

7. The existence of a variety of homogeneous areas of distinct character increases choice at the urban scale.

8. Homogeneity provides mutual support at times of stress and rapid culture change. Through the ability to share meanings, various institutions, language, food, festivals, rituals and religion, family and kinship, environmental stress can be greatly reduced. The use of all such institutions for mutual support can help in the success of immigrant groups in new environments. Again, the effects vary for different groups, depending on the degree of stress, the differences among groups and hence rapidity of culture change necessary, whether the group is space-bound or not.

The fear is often expressed that allowing such clustering to occur will lead to the isolation of groups, whereas heterogeneous neighbourhoods will maximise interaction. In fact, it appears, although it seems counter-intuitive, that people (like other animals) interact most if they have a secure 'private' area which they 'own', and to

which they can retreat. They can then emerge to interact. Of course, to interact they must have something in common; propinquity does not necessarily lead to interaction — it may lead to avoidance or conflict. Environments are not determining in that sense, but rather facilitating or inhibiting: one may lead a horse to water, but can't make it drink.

This question of interaction among groups introduces two requirements. First, the scale of homogeneous areas must be small enough to allow people to be aware of others; at the same time people in adjoining areas should not be too different. The second is that there need to be what could be called 'neutral' settings in which interaction can occur. These, once again, tend to be subjectively defined, in terms of location, their nature and use, and the cues that indicate neutrality. For example, parks are frequently proposed as such areas, but in many cases have not worked because of not being seen as neutral by the intended groups. Schools are even less likely to work, since they are crucial in lifestyle definition involving, as they do, the upbringing and enculturation, of children; their behaviour, language, attitudes to study and work and so on. They are also often, at least in the U.S., a major concern when people choose neighbourhoods, which means that schools help define homogeneity. Shopping activities (markets, shops or supermarkets) and work-places often do function as neutral ground. The specifics are, once again, culturally variable and specific but reflect certain general, basic processes and behaviours.

It should also be pointed out that if one considers social interaction, as well as systems of activities, in relation to neighbourhood, two very different polar possibilities exist (in addition to a range of intermediate forms). In one, the interactions, social networks and activity systems predominantly occur in a geographically defined area surrounding key institutions. In the other the networks and activities cover extensive areas — although frequently also centred on key institutions (fig. 5.4), as for example in Los Angeles in the case of a Samoan community,[136] or a Serbian church visited by the author.

IMPORTANCE OF NEIGHBOURHOOD
FOR DIFFERENT GROUPS

It was suggested above that the concept of neighbourhood has differential importance for different groups, depending on culture, context, age, sex, ethnicity, social rank, stage in life-cycle and household composition, occupation, 'competence',

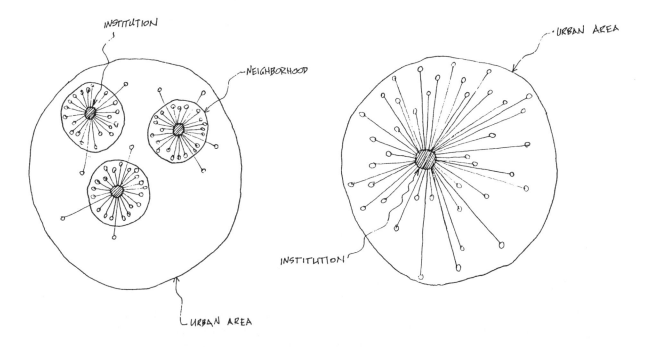

fig. 5.4 Key institutions inside and outside neighbourhoods.

dependence on local social networks and support and, hence, mobility. For example, it has been shown that some populations will accept unemployment rather than to leave neighbourhoods for guaranteed, and better jobs.[137] This means that the importance, or salience, of neighbourhood varies among groups in terms of its lifestyle and activity systems. For example, in Sydney, Los Angeles and other cities, some groups only know a few city blocks in their neighbourhoods, whereas others have detailed knowledge of extensive areas.[138] Clearly, the salience of neighbourhood to those groups is very different. In U.S. cities those familiar only with their immediate locality tend to be recent immigrants, ethnic minorities, the uneducated, while those with an extensive knowledge are their opposites. In many Third World countries the reverse tends to be the case.

There is increased awareness of such group-specificity and diversity in many domains, and increasing sophistication in defining them for marketing and advertising.[139] As a result the number of such lifestyle groups identified has increased. In the 1970's the categories were based on two main groups — localites and cosmopolites (or urbanites), with the former more dependent on neighbourhood; or four lifestyle groups — consumption oriented, social prestige oriented, family oriented and community oriented, each with a very different set of wants and values, making particular residential choices so that neighbourhood had distinct salience for each.

Currently a large industry has emerged providing multiple lifestyle group profiles, ranging from 8 to 40, 44 or 47 categories.[140] These profiles also identify where such groups live, assigning neighbourhoods to distinctive lifestyle clusters, and can predict consumer behaviour regarding cars, clothing, food, drink, reading materials, leisure and recreation, whether houses are bought or rented, the type of dwelling and its furnishings and also the areas of cities in which they are found, that is the neighbourhoods and their attributes of positive or negative environmental quality.

These groups are defined on the basis of their demographic, socio-economic, educational, ethnic and other characteristics at the block level, with highly distinct and diverse wants and preferences. Each such area is homogeneous within its market segment and very different to other such segments. Neighbourhoods based on lifestyle are clearly alive and well, indeed thriving.

Wants and preferences, as already pointed out, imply some image of an ideal life — and with it an image of an ideal setting, social and physical. Hence the importance of the socio-spatial schema as the basis for neighbourhood in that it represents a social and physical milieu that is congruent with lifestyle, and hence the image of an ideal life. The importance of ideals, often expressed in images, is clear from the way new housing is sold. The naming of developments or estates, and advertising, together with what it emphasises, states or leaves out, are most enlightening. The dwelling itself is rarely shown, or even mentioned, the emphasis being on the larger setting, the neighbourhood, people and their attributes. These advertisements emphasise lifestyle and neighbourhood — and 'sell dreams'.[141]

THE NEIGHBOURHOOD IS NO LONGER THE SETTING FOR ALL OF LIFE (IF IT EVER WAS)

Whether neighbourhoods still exist, and whether they are still important, seems really to be a non-argument. However, arguments for the reduced importance of neighbourhood in contemporary developed countries and in developing countries with modernization (understood as a form of culture change) make one important point. Rarely is neighbourhood, however salient, the setting for all of life, in spite of its significance for certain activities and aspects of life for particular groups at specific times — depending, in part, on their need for local, supportive networks. With urban areas increasing in size, becoming metropoli and megalopoli, people can neither know nor use such areas, or identify with them. The neighbourhood then acts as an area intermediate between the dwelling and the whole urban area, it is an area which is better known and with which one has more identification (however minimal) than the larger, often unknown (or even feared) urban area.[142] The neighbourhood becomes a figure that stands out against the ground of the city[143] In this sense also it is a cognitive construct, adding to importance of its subjective, cognitive definition. It should, however be questioned, in light of the previous discussion of activity systems occurring in systems of settings, whether neighbourhoods were ever the setting for all of life, even in the most traditional settlements.[144] The change may thus be more one of degree not of kind.

The importance of 'a sense of community', its relation to satisfaction[145] and, in turn, to perceived homogeneity, can be interpreted in these terms.[146] People seem to need to be able to identify with such a unit.[147] A similar argument has increasingly been made for the general importance of what have been called 'intermediate institutions' and 'mediating structures, often requiring supportive spatial units.[148] As already suggested, the clearer these are the better they work and, moreover, clear identities and images of such intermediate areas lend themselves more easily to manipulation and change by designers and by the public, as in the case of gentrification.[149] In the present context whether or not 'a sense of community' can be generated or at least facilitated by design is not under discussion.

Territorial behaviour

Even when one considers the disagreements about the scale at which territoriality applies[150] neighbourhoods (and certainly micro-neighbourhoods) have clear and potentially important links with notions of territory. The nature, importance and use of the territory can be clarified by such links as well as with related concepts such as core areas and home ranges,[151] which in turn relate to systems of activities in systems of settings, and hence the interaction of people with the overall urban environment. Territories also represent areas within which the actual systems and sub-systems of settings are found[152] and vary both for different groups and different sizes of cities.[153] They also vary with crime (or the fear of crime) and can be traced over time. Thus Gaster[154] shows that a major reduction in children's access to the neighbourhood (their home range) has occurred over time. These studies correspond to, and confirm earlier work by Parr, Gump and others.[155]

Altogether, neighbourhoods remain part of the city whether as a series of social worlds, or as units of intermediate scale, and continue to be important in terms of one more aspect — their meaning or symbolic importance.

Meaning and symbolic importance

Meaning is central to the way people interact with all environments.[156] Clothing, furnishings, buildings and their layouts, gardens, streets, and neighbourhoods are all used in establishing both group and individual identity, and in the enculturation of children. Like it or not, *you are where you live* particularly in contemporary, large-scale, heterogeneous societies such as in the U.S.[157] This is partly because we make inferences about the kinds of people who live in areas from the attributes of these areas — levels of maintenance, cleanliness, types of shops and what they sell, signs, colours, planting, types of dwellings and personalisation, from what is visible through windows, the cars, people, sounds, graffiti or its absence.[158] This process is becoming increasingly common and important as heterogeneity increases and traditional social categories become less recognisable or less rigid.

The nature, character, ethnicity and status of urban areas, including neighbourhoods, can be read and provide cues for behaviour; they guide, facilitate and modify social interaction and behaviour. The physical environment communicates various identities, defines situations and thus constrains and guides behaviour.[159] This works best when people share cues and understand their meaning. They then communicate easily, almost effortlessly — hence the importance of clustering and homogeneity. Also, as we have seen, under such conditions the cues becomes clearer, since they 'add up, rather than cancelling out.'

It follows that meaning is not something apart from function but a central and most important aspect of function. Thus the appearance of the housing and other components of the area not only communicates these meanings, but also identifies, reflects values, embodies beliefs and expresses ideals. While the way this happens varies cross-culturally and in different places and periods, it becomes particularly significant in less hierarchical, socially mobile, large scale and heterogeneous societies. Since one cannot know people because of large scale and social mobility, and the old clues such as accent and clothing no longer communicate social status clearly, or at all, where one lives, that is locations in urban space, become instrumental for locating people in social space: one is judged by one's neighbourhood, which may reinforce or negate the message of one's dwelling. Once again, we see the role of redundancy, and consequently strong, clear, easily communicated messages about the extent and boundaries of the neighbourhood and about those who live in it.

In this connection a number of recent developments become significant. For example, so-called 'neo-traditional development' has much to say about the importance of neighbourhood and 'community'.[160] Much the same message is communicated by the increasing 'gating' of existing urban areas in the U.S. where numerous gated communities now exist and have been analyzed.[161] Among examples discussed are the Clason Point public housing project in the South Bronx, N.Y., Yonkers, N.Y. and especially the Five Oaks area of Dayton, Ohio, where a half square mile, 2,000 household area was divided into ten mini-neighbourhoods, all gated, and typically comprising 400-500 single family houses. Not only does this confirm the continued significance of neighbourhoods and clear boundaries but also that they tend to be small[162] and that 'defending' such neighbourhoods is a consideration.[163]

THE FUTURE

It has been argued here that it is more than likely that not only will neighbourhoods continue to play a primary role in urban life but may, in fact,

increase in significance. The importance of perceived homogeneity of populations and their stability, which leads to social cohesion and identification with specific neighbourhoods or neighbourhood types, and the way these, in turn, are linked to values, norms, standards, ideals, and hence physical as well as social cues has been stressed. These factors, through differences in environmental preferences of different groups, have led to increased neighbourhood participation, through direct action, neighbourhood-based design boards or consultation on growth, and the growing emphasis on community participation in urban design exemplified by the work of Sanoff and others in the U.S. and overseas and also the frequent use of the terms 'urban village' and 'neighbourhood' in such work, for example that of John Thompson and Partners in the U.K. and continental Europe.

Cultural specificity, however, means that there will be different futures and different trajectories for implementing ideas about neighbourhood, which will depend partly on policy, allowing (or even encouraging) clustering as opposed to making it difficult or impossible. Their persistence may perhaps also be encouraged by retaining and reinforcing the use of established names, traditions and history, making administrative boundaries coincide with subjectively defined areas, and planning and designing to strengthen redundancy and hence clearly noticeable differences, and distinct character and ambience of different urban areas.

Whether policy is pro- or anti-neighbourhood, the meaning of 'neighbourhood', and the complex processes involved have to be understood for establishing data and carrying out research. One needs to know what it is, how it occurs, how it is construed in people's minds, how it coincides with what administrators, planners and designers do, and hence what they can do, to strengthen or enhance or alternatively to weaken or inhibit neighbourhoods.

Although one is often dealing with the subjective definition of variables, this does not undermine the assessment, as it is the subjective environment that influences behaviour. That subjective environment, moreover, is far from arbitrary, and does not spring full-grown in the mind. It is constructed on the basis of the environment 'out there', to which it is ultimately related — it is the objective environment which is so transformed. The administrators', planners' and designers' task, then, seems to be to understand these transformations, and the mechanisms involved, and to provide those environmental attributes that will help people construct mentally those environments which are appropriate, which they desire, which match their images and ideals. Only such environments are supportive for people's lifestyles and activities. The role of administration, planning and design needs to be to make more predictable and effective the relations and congruence between the 'objective' and 'subjective' environments.

All such actions should aim to help people define neighbourhoods that are salient for them. This is partly because there are often good reasons for patterns, and partly because when the natural processes of selection by perceived homogeneity, and ability to define an appropriate area, are blocked, other forms of homogeneity will tend to emerge which may be less desirable, because artificial rather than natural. These may be based on imposed and arbitrary, rather than subjectively defined criteria, and hence not work as well — if at all.

Milwaukee

An interesting case which bears on all these matters is provided by recent developments in the city of Milwaukee, Wisconsin, with a population of about 600,000 in a Metropolitan area of about 1.5 million. It was unusual in that compared to other cities (e.g. Baltimore with its 249 neighbourhoods, let alone other cultures), it had relatively few named and widely known neighbourhoods.[164]

In 1989 the organization Future Milwaukee produced a map proposing 75 named neighbourhoods.[165] In that proposal large areas of the city did not have such neighbourhoods, but by 1993 the whole city was covered by 189 named neighbourhoods (fig. 5.5).[166] The City of Miwaukee has produced neighbourhood designation signage for a number of neighbourhoods including Arlington Heights, Borchert Field, Brewers Hill, Clarke Square, Concordia, Franklin Heights, Jackson Park, Lincoln Village, Parkwest, Rufus King, Story Hill, Walker's Point, Washington Heights, and Garden Homes, while private signage already exists for some others. Figures 5.6-5.16 give examples of the signs in their settings. Although the neighbourhoods vary in size, their average can be determined given that the urban area is approximately 96 sq. miles (Huxtable, personal communication), as approximately half a square mile, not too different to the figure for the U.S. given above.[167] This is, however significantly larger than the gated communities being created, for example in Cleveland.[168] There, a half square mile area was divided into ten micro-neighbourhoods. The average size also seems larger than that found in a study of residents' subjective definition of Milwaukee neighbourhoods, where

fig. 5.5 Map of 189 Miwaukee neighbourhoods, August 1996 (City of Milwaukee, Department of City Development). Key:

1 North Granville, 2 North Meadows, 3 Ridgeview, 4 Hilltop Parish, 5 Northridge, 6 Northridge Lakes, 7 Dretzka Park, 8 Granville Station, 9 Pheasant Run, 10 Riverton Heights, 11 Land Bank, 12 Servite Woods, 13 Whispering Hills, 14 Freedom Village, 15 Granville Woods, 16 Pollber Heights, 17 Buchel Park, 18 Melody View, 19 Calumet Farms, 20 Park Place, 21 Mill Valley, 22 Heritage Heights, 23 Mack Acres, 24 Golden Gate, 25 Menomonee River Hills, 26 Menomonee River Hills East, 27 Brynwood, 28 Bradley Estates, 29 Tripoli Park, 30 Brown Deer Park, 31 Town and Country Manor, 32 Wyrick Park, 33 Graceland, 34 Fairfield, 35 Havenwoods, 36 Silver Spring, 37 McGovern Park, 38 Thurston Woods, 39 Maple Tree, 40 Park Knoll, 41 Florist Highlands, 42 Little Menomonee Parkway, 43 Parkway Hills, 44 Silver Swan, 45 Timmerman West, 46 Timmerman Airport, 47 Valhalla, 48 Vogel Park, 49 Long View, 50 Hampton Heights, 51 Wahl Park, 52 Old North Milwaukee, 53 Lincoln Park, 54 Milwaukee River Parkway, 55 Eastbrook Park, 56 Grover Heights, 57 Rufus King, 58 Garden Homes, 59 Lincoln Creek, 60 Capitol Heights, 61 Columbus Park, 62 Arlington Gardens, 63 Lindsay Park, 64 Grantosa, 65 Golden Valley, 66 St. Aemuan's, 67 Nash Park, 68 Kops Park, 69 Mount Mary, 70 Cooper Park, 71 Dineen Park, 72 Enderis Park, 73 Grasslyn Manor, 74 Sunset Heights, 75 St. Joseph's, 76 Roosvelt Grove, 77 Sherman Park, 78 Franklin Heights, 79 Park West, 80 Arlington Heights, 81 Borchert Field, 82 North Division, 83 Williamsburg Heights, 84 Harambee, 85 Riverwest, 86 Cambridge Heights, 87 Riverside Park, 88 Downer Woods, 89 Upper East Side, 90 Murray Hill, 91 Lake Park, 92 North Point, 93 Lower East Side, 94 Yankee Hill, 95 Brewers Hill, 96 Schlitz Park, 97 Haymarket, 98 Halyard Park, 99 Hillside, 100 Triangle North, 101 Triangle, 102 King Park, 103 Park View, 104 Midtown, 105 Walnut Hill, 106 Metcalfe Park, 107 Uptown, 108 Washington Heights, 109 Washington Park, 110 Hawthorne Glen, 111 Wick Field, 112 Valley Forge, 113 Martin Drive, 114 Cold Spring Park, 115 Miller Valley, 116 Concordia, 117 Avenues West, 118 Marquette, 119 Kilbourn Town, 120 Juneau Town, 121 Historic Third Ward, 122 Jones' Island, 123 Menomonee River Valley, 124 Merrill Park, 125 The Valley, 126 Story Hill, 127 Bluemound Heights, 128 Honey Creek Parkway, 129 Cannon Park, 130 Zoo, 131 Fair Park, 132 Johnson's Woods, 133 Veteran's Affairs, 134 Silver City, 135 National Park, 136 Mitchell Park, 137 Clarke Square, 138 Walker's Point, 139 Harbor View, 140 Clock Tower Acres, 141 Historic Mitchell Street, 142 Muskego Way, 143 Burnham Park, 144 Layton Park, 145 Forest Home Hills, 146 Lincoln Village, 147 Baran Park, 148 Bay View, 149 Fernwood, 150 Tippecanoe, 151 Saveland Park, 152 Morgandale, 153 Polonia, 154 Southgate, 155 Southpoint, 156 Mount Olivet, 157 Harder's Oaks, 158 Jackson Park, 159 White Manor, 160 Fairview, 161 Lyons Park, 162 Hawley Farms, 163 River Bend, 164 Highwood Estates, 165 Euclid Park, 166 West View, 167 Alcott Park, 168 Morgan Heights, 169 Rolling Green, 170 Wedgewood, 171 Root Creek, 172 Woodland Court, 173 Red Oak Heights, 174 Green Moor, 175 Honey Creek Manor, 176 Alverno, 177 Wilson Park, 178 Castle Manor, 179 Town of Lake, 180 Mitchell West, 181 Holler Park, 182 Mitchell Field, 183 New Coeln, 184 Maitland Park, 185 Clayton Crest, 186 Gra-ram, 187 Copernicus Park, 188 Goldman Park, 189 College Heights.

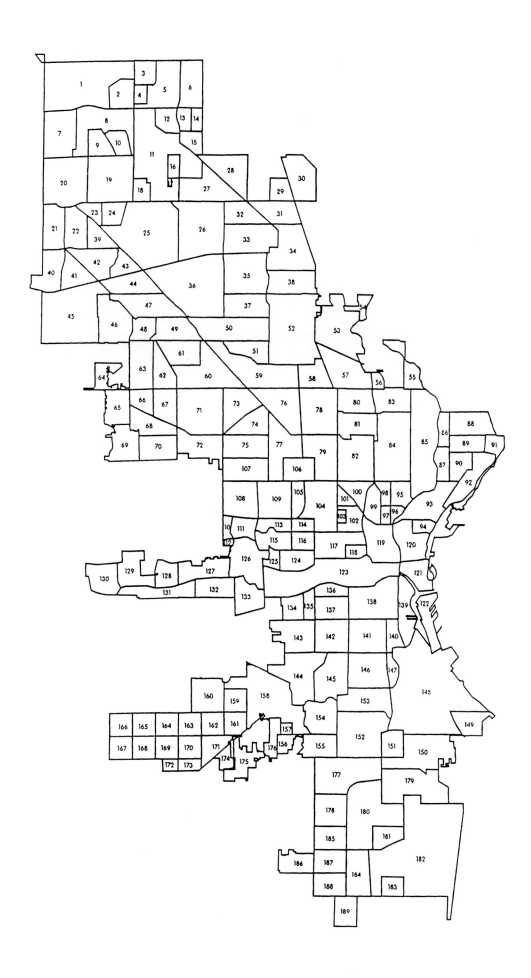

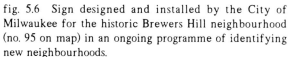

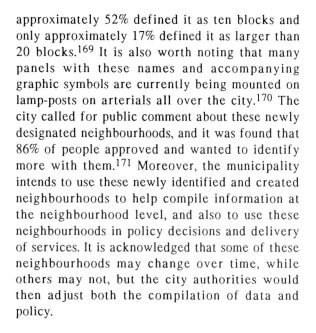

fig. 5.6 Sign designed and installed by the City of Milwaukee for the historic Brewers Hill neighbourhood (no. 95 on map) in an ongoing programme of identifying new neighbourhoods.

fig. 5.7 Sign for the Washington Heights neighbourhood, Milwaukee (no . 108 on map).

approximately 52% defined it as ten blocks and only approximately 17% defined it as larger than 20 blocks.[169] It is also worth noting that many panels with these names and accompanying graphic symbols are currently being mounted on lamp-posts on arterials all over the city.[170] The city called for public comment about these newly designated neighbourhoods, and it was found that 86% of people approved and wanted to identify more with them.[171] Moreover, the municipality intends to use these newly identified and created neighbourhoods to help compile information at the neighbourhood level, and also to use these neighbourhoods in policy decisions and delivery of services. It is acknowledged that some of these neighbourhoods may change over time, while others may not, but the city authorities would then adjust both the compilation of data and policy.

CONCLUSION

A variety of disciplinary sources and reference to other countries may be employed for future assessments of the phenomenon, but from the limited portion of the literature under review a broad picture emerges about the continuing importance of neighbourhood: the fact that it is defined subjectively, that it is smaller than usually assumed, that names are important, and that agreement about boundaries can be increased by using a great variety of strong cues and high levels of redundancy. This last point bears on the fact that for clear cognitive schemata to develop, objective physical environments require certain attributes, and that these are perhaps the only variables designers can manipulate. Of course, walls and gates are the strongest possible cues, hence the significance of both walled and gated areas as a response to the physical and psychological pressures of the world 'out there', although at the instrumental level they may also provide increased security.

In addition, while neighbourhoods may be growing in importance, it appears that fewer of them are probably the setting for most of life, so that they may be tending towards becoming home grounds, or areas around one's dwelling intermediate in scale between it and the urban area; they represent socio-spatial schemata; and they

fig. 5.8 Private sign for University Square, subdividing the city-defined Lower East Side neighbourhood, Milwaukee (no. 93 on map).

fig. 5.9 Private sign on the same street as University Square, Lower East Side.

fig. 5.10 Private sign for 3rd Street, Downtown.

fig. 5.11 Private sign, Westown, Downtown.

fig. 5.12 Private sign, East Town, Downtown, Milwaukee.　　fig. 5.13 Historic Third Ward, Milwaukee.

fig. 5.14 Gateway to Third Ward neighbourhood.

fig. 5.15 Walker Square, Milwaukee.

fig. 5.16 Walker Square, Milwaukee.

differ depending on the nature of the groups involved, their values, ideals, lifestyles, systems of activities and the nature and arrangement of

systems of settings (such as various services and their use). Thus, while implying identity and familiarity they do not necessarily imply neighbouring, 'community' and the like in the traditional sense. While standing out in relation to the centre, other neighbourhoods and the larger urban context, they also differ in the nature of their cultural landscape and ambience .

One outcome is that there are different ideal neighbourhoods that people try to find and create, and new technologies tend to increase choice. With all these commonalties, neighbourhood is not a single 'thing'; these ideals, evaluations of environmental quality, and hence choices may result in the differential distribution of people in urban space, changes in the social geography of the city, with its differing ambiences, and hence the diverse character of the neighbourhoods.

In a recent paper by Webber[172] he admits that traditional cities have proven 'tenacious and are not about to disappear.' He acknowledges the 'persisting power of propinquity' and implicitly also concedes the persistence of neighbourhoods when he remarks that 'most people still live out their lives in the locales where they reside', and that 'daily life is largely local'. Since Webber's earlier work was the jumping off point for this review, his latest contribution brings us, as it were, full circle.

Amos Rapoport
University of Wisconsin, Milwaukee

NOTES

1 A. Rapoport, *Human Aspects of Urban Form*, (Pergamon Press) Oxford, 1977; 'Neighborhood homogeneity or heterogeneity', *Architecture and Behaviour*, vol. 1, no. 1, 1980/81, 67-77.
2 P. Olson, 'Urban neighbourhood research, its development and current focus', *Urban Affairs Journal*, vol. 17 no 4, 1982, 491-518.
3 M. M. Webber, 'Order in diversity: community without propinquity', in L. Wingo (ed.), *Cities and Space*, (Johns Hopkins University Press) Baltimore, 1963, 25-54; 'The urban place and the non-place urban realm', in M. M. Webber (ed.), *Explorations into Urban Structure*, (University of Pennsylvania Press) Philadelphia, 1964, 19-41.
4 See for example C. S. Fischer et al., *Networks and Places*, (The Free Press) New York, 1977; K. Robins and M. Hepworth, 'Electronic spaces: new technologies and the future of cities', *Futures*, April 1988, 155-176; M. Sorkin, (ed.), *Variations On a Theme Park: The New American City and the End of Public Space*, (The Noonday Press) New York, 1992; W. Mitchell, *City of Bits: Space, Place and the Infobahn*, (MIT Press) Cambridge, MA., 1995; W. Rybczynski, *City Life: Urban Expectations in a New World*, (Scribner) New York, 1995; G. Gumpert, 'Communications and our sense of community: a planning agenda', *Intermedia*, vol. 24 no 4, 1996, 8-11; G. Gumpert and S. J. Drucker, 'Communication and the built form: the changing social landscape', in J. L. Nasar and B. B. Brown (eds.), *Public and Private Spaces*, (EDRA 27), Edmond, Oklahoma, 1996, 34-38.

5 R. Sennett, *The Fall of Public Man*, (Knopf) New York, 1977; c.f. Gumpert, *Intermedia* vol. 24, no. 4, 1996, 8-11.
6 A. Rapoport, *Human Aspects of Urban Form*, 1977, 15-20, 48-107; 'Thinking about home environments: a conceptual framework', in I. Altman and C. M. Werner (eds.), *Home Environments*, (Plenum) New York, 1985, 255-286; 'Environmental quality and environmental quality profiles', in A. Rapoport *Thirty-Three papers in environment behaviour Research*, (Urban International Press) Newcastle, 1995, 471-488; M. P. Baumgartner, *The Moral Order of the Suburb*, (Oxford University Press) New York, 1988.
7 J. Gottmann, *The Coming of the Transactional City*, (University of Maryland Institute for Urban Studies) College Park, Maryland, 1983.
8 Gottmann, op. cit., 1983, 77.
9 S. B. Ahrentzen, Blurring Boundaries: cocio-spatial consequences of working at home (Research Report), Milwaukee, University of Wisconsin-Milwaukee, Centre for Architecture and Urban Planning Research, 1987; 'Managing conflict by managing boundaries: how professional homeworkers cope with multiple roles at home', *Environment and Behaviour*, vol. 22, no 6, Nov 1990, 748.
10 T. R. Lee, 'Urban neighbourhood as socio-spatial schema', *Human Relations*, vol. 21 no. 3, Aug 1968, 53-61.
11 Hargreaves and Robillard 1979, cited in A. Rapoport, 'Thinking about home environments: a conceptual framework'. in I. Altman and C. M. Werner (eds.), *Home Environments*,

(Plenum) New York, 1985, 255-286.

12 B. Badura, 'Social networks and the quality of life', in D. Frick (ed.), *The Quality of Urban Life: Social, Psychological and Physical Conditions*, (de Gruyter) Berlin, 1986, 55-60.

13 W. Sodeur, 'Social networks in urban neighbourhoods', in Frick (ed.), op. cit., 1986, 61-74, especially 61-64.

14 Olson, op. cit., 491-518.

15 c.f. A. Rapoport, 'Development, culture change and supportive design', *Habitat International*, vol. 7, nos. 5/6, 1983, 249-268, especially 255.

16 P. L. Clay & R.M. Hollister (eds.), *Neighborhood Policy and Planning*, (Lexington Books) Lexington, MA., 1983; H. Hellman, *Neighborhoods: Their Place in Urban Life*, (Sage) Beverly Hills Ca., 1984; R. S. Ahlbrandt Jr., *Neighborhoods People and Community*, (Plenum) New York, 1984; R. B. Taylor (ed.), *Urban Neighborhoods (Research and Practice)*, (Praeger) New York, 1986; D. P. Varady, 'Neighborhood confidence: a critical factor in neighborhood revitalization', *Environment and Behaviour*, vol. 18, no. 4, July 1986, 480-501; 'Neighborhood upgrading', *Journal of Planning Literature*, vol. 1 no 3, Summer 1986, 271-293; *Neighborhood Upgrading (A Realistic Assessment)*, (SUNY Press) Albany, NY, 1986; I. Altman & A. Wandersman (eds.), *Neighborhoods and Community*, (Plenum) New York, 1987; A. M. Guest, et al., 'Changing locality identification in the metropolis: Seattle', *American Sociological Review*, vol. 48 no. 4, August 1983, 543-549; L. Hamilton, 'The evolution of neighborhood identities: competing images of a Chicago community', *Urban Resources*, vol. 1, no. 4, Spring 1984, 3-8.

17 S. Wellman, 'The boundaries of race: process of ethnicity in England', *Man*, vol. 13, no. 2, June 1978, 200-217; P. Jackson, *Ethnic Groups and Boundaries*, (Oxford University Press) Oxford, 1980; P. Jackson & S. Smith, *Exploring Social Geography*, (Allen and Unwin) London, 1984; M. J. Weiss, *The Clustering of America*, (Harper and Row) New York, 1988.

18 A. J. Brown and H. M. Sherrard, *Town and Country Planning*, (Melbourne University Press) Melbourne, 1951, 225-257.

19 cf. review in Rapoport, *Human Aspects of Urban Form*, 1977, 157-69.

20 A. Rapoport,'The use and design of open spaces in urban neighbourhoods', in Frick, *The Quality of Urban Life*, 1986, 159-175; 'Systems of activities and systems of settings', in S. Kent (ed.), *Domestic Architecture and the Use of Space*, (Cambridge University Press) Cambridge, 1990, 9-20; M. Bonaiuto et al., 'Pragmatics of urban places according to the size of the city', in S. J. Neary et al., (eds.), *The Urban Experience: a People-Environment Perspective*, (IAPS 13), (Spon) London, 1994, 335-349; M. Bonnes, (ed.), *UNESCO-MAB Project 11 - Urban Ecology Applied to the City of Rome*, (Institute of Psychology, National Research Council) Rome, 1987; M. Bonnes et al., 'The City as a multi-place system: an analysis of people-urban environment transactions', *Journal of Environmental Psychology*, vol. 10, 1990, 37-65.

21 R. Nisbet, *Sociology as an Art Form*, (Oxford University Press) Oxford - New York, 1976; P. L. Berger, 'Speaking to the Third World', *Commentary*, vol. 12, no. 4, Oct 1981, 29-36; A. Rapoport, 'Development, culture change and supportive design', 1983, 256-7.

22 T. R. Lee, 'Urban neighborhood as socio-spatial schema', 1968, 53-61.

23 Rapoport, *Human Aspects of Urban Form*, 1977, 157-69; 'Neighborhood homogeneity or heterogeneity', 1980/81, 67-77.

24 K. S. Blake, & D. D. Arreola, 'Residential subdivision identity in Metropolitan Phoenix', *Landscape Journal*, vol. 15, no. 1, Spring 1996, 23-35.

25 B. H. Stanton, 'The incidence of home grounds and experiential networks: some implications', *Environment and Behaviour*, vol. 18, no. 3, May 1986, 299-329.

26 e.g. Baumgartner, op. cit., 1988.

27 'Neighborhood confidence', 1986, 480-501; 'Neighborhood upgrading', 1986, 271-293.

28 cf. J. Covington & R. B. Taylor, 'Gentrification and crime: robbery and larceny changes in appreciating Baltimore neighbor-

hoods during the 1970's', *Urban Affairs Quarterly*, vol. 25, no. 1, September 1989, 142-172; L. W. Kennedy & R. A. Silverman, 'Perception of social diversity and fear of crime', *Environment and Behaviour*, vol. 17 no. 3, May 1985, 275-295.

29 op. cit., 53-61.

30 e.g. S. Raju, 'The social meaning of "Urban neighborhood"', *Ekistics*, vol. 47 no. 283, July/August 1980, 286 ff; S. E. Merry, 'Racial integration in an urban neighborhood: the social organization of strangers', *Human Organization*, vol. 39, no. 1, Spring 1980, 59-69; D. Pellow, 'The new urban community: mutual relevance of the social and physical environments', *Human Organization*, vol. 40, no. 1, 1981, 15-26; S. D. Greenbaum & P. E. Greenbaum, 'The spatial ecology of social networks in four urban neighbourhoods', in A. E. Osterberg et al., (eds.), *Design Research Interactions* (EDRA 12), Washington, D.C., 1981, 443 (abstract only); P. E. Greenbaum & S. D. Greenbaum, 'Territorial personalisation: group identity and social interaction in a Slavic-American Neighborhood', *Environment and Behaviour*, vol. 13, no. 5, September 1981, 574-589; D. E. Gale, *Neighborhood, Revitalization and the Postindustrial City*, (Lexington Books) Lexington, MA., 1984; Frick, *The Quality of Urban Life*, 1986, 151-218; Rapoport, *The Meaning of the Built Environment*, 1990, 137-176.

31 W. G. Haney & E. S. Knowles, 'Perception of neighborhood by city and suburban residents', *Human Ecology*, vol. 6, no. 2, 1978, 201-214.

32 cf. Rapoport, *Human Aspects of Urban Form*, 1977, 157-69.

33 Sauer, L., 'Joining old and new: neighborhood planning and architecture for city revitalization', *Architecture and Behaviour*, vol. 5, no. 4, 1989, 305-338.

34 In fact, there are 249 (Brower, personal communication).

35 Lee, op. cit., 53-61.

36 e.g. Rapoport, *Human Aspects of Urban Form*, 1977, 157-169; 'On regions and regionalism', in N. C. Markovich et al. (eds.), *Pueblo Style and Regional Architecture*, Paperback Edition (Van Nostrand Reinhold), New York, 1992, 272-294; 'On cultural landscapes', *Traditional Dwellings and Settlements Review*, vol. 3, no. 2, Spring 1992, 33-47; B. Sims, 'Neighborhood boundaries', (Dept of City and Regional Planning, Ohio State University) Columbus, OH., (Mimeo) n.d., 1-26.

37 L. G. Rich et al., *Neighborhood — a State of Mind*, Baltimore, Johns Hopkins University Press, 1981.

38 J. F. Wohlwill, 'The environment is not in the head', in W. Preiser (ed.), *Environmental Design Research*, (EDRA 4), vol. 2, (Dowden, Hutchinson and Ross) Stroudsburg, PA., 1973, 166-181.

39 cf. S. Brower & R. B. Taylor, 'Qualities of ideal and real-world environments', paper given at the 14th IAPS Conference, Stockholm (Unpublished), July 30-Aug 3, 1996.

40 Rapoport, 'On regions and regionalism', 1992, 272-294; cf. Brower, *The Design of Neighborhood Parks*, 1977, 1-54.

41 Rapoport, 'On regions and regionalism', 1992, 272-294.

42 Rapoport, *Human Aspects of Urban Form*, 1977, 62-64; 'Indirect approaches to environment behaviour research', *The National Geographical Journal of India*, vol. 36, pt. 1-2, March-June 1990, 30-46 (also in R. L. Singh & R. P. B. Singh (eds)., *Literature and Humanistic Geography*, (National Geography Society of India Research Publication Series, Banaras Hindu University) Varanasi, No. 37, 1990, 30-46); 'Thinking about home environments', 1985, 255-286; 'On diversity' and 'Designing for diversity', 1985, 5-8 and 30-36 respectively; *The Meaning of the Built Environment*, 1990, 137-176.

43 Blake & Arreola, 1996, op. cit, 23-35; 'Thinking about home environments', 1985, 255-286.

44 W. R. Janz, 'The extension of identity into home fronts: two Milwaukee, Wisconsin neighborhoods', *Journal of Architectural and Planning Research*, vol. 9, no. 1, Spring 1992, 48-63.

45 M. Rohde, 'Going by another name: Glendale's N. 26th St. to become Braeburn Lane', *Milwaukee Journal*, March 28, 1995, 131 and 134.

46 Rapoport, *Human Aspects of Urban Form*, 1977, 159.

47 Bonnes, *Urban Ecology Applied to the City of Rome*, 1987, 23-25.

48 Stanton, op. cit., 1986, 299-329.

49 Rapoport, *The Meaning of the Built Environment*, 1990, 137-176; 'On regions and regionalism', 1992, 272-294.

50 Rapoport, *Human Aspects of Urban Form*, 1977, 98, 331; 'Environmental quality and environmental quality profiles', 1985, 471-488; 'Sustainability, meaning and traditional environments', *Traditional Dwellings and Settlements Working Paper Series*, vol. 75, IASTE 75-94, (University of California, Centre for Environmental Design Research) Berkeley, 1994; S. Brower, 'Residents' and outsiders' perceptions of the environment', in S. M. Low & E. Chambers (eds.), *Housing, Culture and Design*, (University of Pennsylvania Press) Philadelphia, 1989, 189-202; Aitken, 'Local evaluation of neighborhood change', *Annals of the Association of American Geographers*, vol. 80, no. 2, 1990, 247-267.

51 e.g. F. Barth, *Ethnic Groups and Social Boundaries*, (Little Brown) Boston, 1969.

52 op. cit., 1968, 53-61.

53 Rapoport, *Human Aspects of Urban Form*, 1977, 150-157.

54 op. cit., 1-26.

55 cf. Rapoport, *Human Aspects of Urban Form*, 1977, 149-169; *The Meaning of the Built Environment*, 1990, 137-176; 'On regions and regionalism', 1992, 275-280; 'On cultural landscapes', 33-47.

56 cf. Rapoport, 'On regions and regionalism', 1992, 276-280.

57 op. cit., 1,26.

58 D. Frick, *Stadtquartier und Qualität der Lebensbedingungen / Quartier Urbain et Qualité de Vie*, (Technischen Universität Berlin, Institut für Stadt-und Regional planung) Berlin, 1990, 1-73.

59 Sims op. cit., 1-26.

60 Rapoport, 'Environmental quality and environmental quality profiles', 1995, 471-488.

61 A. M. Al-Abed & F. H. Mustapha, 'Satisfaction level with neighbourhoods in low-income public housing in Yemen', paper given at the 14th IAPS Conference, Stockholm (Unpublished), July 30-Aug 3, 1996.

62 C. Rutheiser, 'Mapping contested terrains: schoolrooms and streetcorners in urban Belize', in R. Rotenberg and G. McDonogh (eds.), *The Cultural Meaning of Urban Space*, (Bergin & Garvey) Westport, CN., 1993, 103-120.

63 cf. Rapoport, *Human Aspects of Urban Form*, 1977, 258-288.

64 A. Rapoport, *Human Aspects of Urban Form*, 1977, 20, 84-91; 'Neighborhood homogeneity or heterogeneity', 1980/81, 70; 'On regions and regionalism', 1992, 276, 284; *Cross-Cultural Studies and Urban Form*, 1993, 16; 'Environmental quality and environmental quality profiles', 1995, 484-6.

65 e.g. M. Abrahamson, *Urban Enclaves: Identity and Place in America*, (St. Martin's Press) New York, 1996; H. L. Margulis 'Asian Villages: downtown sanctuaries, immigrant reception areas, and festival marketplaces', *Journal of Architectural Education*, vol. 45, no. 3, May 1992, 150-160.

66 Rapoport, 'On regions and regionalism', 1992, 276-80; 'On cultural landscapes', 1992, 38.

67 e.g. references in Rapoport, *Human Aspects of Urban Form*, 1977, 258; *The Meaning of the Built Environment*, 1990, 173-4; 'On cultural landscapes', 1992, 38-9.

68 e.g. P. E. Greenbaum and S. D. Greenbaum, 'Territorial personalization', 1981, 574-589; D. D. Arreola, 'Fences as landscape taste: Tucson's barrios', *Journal of Cultural Geography*, vol. 2, no. 1, 1993, 96-105; 'House colour in Mexican-American barrios', paper presented at conference on Built Form and Culture Research, University of Kansas, Lawrence, October 18-20, 1984, (Mimeo); 'Mexican-American townscapes', *Geographical Review*, vol. 78, no. 3, 1988, 299-315.

69 D. D. Arreola & J. R. Curtis, *The Mexican Border Cities (Landscape Anatomy and Place Personality)*, (University of Arizona Press) Tucson, 1993.

70 S. O'Donnell, 'Towards urban frameworks (Accommodating change in urban cultural landscapes', M.Arch. Thesis, Dept of Architecture, University of Wisconsin-Milwaukee (unpublished), 1995.

71 e.g. Rapoport, 'On regions and regionalism', 1992, 276-280.

72 Rapoport, 'On regions and regionalism', 1992, 273-5.

73 e.g. Barth, op. cit., 1969; Jackson, *Ethnic Groups and Boundaries*, 1980.

74 Rapoport, *Human Aspects of Urban Form*, 1977; *Cross-Cultural Studies and Urban Form*, 1993; *History and Precedent in Environmental Design*, New York, Plenum, 1990, 1-120.

75 N. Fiévé, N., 'Espace architectural dans le Japan des époques classique et médiévale: l 'example des residences de l'aristocratie et de la caste militaire', *Architecture and Behaviour*, vol. 7, no. 3, September 1991, 273-299.

76 cf. Rapoport, 'The use and design of open spaces in urban neighborhoods', 1986, 159-175; 'Systems of activities and systems of settings', 1990, 9-20; 'On cultural landscapes', 1992, 37-9; *Cross-Cultural Studies and Urban Form*, 1993, 17-19.

77 e.g. Blake & Arreola, op. cit., 1996, 23-35; C. M. Anders, 'Demographics influence home sales techniques', *Honolulu Sunday Star-Bulletin and Advertiser*, July 14, 1991; cf. Rapoport, *Human Aspects of Urban Form*, 1977, 48-91; 'Thinking about home environments', 1985, 260-66; 'Designing for diversity', 1985, 30-33; 'The use and design of open spaces in urban neighborhoods', 1986, 159-75; *The Meaning of the Built Environment*, 1990, 123-176.

78 e.g. Rapoport, *Human Aspects of Urban Form*, 1977, 62-81; 'Designing for diversity', 1985, 30-36; *The Meaning of the Built Environment*, 1990, 56-176; 'Indirect approaches to environment behaviour research', 30-46.

79 S. Greenleaf, *Flesh Wounds*, (Scribner) New York, 1996, 84.

80 Guest, op. cit., 1983, 543-549.

81 cf. Rutheiser, 'Mapping contested terrains', 1993, 103-120.

82 e.g. Rapoport,'Thinking about home environments', 1985, 262-276; 'On diversity' and 'Designing for diversity', 1985, 5-8 and 30-36 respectively.

83 e.g. S. Chira, 'Hispanic families avoid using day care, study says', *New York Times*, April 6, 1994, 49.

84 Rapoport, 'Sustainability, meaning and traditional environments', 1994; 'Environmental quality and environmental quality profiles', 1995, 471-488; cf. O. Khattab, 'Environmental quality assessment: an attempt to evaluate government housing projects', *Open House International*, vol. 18, no. 4, 1993, 41-47.

85 D. M. Hummon, *Commonplaces: Community Ideology and Identity in American Culture*, (State University of New York Press) Albany, 1990; R. M. Feldman, 'Settlement-identity: psychological bonds with home places in a mobile society', *Environment and Behaviour*, vol. 22, no. 2, March 1990, 183-229; 'Constancy and change in attachments to types of settlements', *Environment and Behaviour*, vol. 28, no. 4, July 1996, 419-445.

86 S. Brower, *Good Neighbourhoods*, (Praeger) Westport, CT., 1996.

87 Rapoport, 'Some thoughts on units of settlement', 1981, 447-453; D. Johnson, 'Influx of newcomers part of a rural upturn', *New York Times*, Sept 23, 1996.

88 'S. Brower, *Good Neighbourhoods*, 1996.

89 Rapoport, 'Some thoughts on units of settlement', 1981; 'Environmental quality, metropolitan areas and traditional settlements', *Habitat International*, vol. 7, no. 3/4, 1983, 42-3.

90 M. Blanchet, 'Images et perception du quartier dans une ville nouvelle', paper given at the 14th IAPS Conference, Stockholm (unpublished), 30th July - 3rd August 1996.

91 M. Abrahamson, op. cit., 1996.

92 Rapoport, *Human Aspects of Urban Form*, 1977, 157-169, 248-315; *The Meaning of the Built Environment*, 1990, 137-176.

93 e.g. Weiss, op. cit., 1988.

94 e.g. D. D. Arreola, 'Fences as landscape taste', 1993, 96-105; 'House colour in Mexican-American barrios', 1984; 'Mexican-American townscapes', *Geographical Review*, vol. 78, no. 3, 1988, 299-315, 1988; Arreola & Curtis, *The Mexican Border Cities (Landscape Anatomy and Place Personality)*, 1993; Greenbaum & Greenbaum, 'Territorial personalisation: group identity and social interaction in a Slavic-American Neighborhood', 1981, 574-589; Hamilton, op. cit., 3-8; Janz, op. cit., 1992, 48-63; Rapoport, 'On regions and regionalism' 1992, 272-294; 'On cultural landscapes', 1992, 35-37.

95 M. Abrahamson, op. cit., 1996.

96 cf. R. W. Stevenson, 'Catering to consumers' ethnic needs', *New York Times*, 23rd January 1992, C-1; Chira, 'Hispanic families avoid using day care, study says', 1994.

97 c.f. discussion of Proposition M in Los Angeles in Rapoport 'Thinking about home environments: a conceptual framework', 1985, 263.

98 e.g. Anders, op. cit., 1991; P. Langdon, 'Lucky Houses', *Atlantic Monthly*, November 1991, 146-151.

99 L. Wheeler, 'Behavioral and social aspects of the Santa Cruz Riverpark project', *Man-Environment Systems*, vol. 7, no. 4, July 1977, 203-205.

100 P. Belluck, 'Turkish mosaic grows in New York', *New York Times*, 2nd April 1996, A-7; cf. 'Stick together, researcher advises immigrants to U.S.', *Milwaukee Journal*, 5th May 1982, 5; 'Only a heartbeat away from the Northwest Frontier', *The Times*, London, 2nd October 1982, 20; S. Spalding, 'The myth of the classic slum: contradictory perceptions of Boyle Heights Flats, 1900-1991', *Journal of Architectural Education*, vol. 45, no. 2, Feb 1992, 107-119; Wellman, op. cit., 1978, 200-217; Merry, 'Racial integration in an urban neighborhood: the social organization of strangers', 1980, 59 - 69; Pellow, 'The new urban community: mutual relevance of the social and physical environments' 1981, 15 - 26; Margulis, op. cit., 1992, 150 - 160.

101 e.g. M. Lisheron, '1000-home subdivision proposed to help preserve Hmong heritage', *Milwaukee Journal*, 25th April 1994, 5, 7.

102 op. cit., 1992, 150 - 160.

103 cf. Badura, op. cit., 1986, 55-60.

104 Rapoport,'On regions and regionalism', 1992, 276-280; 'On cultural landscapes', 1992, 37-9.

105 Rapoport, 'Flexibility, open endedness and design', 1995, 529-539, 547-9; O'Donnell, op. cit., 1995.

106 op. cit., 1992, 159-60.

107 Rapoport, *Human Aspects of Urban Form*, 1977; 'Neighborhood homogeneity or heterogeneity', 1980/81, 70-76.

108 T. Andreadou, 'Transformation of a low-income into a middle class housing area', paper given at the 14th IAPS Conference, Stockholm (unpublished), July 30-Aug 3, 1996.

109 Blanchet, op. cit., 1996.

110 Rapoport, 'Neighborhood homogeneity or heterogeneity', 1980/81, 72-3; *The Meaning of the Built Environment*, 1990, 65-86.

111 D. Halle, *America's Working Man: Work, Home and Politics among Blue-Collar Property Owners*, (University of Chicago Press), Chicago, 1984, xi-xviii and 3-33.

112 cf. R. B. Taylor and Covington, 'Neighborhood changes in ecology and violence', *Criminology*, vol. 26, no. 4, November 1988, 553-589; K. Teltsch, 'Stable neighborhoods help aging New Yorkers', *New York Times*, 6th November 1993, 9.

113 e.g. Badura, op. cit., 1986, 55-60; Teltsch, op. cit,. 1993.

114 Halle, op. cit., 1984, 10, 24-40.

115 M. M. Gordon, *Human Nature, Class and Ethnicity*, (Oxford University Press), Oxford, New York, 1978.

116 Op. cit., 1988, 557.

117 c.f. Varady, 'Neighborhood confidence', 1986, 480-501; 'Neighborhood upgrading', 1986, 271-293; Teltsch, op. cit., 1993.

118 cf. Rutheiser 1993, 103-120.

119 e.g. M. G. Holli & P. d'A. Jones (eds.), *The Ethnic Frontier*, (Eerdmans) Grand Rapids, Mi., 1977; 'Stick together, researcher advises immigrants to U.S.', *Milwaukee Journal*, 5th May 1982, 5; Wellman, op. cit., 1978, 200-217; Merry, op. cit., 1980, 59-69; 'Bronx area fights outside threats', *New York Times*, Aug 20, 1981, A-14; Belluck, op. cit., 1996, A-7.

120 e.g. S. P. Schoenberg & P. L. Rosenbaum, *Neighborhoods that Work*, (Rutgers University Press) New Brunswick, N.J., 1980; D. D. Moore, *At Home in America*, (Columbia University Press) New York, 1981; Pellow, op. cit., 1981; Kennedy & Silverman, op. cit., 1985, 275-295.

121 e.g. Gale, op. cit., 1984.

122 Rapoport, *The Meaning of the Built Environment*, 1990, 137-176.

123 Rapoport, *History and Precedent in Environmental Design*, 1990, 1-120, 243-467.

124 e.g. A. Gibbons, 'Rain forest diet: you are what you eat', *Science*, vol. 255, no. 5041, 10th January 1992, 163.

125 Rapoport, 'Culture and built form — a reconsideration', 1995, 406-7.

126 Rapoport, 'Indirect approaches to environment behaviour research', 1990, 30-46.

127 e.g. Rapoport, *Human Aspects of Urban Form*, 1977, 249-265; 'Neighborhood homogeneity or heterogeneity', 1980/81, 71-5.

128 Rapoport, *Human Aspects of Urban Form*, 1977, 256.

129 W. Michelson and P. Reed, *The Theoretical Status and Operational Usage of Lifestyle in Environmental Research*, Research Paper no. 36, Centre for Urban and Community Studies, University of Toronto, Sept. 1970 1-31.

130 Rapoport, 'Environmental quality and environmental quality profiles', 1995, 484-6.

131 e.g. Kramer op. cit., 1980.

132 Kennedy and Silverman, op. cit., 1980, 275-295; Varady, 'Neighborhood confidence', 1986, 480-501.

133 Taylor & Covington, 'Neighborhood changes in ecology and violence', 1988, 553-589; Covington & Taylor, 'Gentrification and crime', 1989, 142-172.

134 e.g. J. Bishop, 'Passing in the night: public and professional views of Milton Keynes', *Places*, vol. 1, no. 4, 1984, 9-16; R. Habe, 'Community growth gaming: a survey method', *Environment and Behaviour*, vol. 21, no. 3, May 1989, 298-322; Arthur E. Stamps III, 'Comparing preferences of neighbors and a neighborhood design review board', *Environment and Behaviour*, vol. 23, no. 5, September 1991, 616-629; Brower, 'Residents' and outsiders' perceptions of the environment', 1989; Janz, op. cit., 1992, 48-63; Spalding, op. cit., 1992, 107-119; Stevenson, 'Catering to consumers' ethnic needs', 1992.

135 Rapoport, *The Meaning of the Built Environment*, 1990, 137-8; 'On regions and regionalism', 1992, 273-6; 'On cultural landscapes', 1992, 35-7.

136 J. Ablon, 'The social organization of an urban Samoan community', *Southwest Journal of Anthropology*, vol. 27, no. 1, Spring 1970, 75-96.

137 I. Cullen et al., *Employment and Mobility in Inner Urban Areas*, (Report to SSRC), (Bartlett School of Architecture and Planning, University College London) London, August 1980, (Mimeo), 1-184; Rapoport, 'Thinking about home environments', 1985, 258-9.

138 See references in Rapoport, *Human Aspects of Urban Form*, 1977, 129-142.

139 e.g. Guest et al., op. cit., 1983, 543-549.

140 e.g. Rapoport, 'Thinking about home environments', 1985, 262-4; 'Designing for diversity', 1985, 31-33; Weiss, op. cit., 1988.

141 Rapoport, 'Thinking about home environments', 1985, 262-276; 'Designing for diversity', 1985, 31-3.

142 e.g. Stanton, op. cit., 1986, 299-300, 305, 316-319, 323-4.

143 e.g. Rutheiser, op. cit., 1993, 106-9.

144 e.g. Fiévé, op. cit., 1993, 286.

145 e.g. G. Wilson and M. Baldassarre, 'Overall "Sense of community" in a suburban region: the effects of localism, privacy and urbanization', *Environment and Behaviour*, vol. 28, no. 1, Jan 1996, 27-43.

146 e.g. Athens Centre of Elistics, 'HUCO: the human community in Athens', *Ekistics*, vol. 47, no. 283, July/Aug 1980, 232-263 (whole issue devoted to neighbourhoods); Rapoport, 'Settlements and energy: historical precedents', in W. H. Itelson et al., (eds.), *Cross-Cultural Research in Environment and Behaviour*, (University of Arizona) Tucson, 1986, 219-237; 'Learning about settlements and energy from historical precedents', *Ekistics*, vol. 54, nos. 325-327, July-December 1987, 262-268.

147 e.g. A. Hunter, *Symbolic Communities (The Persistence and Change of Chicago's Local Communities)*, (University of Chicago Press) Chicago, 1974.

148 Rapoport, 'Development, culture change and supportive design', 1983, 254-8.

149 e.g. Gale, op cit., 1984; Hamilton, op. cit., 1984, 3-8.

150 e.g. R. D. Sack, *Human Territoriality*, (Cambridge University Press) Cambridge, 1986; R. B. Taylor, *Human Territorial Functioning*, (Cambridge University Press), Cambridge, 1988, especially 80, 314-321.

151 e.g. Rapoport, *Human Aspects of Urban Form*, 1977, 277-289.

152 e.g. Rapoport, 'The use and design of open spaces in urban neighborhoods', 1986, 159-175; 'Systems of activities and systems of settings', 1990, 11-18; Bonnes, *Urban Ecology Applied to the City of Rome*, 1987; Bonnes et al., 'The city as a multi-place system', 1990, 37-65.

153 e.g. Bonaiuto et al., op. cit., 1994, 335-349.

154 S. Gaster, 'Urban children's access to their neighborhood: changes over three generations', *Environment and Behaviour*, vol. 23, no. 1, January 1991, 70-85.

155 References in Rapoport, *Human Aspects of Urban Form*, 1977.

156 Rapoport, *The Meaning of the Built Environment*, 1990, especially 11-34.

157 e.g. Hunter, op. cit., 1974.

158 Rapoport, 'On regions and regionalism', 1992, 276-280.

159 Rapoport, *The Meaning of the Built Environment*, 1990.

160 e.g. A. Christoferidis, 'New alternatives to the suburb: neo-traditional development', in J. L. Nasar & B. B. Brown (eds.), *Public and Private Spaces*, (EDRA 27), Edmond, OK., 1996, 3-17.

161 O. Newman, 'Defensible space: a new physical tool for urban revitalization', in J. L. Nasar and B. B. Brown (eds.), *Public and Private Spaces*, (EDRA 27), Edmond, OK., 1996, 18-25; K. A. Franck, 'Interview with Oscar Newman', ibid., 26-33; M. Owens, 'Saving neighborhoods one gate at a time', *New York Times*, 25th August 1994, B-1.

162 cf. Franck, op. cit., 1996, 26-9.

163 'Bronx area fights outside threats', *New York Times*, 20th August 1981, A-14.

164 Rapoport, *Human Aspects of Urban Form*, 1977, 144-5.

165 K. Hendrickson et al., *The Neighborhood Identity Project*, [Milwaukee], 25th April 1989, (Mimeo), 1-27.

166 E. S. Tijerina, 'A map for all places: now there's a name for every neighborhood', *Milwaukee Journal*, 4th March 1993, A-4.

167 *Human Aspects of Urban Form*, 1977, ch. 3.

168 Owens, 'Saving neighborhoods one gate at a time', *New York Times*, 25th August 1994; Franck, op. cit., 1996, 26-9; Newman, 'Defensible space', 1996, 18-25.

169 G. R. Meadows & S. T. Call, 'Property value trends and resident attitudes as guides to neighborhood revitalization planning: a case study of Milwaukee', in J. P. Blair and R. S. Edari (eds.), *Milwaukee's Economy*, (The Federal Reserve Bank of Chicago) Chicago, 1978, 60-85, especially 78-82.

170 On the importance of arterials see A. Pred, 'Business thoroughfares as expressions of urban Negro culture', *Ecnomic Geography*, vol. 39, July 1963, 217-233; H. P. Chudakoff, *Mobile Americans*, (Oxford University Press) Oxford, New York, 1972; 'A new look: residential depression and the concept of visibility in a medium sized city', *Journal of American History*, vol. 60, June 1973, 77-91; Y. Ginsberg, *Jews in a Changing Neighbourhood*, (Macmillan) New York, 1975; cf. Rapoport, 'On cultural landscapes', 1992, 37-9.

171 Tijerina, op cit., 1993, A-4.

172 M. M. Webber, 'Tenacious cities', paper presented at Conference on Spatial Technologies, Geographic Information and the City, Baltimore, Md., 8th - 11th September 1996, (Mimeo), 2.

WHATEVER HAPPENED TO THE GRAND LADY OF BOYLE HEIGHTS: TEENAGERS IN EAST L.A.

GRETTA MADJZOOB

In 1897 the burgeoning Catholic community of Boyle Heights decided that the time had come to build a splendid church.[1] Boyle Heights was one of the earliest subdivisions of the city, situated on pasture land on the east of the Los Angeles River; in the early 19th century few people lived there, anything of importance taking place in the plaza of the pueblo of La Reyna de los Angeles, a sleepy little town of unpaved streets and adobe houses populated by the descendants of the original settlers and a dwindling number of impoverished Indians. After 1848 and the American conquest of Mexico,[2] in 1850 California became the 31st State and Los Angeles found itself to be one of the largest cities in area in the United States, also considered by some to be the roughest.

The development of the east side of the river was closely connected with the activities of entrepreneurs and settlers, and in particular Andrew A. Boyle, who moved there from New Orleans, and his son-in-law William H. Workman, later Mayor of Los Angeles. The two families purchased flat land by the river as well as high unirrigated land on the mesa, and developed vineyards, fruit and walnut orchards. As this was not possible without irrigation, Workman ran his own aqueduct to the mesa, as well as laying out streets, building a bridge, and providing public transportation by horse trams. In 1871 Workman sold some acreage near his home and renamed his development Boyle Heights, described as being 'within a fifteen minute ride from the centre of the city ... healthy beyond dispute; free of malaria'. In 1886 after the development of the Santa Fe Railroad land values in general soared by 400-500%, and, to attract more people to Boyle Heights Workman donated land for schools, public parks, and eventually for five churches. In spite of fluctuations in the market other real estate speculators and developers continued developing Boyle Heights, and in 1896 it was made a separate parish, and plans and fund raising for the construction of the original building of St Mary's Church (figs. 6.1 and 6.2) got under way.

By the turn of the century the eastern part of Boyle Heights, known as Belvedere, marked the eastern extent of Los Angeles city growth, with the city of Vernon to the south, and farmland beyond. Within the parish of St Mary were an orphanage and school, and to its south, Pico Heights, a convent and boarding school associated with St Mary's. According to the 1899 diocesan census St Mary's parish recorded some 200 families, with Hispanic names outnumbering Irish names almost two to one. Beside Americans, the early church records show Irish, Mexican, German, Basque, Italian, Austrian, French, Canadian, Peruvian, Chilean, Philippine and Swiss parishioners. There were also Russians, who eventually moved to the West Side. Reflecting the demography of Los Angeles in general, the Americans were mostly not native Californians, and the political and social turmoil in Mexico brought an influx of Mexicans. The proximity of unskilled work and the efficient public transport system of Boyle Heights also attracted considerable numbers of Mexicans from the central city. The area continued to prosper, and in the 1920s-40s was a centre for the Jewish Community, almost exclusively from Eastern Europe, a number of whom moved from the Brooklyn area of New York and established businesses on Brooklyn Avenue (now renamed Cesar Chavez Avenue), with residences nearby in the City Terrace area on the hills in East L.A. In the 1940s it was the largest Jewish community — numbering some 75,000 — west of Chicago, and the only one of its kind on the West Coast. Today there are less than 10 Jewish families in Boyle Heights and City Terrace.[3]

THE DOWNTURN

This formerly thriving prosperous, forward looking area, is now considered deprived, run down and 'dangerous', with social problems connected with unemployment, overcrowding, crime, juvenile delinquency and street gangs. We will consider here the interaction of urban space and

fig. 6.1 Church of St Mary of the Annunciation, Boyle Heights, founded in 1897 on the corner of 4th and Chicago Streets, in the fifth oldest Catholic parish in Los Angeles, built with the aid of funds raised from the parishioners by Fr. Joseph Doyle (photo: R. Ruiz).

fig. 6.2 Interior of St Mary's Church showing embellishments donated by benefactors, and children from St Mary's School preparing for Easter celebrations (photo: R. Ruiz).

social factors and their role in the quality of life in this particular locality situated in one of the wealthiest parts of the developed world.

The infrastructure and communications of a major metropolis like Los Angeles, with its opportunities for employment and improvement act as a magnet; Boyle Heights has hospitals, schools, parks (fig. 6.3) and recreation facilities, and a community with strong cultural identity, but in spite of this could be described as a third world pocket in a first world city.

Neighbourhoods in American cities are known for being subject to change, and one of the most important causes of downgrading is usually considered to be the influx of relatively poor people. In the 'middle class' public conscience, ethnic minorities in general fall into this bracket, with a consequence that characteristic signs of a minority population may be seen as unfavourable, even if the people in question are prospering. Many subjective factors determine where people choose to live, and influence house prices, to the extent that in the past rumours or allegations that speculators were letting property to poor people could be an effective way of persuading better off people to move to new developments. Conversely real estate agents may aim to enhance the

appeal of an area by hinting to clients that members of ethnic minorities would not be shown properties there — although it is, of course, against the law to discriminate. Many other factors to do with employment, services, amenities and size of living space have contributed to people moving away from the old centres of cities to more spacious suburbs — the doughnut effect. In Los Angeles strenuous efforts are being made to reverse the impoverishment and downgrading which has occurred in the administrative quarter of the Downtown area because of these shifts of population, but Boyle Heights is no longer an important commercial area, and has all the visible signs of the doughnut effect. These include boarded up business premises, barricades and graffiti, as well as the invisible barriers associated with the reputation of the area.

DEMOGRAPHIC PROFILE

East Los Angeles, located approximately 4 miles east of Los Angeles civic centre, is an unincorporated community of about 171,000 people with a median age of 24.6.[4] The 1990 Census figures for Boyle Heights,[5] situated within East L.A., give a total population of 57,494 with 90.8% Hispanic,

fig. 6.3 St Louis Street with Hollenbeck Park on the right and housing near the Linda Vista Community Hospital (photo: R. Ruiz).

and a median family income of $17,100 p.a. A large number (2,585) of people under the age of 17 are noted as not speaking English well, with an even larger number (16,521) in the over 18 years old age group. It should be born in mind that Spanish is used as a second language for administrative purposes in L.A., but lack of English is certainly a disadvantage from the point of view of skilled employment. From the point of view of the authorities, the figures for Boyle Heights show it as one of the largest Latino communies of L.A., and put it into the category of a relatively poor Hispanic neighbourhood, with a disadvantaged population. Whether or not this of itself makes it a 'bad' neighbourhood is perhaps not the point, but it is important for the way it is perceived.

HOUSING

Home ownership is an important goal in American society, and a high proportion of rented accommodation in a neighbourhood tends to indicate a less well-off, mobile or transient population. This is now the case in Boyle Heights, where 11,354 households are noted as living in rented accommodation, with a median rental of $418

p.m.[6] Apart from privately rented apartments, Boyle Heights also has one of the earliest Public Housing Projects (figs 6.5, 6.6) funded by the City of Los Angeles. It consists of nine blocks of low rise apartments with communal spaces in between. The 'Projects' are divided into three sections, Aliso Village, Aliso Extension, and Pico Park.

The complex is set between 1st and 4th Streets, and the apartments look over communal spaces which are open to the public road (figs. 6.6 and 6.7). There are no balconies or private outdoor spaces, and the communal space is either grassed over and provided with washing lines, or left bare with some minimal facilities for children to play. The buildings and exterior space are maintained by the Housing Authority and present a neat aspect, but the lack of seclusion in the semi-public open space means that there is little activity compared to what would be seen in a private complex. Where such complexes are similar in general plan but are privately owned and let (apartments) or owner occupied (condominiums), they are normally subdivided, fenced and gated, and have small private gardens or patios outside the units, while the landscaping and planting of semi-private circulation and parking areas is also

fig. 6.4 Back street behind St Mary's Church and School (photo: R. Ruiz).

fig. 6.5 Los Angeles Housing Authority Housing Project with nine low-rise blocks of apartments. The space between is planned as communal, but is marked off as territory by local street gangs (photo: R. Ruiz).

fig. 6.6 Children's' play area in the Housing Project (photo: R. Ruiz).

designed to give seclusion and cut direct views into ground floor units. Maintenance, sometimes including closed circuit television cameras and security staff, is paid for by fixed contributions to Home Owners Associations, and may involve substantial sums. In the Boyle Heights Housing Projects on the other hand, the semi-public space comes right up to the ground floor windows, and a number of these units are unoccupied and boarded up, presumably because of the obvious problems associated with the lack of security this configuration produces. 'Village' scenes of people sitting outside their doors or gathering in the squares are not a feature of life in the Projects. The circulation areas are just that, and their emptiness means people have no inclination to reclaim them for social use.

There are 12 units to each three storey building, with the size of the apartments varying between one to two bedrooms in Aliso Village, the thee blocks to the north, two bedrooms in Aliso Extension in the centre, and two to five bedooms, with larger kitchens, in Pico Park, the three blocks to the south of the complex on 4th St. The rent ranges from $50-$300 per month, and is dependent on income, rather than the size of the apartment. The size of the rooms in the units is minimal, in the two bedroom units, for example, living rooms are about 8x10' (2.50x3.00m) and the bedrooms this size or smaller, with a 7x5' (2.15x150m) kitchen. These are unusually small for Californian dwellings even in the least affluent neighbourhoods, such as the area adjacent to the Projects (fig. 6.7). The units are designed for three or four people, but residents interviewed pointed out that people who do not qualify for social housing move in with partners who do, such as women with dependent children,[7] so their are far more people living in the Projects than planned.

LIFE IN THE PROJECTS

According to community workers and residents the design of the Projects has created social problems associated with dense housing and lack of recreation space. In addition there is a high level of gang activity in the neighbourhood. In the Projects each section has a gang, and therefore groups from other buildings are considered to be rivals, and infringements of 'territory' not tolerated. Residents do not therefore have full use of the open space which does exist, even with the shortcomings mentioned above, and children

fig. 6.7 Houses on 3rd Street opposite the Housing Project (photo: R. Ruiz).

have little room to play. According to three young males interviewed, the dominant gang is known as TMC (The Mob Crew) after a break-dance group. The interviewees had lived in the projects most of their lives, and were unemployed. They appeared to act as community gate keepers, and their permission was acquired for taking photographs. The pattern is for teenagers to be recruited as gang members from the age of about 11, and grow out of gang activities as they get older and have children.

In spite of all these drawbacks, the residents have some attachment to the Projects. The City had plans to demolish them in 1997 so that they could be rebuilt with two storey buildings and some townhouses. The families were to be relocated, but many had lived in the projects all their lives, and did not want to move, so a court order was acquired by the residents to put a hold on demolition. The low rents and cohesive community proved to be overriding factors, especially as alternative accommodation in the neighbourhood is also likely to be overcrowded, to make it affordable. In a similar way, as far as schooling is concerned, while there is dissatisfaction about the quality of schooling available locally, the maj-

ority of parents did not favour bussing children to schools in other districts.[8]

VISIBLE AND INVISIBLE BARRIERS

The general environment of Boyle Heights is stigmatised by numerous visible barriers in the form of barricades around the police station and other institutions, such as school yards (fig. 6.4) and the Synagogue. The need for security is not of course exclusive to run down areas, but for prestigious new administrative shopping and housing complexes in L.A. the gates and fortifications are part of the architectural planning, rather than obvious ad hoc arrangements added to buildings. Commercial premises in Boyle Heights lack openings on the street or exposed sides, and vulnerable points are likely to be boarded up to deter thieves (fig. 6.8). The long expanses of blank wall are targets for graffiti, tags and slogans associated with gangs, and to counteract this some premises have large murals with themes relating to the community (fig. 6.9). However, the number of empty premises and lack of public street life give an overall aspect that is threatening, especially to outsiders. The deformed

125

grid pattern of the streets and combination of main thoroughfares with residential side streets is typical of L.A., but as with the blocks in the Housing Projects the reasons for areas being underused are connected with the social life of the area rather than its physical design.

The invisible barriers which stigmatise an area like this are harder to quantify. They may indicate to outsiders that the area is undesirable or unsafe, and divide it up for residents. Los Angelenos are accustomed to avoiding unknown areas considered as unsafe, and the perceived danger of entering 'bad' neighbourhoods is of course an extremely important deterrent for outsiders, who have no particular reason to emerge from the freeway system which runs to the north, west and south of the core area, as there are few specific attractions or facilities which are not available in other districts. The danger of entering run down areas may or may not be justified by the level of crime or gang activity and control, but it is usually considered advisable for people unfamiliar with such an area to avoid it at night, and in the case of Boyle Heights, this researcher was cautioned by local community workers that it would be unadvisable to walk about taking photographs without a companion acceptable to the local people.

These barriers to do with reputation are perhaps the most difficult to discard in the context of improving urban areas in L.A. Efforts may be made to remedy the social problems, but the name alone will be enough to dissuade outsiders from moving there or even taking a job. Many health services, for example, have difficulty retaining their professional staff due to a combination of low salaries and the possibility of gang violence, especially for clinics operating in the evenings.[9] These negative views may, however, have little relevance to the people of the area, who may have an entirely different perception of what it has to offer, as has been seen by the reaction to the proposed demolition of the Projects.

THE TEENAGE BIRTH RATE

When assessing the quality and causes of change in an urban area, no factor can be considered in isolation, but it may be useful to consider a particular phenomena in some detail to establish the extent to which it reveals salient factors. Boyle eights has a young population with approximately 20% in the 10-19 year age range.[10]

Among the social problems which effects the population is the high incidence of teenage pregnancy. The area has one of the highest birth rates

in Los Angeles County, and a high rate of teenage pregnancy. The number of teenage live births for 1993 was 7 for under age 15, 111 for 15-17 age group, and 160 for 18-19 year age group.[11] A recent study carried out concerning teenagers in Boyle Heights[12] with the aim of finding an appropriate educational model to address the problem, provided detailed data on housing and use of urban space, as well as insights on how this subgroup viewed their physical environment.

Over one million teenage girls in the US become pregnant every year, the highest rate for western industrialised countries,[13] with California having the highest proportion.[14] According to the Children's Defence Fund, young mothers from minority groups, whether black or Hispanic, are four to five times more likely to become unwed mothers dependent on the welfare system.[15] Teenage pregnancy also contributes to a large number of school drop outs in both male and female students, leading to inadequate education and job skills. Approximately 70% of teenage women who give birth finish high school before the age of 40 compared to 90% of women who have children later in life. Furthermore nearly 60% of teenage mothers live in poverty at the time they give birth.[16] Lack of education and poverty are associated with low birthweight babies, Sudden Infant Death Syndrome, accidents and developmental delays, as well as inadequate immunization of the babies. By the age of two 72% of babies born to teenage parents in California are not up to date on their immunizations.[17] Furthermore one third of teenage mothers receive inadequate pre-natal care, resulting in poor health outcomes for mother and child, and contributing to high public health costs.[18] Early sexual activity and lack of appropriate education is also responsible for the high rates of sexually transmitted diseases among young adults. According to the Centers for Disease Control three million teenagers contract an STD each year, accounting for a quarter of the cases reported annually.[19] These figures again present a picture of the young people of Boyle Heights as a disadvantaged population likely to remain so.

However, the study of Boyle Heights teenagers revealed that contrary to the view of the authorities, teenage pregnancy was not viewed by this group as a particularly stigmatized or negative event in the girls life. Hispanic-American values are assumed to be significantly different from those of Anglos in terms of the way large numbers of children are perceived, and two concepts often emphasised are 'familism' — the Hispanic woman defining herself almost exclusively in a

fig. 6.8 Mural incorporating images related to the local community on the blank walls of a pharmacy with windows shuttered to deter thieves (photo: R. Ruiz).

fig. 6.9 The Homeboy Bakery and Printing Company, started by Fr. Greg Boyle of the Dolores Mission to generate employment in the community (photo: R. Ruiz).

maternal role, and machismo — the Hispanic man's self-esteem conceptualised as being determined by the number of children he procreates.[20] In the past, many teenagers and their parents welcomed the option of teen motherhood since the child would bring additional income to the household in the form of welfare payments.[21] Older relatives were also available to help with child care, so the mother did not face the prospect of rearing the child in isolation.

During pregnancy, whether married or not,[22] a teenager is given extra care and space at home, and many view pregnancy as a way to gain status, respect and attention within the family and the community, or may see it as a way to achieve stability in a relationship, or even as a means of dropping out of school and 'taking a break'. The short term advantages for the young woman are likely to be heavily outweighed by the disadvantages and restrictions of having to bring up a child on a low income with inadequate housing, and before she has finished her own education. However, many of the people who find themselves in this position have themselves been brought up in an impoverished single parent household, and the majority do not take the option of terminating the pregnancy, or of having the child adopted, partly perhaps because living with these difficulties is the norm. The cycle therefore continues.

The links between this phenomenon and the living space — public and private — in Boyle Heights, and in other similar areas, are not, of course, tenuous. The type of social profile this phenomenon produces leads to an on-going situation in which residents are not in a position to improve their existing living environment or move on to a better one, and if they do manage to, there are people ready to take their place. In this situation, improvements for example to the layout and circulation in the Projects to increase security might be unwelcome, and seen as an invasion of privacy, as these would make control and enforcement of regulations more feasible, while at present the families are in a position to keep living expenses to a minimum by crowding together. Improvements and upgrading of particular buildings and control of occupancy levels would therefore be likely to move the problem somewhere else, rather than make a fundamental difference.

COSTS TO GOVERNMENT

In an urban area, a large proportion of people living on welfare is a contributing factor to general downgrading. As well as the implications for the individuals concerned, teenage parenthood is a matter of concern for government because of the public cost. Due to a teenage parent's lack of education and job skills she is likely to become dependent on the welfare system. An estimated 53% of funds dispensed by the Aid to Families with dependant children programme is for families formed through teenage birth. The public cost over a 20 year period for first births to teenagers in California was $717 million,[23] and for the whole country the US spent $16.65 billion on families which had started with teenage mothers.[24]

There is growing concern in government that welfare payments should provide a safety net, but not lead to dependency. However the situation remains that cities develop pockets where people are caught in the poverty/welfare trap, as has happened in many parts of L.A. Following recent reforms to the welfare system by the Clinton administration, many children born to teen-age mothers after March 1st 1997 will not qualify for welfare. Young men interviewed at the time of the announcement of these changes were of the opinion that they would be likely to lead to a drop in the number of teenage mothers.[25] In addition, more grandmothers have joined the paid labour force, and are not therefore available for child care. This has already forced young mothers to put up their children for adoption.

The urban poor, however, may not necessarily react to changes in the Welfare system in the desired fashion, by becoming productive citizens conforming overnight to the work ethics and norms of American society. Being a fully fledged member of mainstream western society tends to mean having cash and spending it. The space in the cities is largely occupied by places for earning money and places for spending it, and tends to become marginal if it does not fit into this pattern, as do people who exist outside this framework. If the people of an area are living near the poverty line commerce is unlikely to thrive or develop, and the public space suffers from the general desolation.

TERRITORY OF TEENAGERS

As far as private space is concerned, in East L.A. living conditions are in many cases extremely cramped, with up to 6 individuals residing in a single bedroom. With members of the household working different shifts all may not be sleeping at the same time, but private space is not an assumed part of the home environment. The teenagers interviewed had various ways of dealing with this, such as letting each other know when apartments would be empty while the occupants were out at work. Many male residents compensate for lack of space by owning spacious vans with tinted glass. When asked about sources of entertainment, gathering at each others apartments to watch TV and 'hang out', and using vacant warehouses as locations for parties at weekends were cited. The males view attending these parties as 'scoring points', and the females as a sign of status and attention. Perhaps more surprisingly, attending Church on Sundays was also viewed as a social event, and useful for 'checking out guys'.

The lack of space does, however, seem to have a direct effect on the way the teenagers manage their personal lives. Many teenagers, for example, feel that possession of contraceptives is not acceptable in the family, and lack of personal space prevents them from retaining and carrying methods of birth control. Most are embarrassed about purchasing means of birth control, and lack knowledge about the resources of the area such as the free clinics in East L.A. and L.A. County. The social profile, and high incidence of young single parents can thus be seen to some extent to have its roots in their living environment.

When it comes to socialising, an important activity for teenagers living in crowded conditions is simply 'hanging out' in the street. While this may be an innocuous activity in itself it has a threatening effect on passers by. In the gang culture of run down areas, claiming territory in this way by establishing pockets where a particular group makes its presence felt may be seen as a reaction to the sense of insecurity felt by the individual in the urban jungle. These pockets can easily become no-go areas both for local people as well as outsiders, simply because when individuals avoid that particular corner, or cross the street, the territory perceived as unsafe becomes empty, and even more threatening. It is far more difficult for such a situation to develop where there is plenty of activity and circulation, but when circulation declines at particular times of day, or because, due to a combination of factors, businesses stop trading and there are areas of shuttered or empty premises this behaviour emerges. For the public, the importance of having a *sense* of security has led to a decline in street life in general in L.A., and the predominance of enclosed shopping malls which also provide facilities for strolling and relaxation. The nearest mall to East L.A. is the Glendale Galleria, one of the largest in L.A., where many teenagers congregate, especially during the school holidays.

For fear of the secure ambience being compromised in any way, many malls, particularly ones situated near areas where gang activity is prevalent, have regulations prohibiting the wearing of colours that may be associated with gangs, or only allow teenagers to stroll around if accompanied by an adult. Some ban groups of teenagers outright. As far as the teenagers are concerned, this kind of control further limits where they can go to socialise, and makes the knots of youths standing about even more of a feature of depressed areas.

SOCIAL PROBLEMS — REDRESSING THE BALANCE

Problem areas naturally become the target of interest by various institutions from Federal to local level. Initiatives and projects are launched, often with substantial funding. How far these have long term effects on the overall quality of an area can be difficult to quantify, but perhaps a reason such areas often retain their run down character despite all the work, is that the relationship between the inhabitants and the space they live in is not really considered. The 'needs' are assumed, and housing, schools, clinics and other facilities may be built, with or without approval and support from the residents, but perhaps without fundamental questions being addressed about what makes the community what it is. Planners and other professionals, including those dedicated to 'community' issues may need to step back from seeing their work only in terms of the goals of a particular discipline, and look at what evolves by its own momentum through the social dynamics of the place.

Tragic incidents such as the shooting of a three year old girl in Cypress Park draw media attention and trigger reactions. For example, following this incident Federal Housing Secretary Henry Cisneros went to the area and listened to residents' accounts of the problems of living with crime and gangs. Speaking in the context of the renovation of a dilapidated 1920's fire station as a community centre, he expressed the view that 'this neighbourhood needs a lot of help, and it needs it from the Federal Government.... It doesn't need a trickle down programme that doesn't trickle down... That's no way we have to live in America... There's no way we can see ourselves a civilised society when parents have to change bedrooms with their children because they're afraid they'll become victims of crimes'.[26]

A BROAD VIEW

In 1990 the Los Angeles Design Action Planning Team carried out an intensive four day public workshop in Boyle Heights to bring to the forefront vital urban issues.[27] The team found that the industrial environment in the area was deteriorating, and that recently enacted environmental regulations would be likely to cause job losses in the furniture manufacturing and metal plating industries, and also dissuade cleaner industries from locating in the area because of the cost of required toxic clean-ups, on top of high land acquisition costs (about $50.00 per sq. ft. for industrial property). Their report pointed out that transportation was geared to efficient distribution of goods and not to the well being of residents and workers, with extensive (illegal) use of residential streets for truck traffic making the streets unsuitable for normal neighbourhood activity. The manner of implementation of previous government projects, such as the Freeway system and L.A. River Aqueduct, had resulted in public controversy and a lack of trust in the authorities.

While existing informal cultural, religious and family networks were seen as strong, the lack of affordable housing was felt to be threatening the stability of the neighbourhood. Families found it difficult to access available funds and loans for rehabilitation or purchase, sometimes because the banks had no loan officer at the local branch, or account and deposit requirements which made borrowing prohibitive. Although many of these problems still remain, forums of this kind do give the community the opportunity to discuss urban issues with members of a variety of concerned professions.

LOCAL INITIATIVES

A number of local bodies are concerned with practical and social issues in the area, some of them based on the six churches. St Mary's is still the largest, with an active congregation, and facilities for adult education and community projects. One of these is the Hope in Youth project set up in 1995 after the Cypress Park shooting. Hope in Youth coordinates activities involving schools, churches, and some 40 agencies and community organisations to do with leadership development training, employment readiness training, parenting, and parent leadership development training as well as projects such as cleaning up particular areas. The aim is to provide support of all kinds to parents and children to develop skills, increase self-esteem and empowerment. In many cases the programme has estimated a change of status in the parents from At-Risk to Safe/Self Sufficient as a result of participation in the programmes.[28]

The Hollenbeck Youth Centre also aims to provide activities for the local youth to do with widening their horizons and looking outside the petty world of gang culture. As the main sports facility in the neighbourhood, the sporting and social activities are seen as part of the initiatives offering alternatives to gang membership, or just hanging around on the streets. Other examples of local strategies which attempt to reduce the impact of gangs include painting murals with images relating to the cultural roots of the people (figs 6.9 and 6.10) on blank walls which would usually be covered with graffiti.

As far as employment is concerned, the 1980 profile of the local economy in East L.A.[29] mentions the great majority of businesses being in the retail trade (44.1%) and services (32%), many being small family run businesses with relatively low turnover. The largest sources of employment are also in retail and services, with a small amount of manufacturing, the local businesses being generally either small, and firmly dependent on the local economy, or large and more interlinked with the region than the local economy. However, only 21% of the active resident labour force was employed within East L.A., and it was found that large local businesses have very weak linkages with the local community. Only 41% of the jobs in East L.A. are held by local residents. Although it is normal for people to travel considerable distances to other areas for work, it is felt that given the high level of unemployment, provision of more jobs within the area could be expected to have positive effects.

The Homeboy Bakery and Printing Company is an example of a local initiative in this direction. The name refers to the concept of neighbourhood, and the Company, started by Fr. Greg Boyle of Dolores Mission Church with the aim of providing opportunities for young people, employs local men and women, and is the main supplier of bread to the White Memorial Medical Centre. While the district is not an attractive commercial proposition because of all the factors discussed above, more small developments of this kind which aim to build up the employment and business prospects of the area from within may have an important contribution to make in its regeneration.

THE DRIVE TO SUCCEED

The present population of Boyle Heights can be seen as being in a direct line with the original migrants to Southern California, in the sense of seeing L.A. as a place to improve their economic position, take advantage of educational opportunities and in general achieve their aspirations in the Land of Opportunity. While it may appear that conditions of life in Boyle Heights do not altogether live up to the American Dream, for migrant workers in particular, it can still be the setting for an improved lifestyle. Although conditions may be well below what is expected in the U.S., communities like Boyle Heights have their own cohesiveness and social networks which make them viable. The population may be seen by outsiders as an underclass, a pocket of the third world, but they themselves are aware of their first world rights. Social and economic im-provement is an achievable aspiration, and there are many role models for people to look to.

Under these conditions, discontent and anger when the door of opportunity appears to be shut, rather than resignation and acceptance of low social status is a predictable reaction. Gang related and criminal activity provides alternative hierarchical structures, 'respect', and status, as well as the proceeds of crime. Giving an individual the means of being self sufficient, so removing the need for this kind of power, is considered a high priority in L.A. and other disturbed urban centres. As far as improving the urban environment is concerned, this point of view is prevalent at all levels from small community based initiatives of the kind mentioned above, to Federal interventions.

SHAPING URBAN SPACE FROM WITHIN

Finding ways of making the best use of the space in such a complex situation is not an easy task for urban designers and planners. Beyond acquiring an understanding of the public space, and its relationship with the surrounding buildings, it is perhaps equally important to understand what is going on inside the buildings.

Understanding the dynamics of physical barriers and circulation patterns is increasingly being seen as crucial for the creation and retention of well integrated environments, as opposed to disparate structures standing in lifeless space. However, the assumption underlying this is that societies are homogeneous, and that people will react in a predictable way to adjustments in the physical characteristics of the particular maze they live in. Los Angeles is an example of a society which does not pretend to be homogeneous, and which is highly segregated according to ethnic and social groupings, particularly as far as residential areas are concerned. America may indeed be a melting pot, but in such a complex society, while people may welcome the opportunity of benefiting from the diversity as far as work is concerned, in many cases they prefer to live in a familiar environment when it comes to their language and culture.

In Los Angeles this is well recognised, and the ethnic composition of a neighbourhood is not a hidden factor. The invisible barriers may expand or contract, but people know where they are. This is not necessarily a negative state. If it is assumed that close communities are of value, and have the capacity to provide social support of all kinds from within, they should perhaps be encouraged. This is particularly the case if the motivation for segregation comes from within, rather than being imposed from outside as with a ghetto.

We have pointed out how the ethnicity of an area can produce the initial territorial barrier, which in turn is reinforced by the area developing as an ethnic enclave. The invisible barriers produced may be stronger than visible or formal administrative ones, but need to be assessed realistically rather than ideologically to find what inner strength is contained within enclaves such as Boyle Heights, and how this can best be fostered to improve the quality of urban life in the city. Los Angeles with its huge diversity of cultures provides a constantly changing view of the interaction of these cultures in urban space, and their role in shaping it, and there are important lessons to be learnt from how this has been and is happening and what it means to the people concerned.

Gretta Madjzoob
California State University, Northridge

NOTES

Acknowledgement. Professor Raul Ruiz, Professor of Chicano Studies, Education Department, California State University, Northridge kindly provided the photographs of Boyle Heights.
1 The information on the development of Boyle Heights and St

Mary's parish is taken from Rev. Robert Delis, S.D.B., *The Grand Lady of Boyle Heights: a history of St. Mary's Church, Los Angeles*, Los Angeles, 1989, vii-viii, 1-12.
2 Rios-Antonio Bustamente, *Mexican Los Angeles: a narrative*

history, Nuestra Historia Series, Monogrpah no. 1, (Floricanto Press) Los Angeles CA., 1992, 146-8.

3 Ellie Kahn, *Meet me at Brooklyn and Soto*, Video (Soutern California Jewish Historical Society), Los Angeles, 1996.

4 Los Angeles County Department of Health Services, *Vital Statistics 1994*, Statistical Report Series 3, 8-9.

5 U.S. Bureau of Census, 1990, *Summery of Key Census Data by Census Tract, L.A. County, Boyle Heights, Zip code 90033*, STF3A Extract, 31.

6 Ibid.

7 Interviews with residents, March 1997. The interviewees preferred to remain anonymous.

8 *Los Angeles County Board of Supervisors Report*, October 1980, 40-45.

9 Ibid.

10 U.S. Bureau of Census, 1990, *Summery of Key Census Data by Census Tract, L.A. County, Boyle Heights, Zip code 90033*, STF3A Extract, 31.

11 Source: L.A. California, Department of Health Services, *Teenage Live Births by Zip Code and Age Range within Zip Code Boyle Heights 90033*, (Maternal and Child Health Epidemiology Section), 1993, 8.

12 Gretta Madjzoob, 'A family planning educational model for junior high school students of the East Los Angeles area', Graduate Project submitted in partial satisfaction of the requirements for the Degree of Master of Public Health, California State University, Northridge, May 1989. Some information has been updated for this paper.

13 California Department of Health Services, Maternal and Child Health, *Release of Facts at a Glance, Data on Teen Fertility in the US*, 1993, 98.

14 Summaries of statistical data published by Planned Parenthood Affiliates of California, *Facts of Life in California*, 1993; cited: Centre for Population Options, *Adolescents, Aids and HIV*, July 1991; State of California Department of Health Services, *AIDS/HIV Update*, April 30th 1992.

15 Children's Defence Fund, *Adolescent Pregnancy*, (Adolescent Pregnancy Prevention), 1992, 55-56.

16 The Alan Guttmacher Institute, *Sex and America's Teenagers*, 1994.

17 U.S. Department of Health and Human Services, Centre for Disease Control, *Monthly Vital Statistics Reports*, April 15th 1992, 5.

18 The Alan Guttmacher Institute, *Sex and America's Teenagers*, 1994.

19 Centres for Disease Control Division of STD/HIV Prevention *Annual Reports*, 1993, 11; L.A. County Department of Health Services, Sexually Transmitted Disease Programme, *Teens and STDs in L.A. County: the quiet epidemic*, November 1995, (summary report) 92.

20 S. J. Andrade, 'Family planning attitudes and practices as a function of degree of cultural identification of female Mexican-American college Students', Ph. D. Thesis, The University of Texas at Austin, 1979, 929.

21 Interview with Jamie P. Ortega, Team Leader, Hope in Youth, Boyle Heights, March 1997.

22 The focus in the literature is usually on out-of-wedlock births. However, by the age of 18 as many as 20% of Hispanic women are married, as compared with 3% of blacks and 4% of whites in the U.S. In addition an unknown percentage may be living with their partners, see K. Fennelly, *El embarazo poecoz: Childbearing among Hispanic teenagers in the United States*, Columbia University School of Public Health, New York, 1988, 15.

23 *Facts of Life in California*, (Planned Parenthood Affiliates of California) 1996, 2.

24 M. R. Butt, *Estimates of Public Costs for Teenage Childbearing*, (Centre For Population Opinions) Washington DC, 1986, 3.

25 Interviews with residents, March 1997.

26 Geoffrey Mohan, 'Cisneros tours site of Cypress Park Killings', *L.A. Times*, Metro, October 15, 1995.

27 *A Los Angeles Design Action Planning Team Report*, co-sponsored by the City of Los Angeles Planning Department and the Urban Design Advisory Coalition, Boyle Heights L.A. CA., May 11th-14th 1990.

28 'Hope in Youth Updates', St Mary's and Sacred Heart, June 1996.

29 *L.A. County Board of Supervisors Report*, October, 1980, 40-45.

Urban Design Studies, Volume 3, 1997

IN DEFENCE OF THE IMAGINATION:
BRIDGING THE GAP BETWEEN PLANNERS AND ARCHITECTS

MELANIE RICHARDSON AND DEREK TROWELL

In an educational climate where many architects still find it difficult to define clearly the field of urban design, it is not surprising to see that students of architecture, and, perhaps even more so, students of town and regional planning — find the subject hard to grasp. Furthermore in the UK, the training of students of planning does not include any design element for either buildings or landscapes. The students are, therefore, less likely to have well developed skills involving visual judgment and graphic presentation. Nevertheless, as with the public they will serve, they may well have strong views on what are at heart aesthetic matters. In such a climate there is a need to direct future — and perhaps even present — planners to be better able to evaluate the form, scale and pattern of proposals for replacement or extension of the fabric of the built environment, and to understand the roots underlying subjective ideas of 'good' and 'bad' design. Planners with personal experience in such areas will, no doubt, be better equipped to evaluate proposals without allowing personal prejudices, or often excessively conservative guide-lines to dominate their views. A further problem in the generation of successful redevelopment of urban areas is the conflict between the professions involved in promoting, or sometimes apparently preventing, the evolution of these areas, and a lack of tolerance or understanding of the viewpoints and responsibilities of members of related professions.

With these issues in mind a teaching programme was developed at Sheffield University for second year students of town and regional planning, which attempts to bridge the perceived divide between architects and planners. The aim was to equip students with sufficient presentation skills and historical background to allow a more philosophical exploration of urban design — an approach unusual within typical planning courses at present. As is usual with planning students, they had very little previous experience of viewing and analysing an area or town in architectural terms, and presenting their ideas visually. An aim was, therefore, to enable the students to develop methods of urban analysis in order to be able to identify and relate aspects of urban development to existing townscape characteristics and visual enhancement. The other aims were to increase their awareness of the way architectural forms reflect philosophical and social concepts, and to develop their skills in presentation techniques.

The main content of the course was practical, and the aim was to avoid an overdose of theory, but theoretical questions, such as Rossi's views with regard to cities were explored in the course of the work especially his view that:

> 'By architecture of the city we mean two different things: first, the city seen as a gigantic man-made object, a work of engineering that is large and complex and growing over time: second, certain more limited but still crucial aspects of the city, namely urban artifacts, which like the city itself are characterised by their own history and thus by their own form'.[1]

The way the form of architecture and patterns of space around and between them is produced by physical and psychological needs and perceptions, and the importance of satisfying these needs by designers of cities was also debated, as well as the way concepts such as zoning develop and are set aside.

BAKEWELL MARKET

In order to give the students an opportunity of working closely with planners, and comparing their work with professional proposals for a site, a real urban regeneration project was selected, concerning the redevelopment of an area within the small market town of Bakewell (fig. 7.1), situated in the Peak District National Park, Derbyshire. The brief had been developed over a long

fig. 7.1 Plan of Bakewell showing the tight urban grain of the settlement, with the market at the core.

period by officers of the Peak Park Joint Planning Board (PPJPB), and had involved consultation with many local interest groups. The town is of historic interest — a livestock market has been held there since 1330, and is situated in an area of Outstanding Natural Beauty, qualities which had to be considered in any proposal. The final document provided concise details of the requirements. We were fortunate to secure the support of PPJPB for our project, who agreed to act as the client. At the various reviews incorporated into the programme a client representative was present to comment on the presentation, answer questions and offer advice. The presentations were both formal and informal, and were held in the University Planning Department, and at the offices of the Planning Board.

STRUCTURE OF THE PROJECT AND THE BRIEF

In structuring the project a comment by Carl Rogers was born in mind:

> 'The evaluation of the extent and significance of the student's learning is made primarily by the learner, although this self evaluation may be influenced and enriched by caring feedback from other members of the group and from the facilitator'.[2]

Such a strategy was appropriate in view of the limitations of time and staffing available for the project. With two staff members teaching 30-35 students one day a week with three hours for all

fig. 7.2 Example of a long narrow grit-stone double aspect dwelling typical of the domestic vernacular architecture of the Bakewell area, and of the Peak District in general, with extensions constructed to blend with the original building in a style acceptable to the planning authorities (drawing: D. Trowell Architects).

work, within 12 weeks of a 15 week semester, practical solutions were needed to cover the necessary ground, which included research; site visit and analysis; development of proposals; model making and graphic presentation; all leading to the final submission and review, with the whole exercise bearing in mind the primary aim of familiarising *planning* students with current *architectural* thinking. The project was also prefaced by a short lecture course, and practical exercises to do with scale, presentation techniques, and the use and interpretation of maps, using collage, photo montage and sketching.

The essence of the project was to re-locate the town market, mindful of the need to preserve the character and urban fabric of Bakewell. The town as it exists today has evolved very largely as a consequence of its historically important weekly livestock market which remains a key to the local economy and to the wider economy of the National Park. Its location, however, in a confined space at the heart of the town of Bakewell is no longer appropriate for a number of reasons, centring on the unacceptable level of traffic congestion that local people, tourists and market traders all have to endure.

The market is considered locally as a cultural and social, as well as an economic asset. The need therefore was to identify a new location within the town for the livestock market, and propose a

commercially viable development for its current site to fund the project. As with many development projects in historic settings, any conflict between 'local needs' and commercial viability needed to be resolved, both from the points of view of the community vis-a-vis the developer, and that of the local planning authority and the developer. In Bakewell there were two clearly identifiable local needs: low cost housing, preferably for rent, and a permanent library to replace the existing temporary facility. Neither of these on their own would be likely to attract proposals from developers, and a scheme which would incorporate benefits to the community with long term commercial prospects was required.

PROJECT CO-ORDINATION AND RESEARCH

For the main research and design aspects the students worked in groups, and reviewed each other's work, each group preparing an initial proposal. The students then voted for one proposal, and concentrated on developing this for the final submission. The winning group became the co-ordinating group, and was responsible for breaking down the proposal into smaller key elements for each group to develop. It was hoped that in this way the students would have the opportunity of working on a far broader and more detailed type of scheme than would have been possible if they were not pooling the resources of the whole team. To help promote a greater exchange of ideas between students with different experiences to contribute, especially where architectural and cultural issues were concerned, students were given roles that equated to planners, architects and developers to accustom them to the possible conflict of ideas which can arise between the professions, and develop collaborative methods of working.

The different groups were each concerned with key topics which included figure ground analysis, theoretical analysis of the site and the construction of models, market research into the viability of specific building types, a study of the local vernacular building traditions (fig. 7.2), and the analysis of the planning policy for Bakewell and the surrounding areas of the National Park. These matters were investigated and formal presentations made to their peers, and a bound reference manual was prepared. Through participating in these presentations each student quickly assimilated a high level of knowledge and understanding of a wide range of relevant topics (about which, previously, most had known nothing)

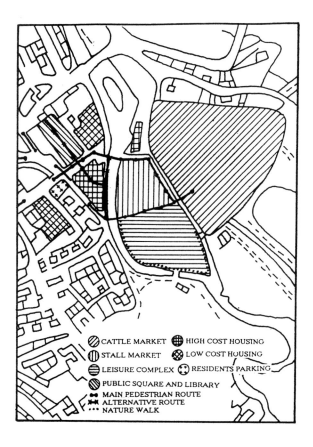

CATTLE MARKET   HIGH COST HOUSING
STALL MARKET   LOW COST HOUSING
LEISURE COMPLEX   RESIDENTS PARKING
PUBLIC SQUARE AND LIBRARY
MAIN PEDESTRIAN ROUTE
ALTERNATIVE ROUTE
NATURE WALK

fig. 7.3 The winning group proposal for the redevelopment of the market area showing both the food and livestock markets relocated away from the centre of the town.

leaving them as well briefed as a professional team might be. Thus the constraints imposed by shortage of time and manpower in the context of the University were exploited to provide a model which could be applied for a real project being carried out with limited resources.

Only one visit to the site was possible, so the groups were again allocated specific tasks: to explore the form of the elevations of the existing buildings around the site from photographs; make sketches to convey the character of Bakewell; produce serial vision images; carry out a site appraisal derived from site reconnaissance; and construct a site model of the existing site. Each group submitted a written document, supplemented with sketches, photographs and other relevant information for a reference handbook, as well as participating in a group presentation to their peers. The method proved rapid and effective for the assimilation of data, and involved a useful element of competition, as well the novelty of supporting or judging their colleagues performance when faced with the daunting task of presenting ideas to an audience, rather than being

lectured at.

Time for preparing the initial proposals and presenting them had been limited to one week. In this way the tortuous debates about proposals which can occur in Schools of Architecture, although this is at odds with practice, were eliminated. The winning scheme would be the one that the group as a whole would develop, so there was a strong incentive to produce proposals which were both exiting and realistic. In addition the democratic selection process made it more acceptable for the students to work on a scheme other than their own.

In the first year that this project was undertaken, five schemes were produced at this stage, three of which opted to retain the food market in the original market location, but move the cattle market to the area on the periphery of the town proposed by the Bakewell Planning Department. This was on the grounds that a market in the centre of the town was an absolute cultural requirement because of people's attachment to it, but that it would be acceptable for it to be a general retail food market. As far as the actual cattle market was concerned, although part of the cultural heritage, changes in technology and transportation meant it would be detrimental to retain it in the town centre.

The two other schemes both hinged on moving both the cattle and the food market out of the centre, leaving a 'heritage town' retaining the old buildings, but without their former function. The scheme selected by the students to be developed and presented was one of these (fig. 7.3). The appeal of this scheme was that the leisure centre required by the brief was placed just outside the town but with good links to the centre and to the new housing on the outskirts, as well as for commuters from neighbouring villages who would be able to reach it without driving through the town. In addition, the leisure centre for the winning scheme was proposed to be mainly underground, and visible only as a bubble rising out of the fields. This choice represented a considerable shift in attitude away from the previously held ideas of many of the planning students with regard to allowing only existing vernacular forms and traditional materials to be used for new structures. This can be seen as part of the result of familiarising some of our future planners with broad concepts of urban design. In *The Concise Townscape*, Cullen points out that the very fact that people gather together means that physical resources will go further:

'A city is more than the sum of its inhabitants. It has the power to generate amenity,

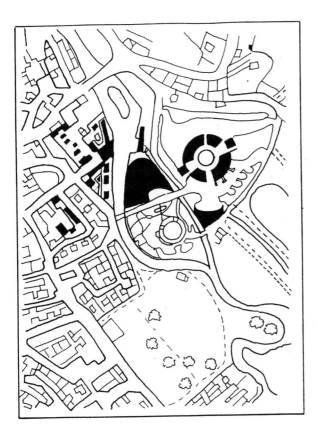

fig. 7.4 Final proposal for the market area with building outline.

which is one reason why people like to live in communities rather than isolation'.[3]
In the choice of design and siting for the leisure centre, the students found a way of combining a bold intervention and new amenity without intruding on the landscape.

FINAL PRESENTATION

In order to achieve the aim of producing a complete piece of work, the group which had devised the winning scheme was allocated the co-ordinating role. This group then had to break down their proposal into smaller elements, such as infrastructure, housing, the new market facility, and recreational facilities. The other groups were then asked to develop these key aspects of the project in discussion with the co-ordinating group, and ourselves as tutors. The co-ordinating group were also responsible for the site model, as well as for setting deadlines and agreeing the format for presentation material in order to ensure a co-ordinated submission from 'one hand'. The final presentation (fig. 7.4) was made to the

Peak Parks Joint Planning Board, and there was no doubt that the quality of the submission was enhanced by the structure of the project.

SUBSEQUENT YEARS

When planning the second year of this course we aimed to address some issues which had arisen with the first set of students. The most striking were a perceived lack of confidence in graphic presentation skills, and an inability to present ideas in a conceptual way, and instead, a tendency to dwell on irrelevant detail. In addition we had found that the students had a surprisingly conservative approach, stemming from a belief that to be adventurous was irresponsible and unacceptable on grounds of reasons of cost and lack of public acceptance. It was felt that the students needed to be more open-minded, and prepared to consider other solutions and not resort as a matter of course to neo-vernacular design ideas because of Bakewell's historic significance.

As far as the use of groups was concerned, there was some distrust of group marking, and occasionally a chauvinistic attitude to communication with peers and tutors. This showed itself in a reluctance on the part of one all-male group of students (mainly rugby players) to discuss their design ideas with the controlling group, who had won the voting, and had an equal number of male and female students. The all-male group presumably felt threatened by 'taking orders' from females, but the problem gradually resolved itself as they got used to working with female tutors in architecture as well as landscape. There also seemed to be a general initial antagonism towards architects in general, which dissipated as the students broadened their viewpoint through being encouraged to discuss their ideas with a representative of the PPJPB and a landscape architect. Finding that we all shared similar views on the built environment rather than being in opposing camps, and that as tutors we were encouraging lateral thinking rather than working to rigid 'accepted' notions improved the working relationship between us to the extent that well after the course finished, the students have consulted us about their project work for the 4th and 5th years in the planning department.

A number of factors made this a particularly rewarding project, and one which can be used as a model for subsequent courses. The creative use of group working, self and peer assessment, task subdivision, and inter-disciplinary co-operation all provide lessons for architecture and planning education. By being able to fragment the project into tasks which the students found manageable, and specifying a varied sequence of presentations, each with different, and sometimes experimental, objectives, but which did not compromise the coherence of the final proposition, the students were able to broaden their perception of their chosen discipline.

Students in the recession struck late 20th century, looking forward to finding rewarding employment, are perhaps becoming sceptical of what they perceive as overdoses of theory, and can relate with enthusiasm to a project which introduces the breadth of practical issues which have to be dealt with in a real work situation. More unexpectedly, through discussing issues with representative of the Peak Parks Joint Planning Board they came to understand that it is not the prerogative of architects to promote examination and analysis of future development in the light of environmental and technical realities of the present age, as well as philosophical ideas and aspirations for the future, but that this is the business of all practitioners in the field of the built environment.

Melanie Richardson
Derek Trowell
University of Sheffield

ACKNOWLEDGEMENTS AND NOTES

We would like to thank Brian Thompson, Joan Sewell and John Keeley of the Peak Park Joint Planning Board for their assistance and participation in the project.

1 Aldo Rossi, *The Architecture of the City*, (MIT Press), Boston, 1989, 29.

2 Carl Rogers, *Freedom to Learn*, (Charles E. Merrivill) Columbus, Ohio, 1983, 189.

3 Gorden Cullen, *The Concise Townscape*, (Butterworth) London, 1988, 7.

138

Urban Design Studies, Volume 3, 1997

HISTORIC MEDWAY TOWNS, A VIEW TO THE FUTURE:
URBAN DESIGN AT THE UNIVERSITY OF GREENWICH 1996-97

MARTIN EYRE AND MEHRDAD SHOKOOHY

Greenwich is known world-wide as a maritime centre, but in the gradual growth of Britain from an island nation to a maritime world power an important role was played by the Medway Towns — a chain of small towns on the bank of a tributary of the River Thames, the Medway River. It was in these towns, and particularly in Chatham, that many of the ships of the Royal Navy were built, repaired and maintained. The towns are located within a region now designated as the Thames Gateway (also known as the East Thames Corridor), and in the heart of the area is the Cathedral City of Rochester, once a Roman settlement on the bank of the Medway River, and in more recent history a market city which provided supplies — and work force — for the dockyards of the satellite settlements (fig. 8.1).

With the decline in ship building and the use of the river as a major commercial route, as well as the final closure of Chatham Dockyards in recent years, the area has suffered not only from unemployment, but also from changes in a long established way of life, with a dramatic effect on the local communities. Large parts of the historic naval shipyards and other industrial sites have been left under-used or unused, leaving vast areas of what are known as 'brown fields'. The renovation of these areas is of national interest, and some plans for their rehabilitation have already been undertaken. A part of the Chatham Dockyards, for example, has been designated as a Heritage Centre, and is open to the public. Within the Historic Dockyard buildings the North Kent Architecture Centre has also been founded, located in the old woodworking shop.

However, for long term revitalisation of the area it is imperative to study the area in detail, and to understand fully the needs of the towns, and the potential role the area can play in future regional development. This is particularly important in the light of the national interest in reviving the river for modern uses. Long term plans have

already changed the character of the old dockyards of East London, and the redevelopment of the towns within the Thames Gateway now needs to be considered.

GREENWICH UNIVERSITY STUDIES

Greenwich University, itself in a historic location with close links with the Medway Towns has a particular interest in the area. Research on some urban aspects of the Medway Towns has already been undertaken by post-graduate students, some of which is hoped to be published in future issues of this journal. In addition, as an urban design exercise a wider study of the area seemed an appropriate project for Diploma students. The North Kent Architecture Centre hosted Greenwich students working on the project, and Barrie Shaw, the Chief Executive of NKAC, provided local briefings and took part in student workshops at Chatham. The result of the students' work was also presented in a public exhibition in the Centre.

While the requirements of the project were for students to produce an urban strategy plan as group work, and detailed design schemes by individuals, the wider aim was to investigate the existing urban conditions, and determine in broad terms the specific needs which would have to be addressed for future development proposals.

First year Diploma students of Architecture worked in groups of three and four as part of the University of Greenwich policy to encourage debate. It also aims to prepare students for working in a similar situation in their professional life. Earlier experience had shown that three or four students to a group is the optimum number for good results. The students take a series of Urban Design Units as a core part of the course, which aims to ground architecture in its context.

The brief was 'open' in that site and buildings were not prescribed. Nevertheless, the study was

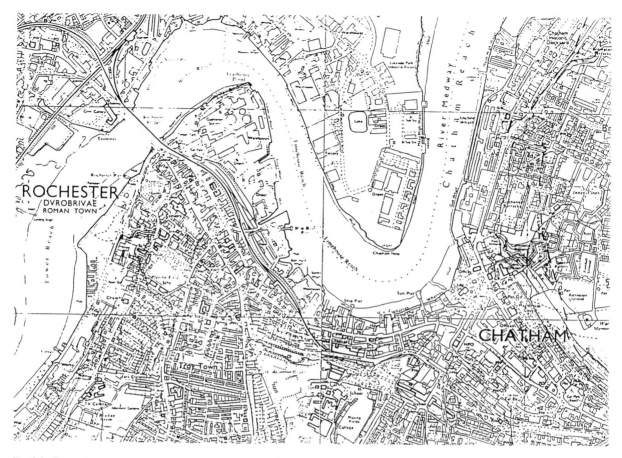

fig. 8.1 River Medway with Rochester to the west and Chatham to the east, and the High Street linking the two areas. The railway makes a classic barrier segregating the High Street from the river and 'brown field' sites (based on Ordnance Survey map).

firmly guided within a framework of Study Units with a progressive structure. Through a process of mapping the programme lead to the definition of areas needing special study. At this stage the students were able to formulate their own briefs, which led to the production of detailed building designs. As a learning device, a major element — perhaps one of the most productive — was the final synthesis stage where the work in each scale was reviewed and students produced a report synthesizing the year's work.

STUDY AREA

A main spatial quality of the area is produced by the river to the north, set in contrast with the sharply rising land to the south — a dramatic setting with the broad sweep of the tidal estuary providing panoramic views which vary with the tides. Between the historic core of Rochester to the west and Chatham High Street to the east lies a built-up ribbon with Victoria Park and the Art College to its south. The figure ground map (fig. 8.2) of the area showing only the footprint of the existing buildings in black against the open space

indicates the density, but, assuming that the buildings are mainly private and most of the open space potentially public, the map also shows the interaction of the public and private space. Although the streets are not shown in the map it is not surprising to see clearly the layout of the historic High Street highlighted by the cluster of densely built up areas.

One of the features of the site is the railway passing through the northern side of the built-up area of Rochester, making a classic urban barrier, segregating in this case the High Street and the commercial heart of Rochester to the south from the river and the run down underused industrial area — the 'brown fields' — to the north. Any future development plan needs to resolve the existing problem of the poor connectivity — almost isolation — of these sites and the rest of the town.

During the course of the study not only were the physical features of the site better understood, but it became apparent that since the decline of the area some of the most important resources have remained underused or ignored; the most important of all, perhaps, being the river itself. Apart from unemployment and a sense of

fig. 8.2 Figure ground map showing the footprint of the existing buildings in black against the open space (S. Lonergan and A. Sweet).

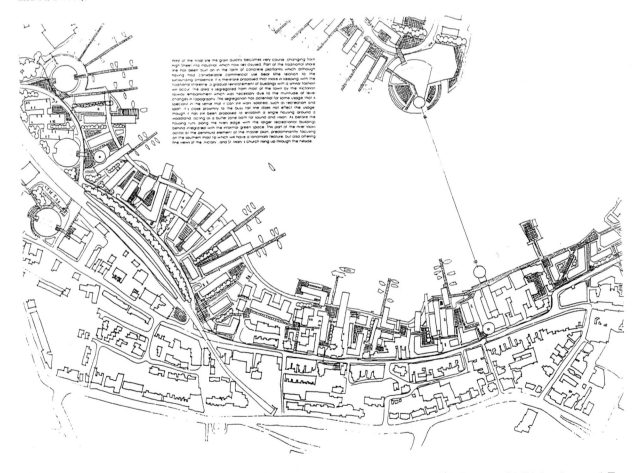

fig. 8.3 An example of a large scale development proposal alongside the river bank (P. Dorman, M. Richardson and T. Wood).

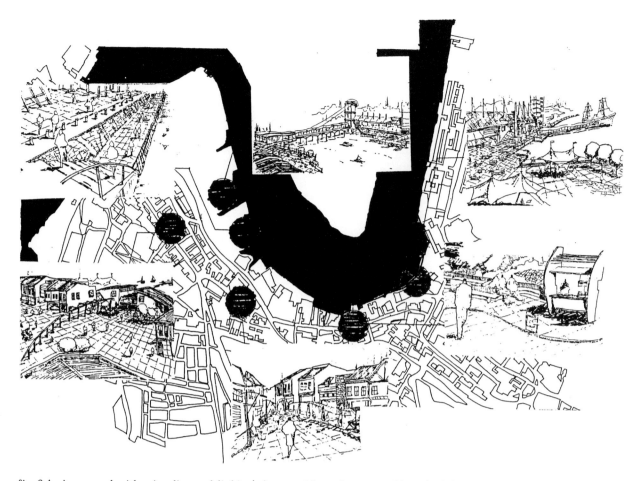

fig. 8.4 A proposal with a 'seeding and linking' theme, with various spots identified for different small scale mixed development, including an integrated urban square (bottom left), a foot bridge over the river (top centre), pedestrianisation of part of the High Street (bottom centre), localised water front developments (top left and top right) (M. S. Rodzi and S. H. Othman).

deprivation due to the closure of the dockyard, which may be seen as a short term problem during a transitory period, it was found that the low density of the area hinders the enhancement of its urban quality. The core of Rochester alone has a strong urban identity; the rest of the Medway Towns form low density urban sprawl of centreless character. The revitalization of brown field sites on the Rochester and Chatham riverside may form an ideal opportunity for not only increasing the density of the area, but perhaps also creating a new centre, well connected to existing facilities.

TRAFFIC

In spite of the low density, traffic congestion and poor public transport are evident in the study area. The lack of adequate local employment has forced many people to seek employment outside the area, and commute to work daily. In addition, as noted, within the area the riverside sites suffer from lack of proper connections with the rest of the area.

The recent records of traffic accidents resulting in personal injury show that most of such accidents occur on the High Street and other major roads with heavy traffic (Star Hill, and part of Medway Street). About 405 of the accidents involved pedestrians attempting to cross the street. One of the contributing factors to the high number of accidents may be the lack of adequate space for pedestrians. The narrow width of parts of the existing pavements seems to bring pedestrians too close to the fast moving traffic. The issues of both motor traffic and pedestrian circulation require appropriate study, but a need for increasing pedestrianised routes was generally acknowledged. Another important issue was felt to be the provision of a cheap and frequent local public transport system, which would minimise the necessity of using cars for short journeys.

A RECENT HOUSING PROJECT AT CHATHAM

The study also produced a critical assessment of the Broadway and Malayan masterplan for the

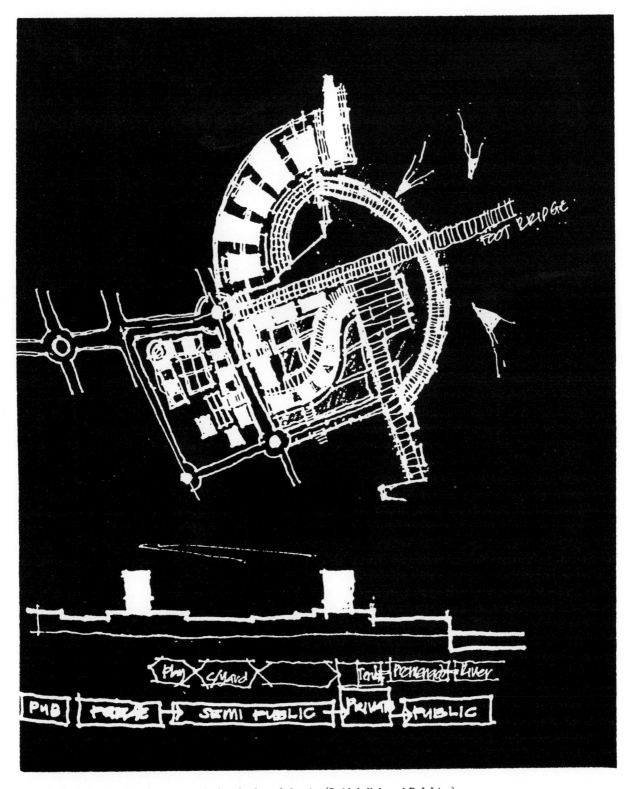

fig. 8.5 High density housing proposal, sketch plan of the site (S. Abdullah and P. J. Liao).

development of 1,700 homes on a 60 hectare site in St. Mary's at Chatham, called Chatham Maritime. Some students concluded that while housing is essential, what Chatham appears to need most is an enhancement of its urban identity, perhaps in the form of a centre, rather than large but isolated housing developments which ignore the host town.

This development, located just north of the Medway Channel aims to be identified as a riverside residential area for commuters to London and other business and industrial centres outside the region. Chatham Maritime already advertises itself as 'close to the Medway tunnel for easy

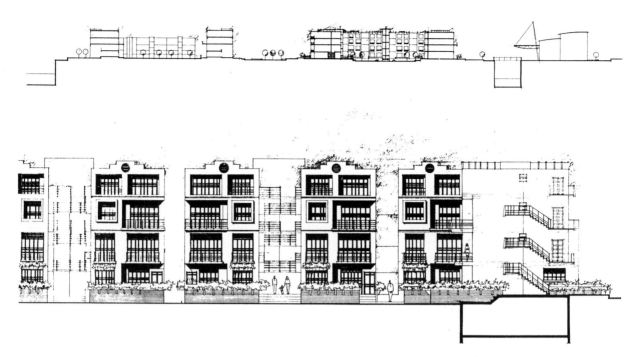

fig. 8.6 High density housing proposal, site section and street view (S. Abdullah and P. J. Liao).

access to London'. Such an approach may bring London dormitory developments closer to Chatham, but will probably contribute little — if anything — towards the urban revitalization of the area.

DESIGN PROPOSALS

In terms of master plan and detailed design proposals, some common themes emerged among the students. As a whole masterplanning was seen as unrealistic, and while some teams suggested large developments along the river bank (fig. 8.3) most strategies proposed some variation on 'seeding and linking'. Mixed development (fig. 8.4) including high density urban housing was seen as an important factor in the revitalization of the area. Housing Density was regarded as a key issue in the urban regeneration debate (figs. 8.5 and 8.6).

Martin Eyre and Mehrdad Shokoohy
University of Greenwich

144

Urban Design Studies, Volume 3, 1997

BOOK REVIEWS

Ali Madanipour, *Design of Urban Space: an inquiry into a social spatial process*, (John Wiley and Sons) Chichester, 1996, 221 pp., 82 illus., bibliog., index, paperback £ 17.99, ISBN 0 471 96673 8; hardback £ 45.00. ISBN 0 471 96672 X

Design of Urban Space takes the form of a review of current writing on the subject, coupled with a series of conclusions by the author. It deals with many aspects of urban design, urban space, and urbanism in general. The book is divided into two parts: Perspectives into Urban Space, and The Making of Urban Space. In the first part the philosophical and structural aspects of urban space are discussed, leading to an analysis of social aspects, an area on which the author places greater emphasis. The Making of Urban Space is concerned with the process, production and regulation of urban space, before outlining current approaches to urban design and ending with a chapter on the actual design of urban space.

The book serves as a useful primer and reference for students and practitioners in that it covers a wide range of topics and authorities, structured in a way to make them easily accessible. It argues strongly for there being two sides to the process — top down and bottom up — which need to be recognised and used together in the design process. The importance of a socio-spatial approach is stressed, but the distinction between spatial and trans-spatial behaviour is not taken sufficiently into account, a concept which could have been used to reinforce many of the author's arguments. The socio-spatial aspect is again emphasised in the last chapter, Design of Urban Space, and some of the imponderables in the nature of urban design are discussed. Here questions of the futility or otherwise of urban design without civic patrons are hinted at. These questions are left open, with an emphasis on the multi-disciplinary nature of the subject, and a warning on the dangers of narrow concentration.

The author presents urban design as a multi-disciplinary field in which many different subjects interact, and no single aspect can be dealt with in isolation. This view is indeed taking prominence among specialists, and can perhaps be taken even further — to include topics such as transport engineering, policing, and also housing and retail management, not given detailed attention in the present work. Nevertheless, given the author's interest in time and change, it can be hoped that in the future he will expand on these matters, as these and many other topics are destined to be incorporated into the general debate.

The book was written to answer three interlinked demands, the first being to address the nature of urban design, in which it succeeds in covering most recognised aspects in sufficient detail. Madanipour's skilful treatment will no doubt act as an stimulus for further thought. Secondly the book aims to respond to the current interest in the field, for which it provides a much needed reference base. The third aim is to indicate possible areas for research. The wide coverage does indeed highlight many areas, but does not aim to establish priorities, as it is for researchers themselves to assess these in the light of their particular work.

PHILIP STRINGER

Colin Rowe and Robert Slutzky, *Transparency*, with a commentary by Bernhard Hoesli and an introduction by Werner Oechslin (tr. Jori Walker), (Birkhauser Verlag) Basel-Boston-Berlin, 1997, 119pp, 153 illus., paperback £17.50, ISBN 3 7643 5615 4

Architects are seldom very precise in the way that they use words or the meanings they assign to them, and often misuse terms in a way that would make an estate agent or realtor blush. The problem is exacerbated when the profession adds to its critical vocabulary by borrowing from other arts and sciences, and subtly (or otherwise) changes the original meaning while still claiming whatever legitimacy is granted by an implied cross disciplinary relationship — witness the confusion that attended recent theoretical forays into semiotics, structuralism, and post-modernism. When such a relationship is deemed seminal to the development of modern architectural principles, then the potential for misunderstanding is immense, and some clarification is required.

In an article written in 1955, Rowe, described in the citation for his RIBA Gold Medal in 1995 as 'the most significant architectural teacher of the second half of the 20th century', and Slutzky, then a colleague of Rowe at the University of Texas at Austin, and a one-time student of Joseph Albers, attempted to correct what they saw as misuse of the term 'transparency' in the written history of modern architecture up to that point. The article achieved cult status in American academic circles, being photocopied and circulated among staff and students long before its eventual publication in 1964 in the Yale architectural journal, *Perspecta*, 8. The delay in publication, according to Hoesli, a colleague of Rowe and Slutzky at Austin and a member of the group of experimental teachers there who came to be known collectively as the 'Texas Rangers', may have been because of the authors' criticism of Gropius, then a demi-god at Harvard. 'But in Austin, a certain poetic licence was welcome, the privilege of a younger generation who not only permit themselves a partisan point of view ... but detect certain advantages in it. If vanity was injured — clearly that of Gropius, for instance — or progressive thinkers rather disdainfully dismissed, they thought little of it' (Oechslin, p. 12).

Such an attitude, combined with the intellectual merits of the article, has a perennial appeal, and the original Transparency text spawned a Swiss edition (with commentary by Hoesli) in 1968; a second part (*Perspecta*, 13/14) in 1971; inclusion in Rowe's collected essays ('The Mathematics of the Ideal Villa') in 1976; a French edition (with an introduction by Oechslin, and an 1982 addendum by Hoesli) in 1992, and, finally the present English edition which includes all the above except Part II. Along the way the thesis expounded in the article also attracted significant criticism, but there can be few pieces in the short history of modern architectural analysis with such longevity.

The article explores the relationship between painting and modern architecture — a well trodden path by that time, but still capable of the odd surprise. Clear tracks had been left by those early 20th century architects who indulged in the odd polemical treatise, especially Oud, Gropius and Le Corbusier, but it was the Museum of Modern Art in New York which set the tone of the subsequent debate. In their companion volume to MOMA's 1932 exhibition of modern architecture, Henry Russell Hitchcock Jr., and Philip Johnson identified Gropius' 1926 buildings at the Bauhaus as having 'profited from ... the aesthetic experimentation of the Dutch Neoplasticists' (later known as De Stijl) and claimed that 'Ozenfant's sort of cubism, called Purism, had perhaps inspired Le Corbusier in his search for sources of formal inspiration' (Hitchcock and Johnson, 'The International Style', 1932). MOMA's later exhibition, 'Cubism and Abstract Art' (1936) also suggested that modern architecture was a 'synthesis of Purism, De Stijl and the Bauhaus' (Oechslin, p. 13). One of the characteristics of the new architecture being an extensive use of glass, it was also firmly in thrall of pseudo-moralists like Bruno Taut.

Fast forward to 1954 and in 'Space, Time and Architecture' Sigfried Giedion 'seems to assume that the presence of an all glass wall at the Bauhaus, with its extensive transparent areas', permits 'the hovering relations of planes and the kind of "overlapping" which appears in contemporary painting', especially in Picasso's *L'Arlessienne* (*Transparency*, p. 34). The 'syllogistic pairing' (Slutzky in *Daidalos*, 33, 1989) of Gropius' Bauhaus and Picasso's *L'Arlessienne*, however ingenious, offended Rowe and Slutzky and their 'semantic dispute' with Giedion over the forms of 'transparency' displayed in the two works prompted the eponymous article.

The title, 'Transparency: literal and phenomenal', defines the parameters of the debate, Rowe and Slutzky relying on a definition of transparency by Gyorgy Kepes in the *Language of Vision* (1944, for which Giedion wrote the foreword) to establish their starting point. For Kepes, transparency 'implies more than an optical characteristic, it implies a broader spatial order. Transparency means a simultaneous perception of different spatial locations. Space not only recedes, but fluctuates in a continuous activity' (p. 77). With this understanding, Rowe and Slutzky assert that 'the transparent ceases to be that which is perfectly clear and becomes instead that which is clearly ambiguous' (p. 23), as exemplified by the 'transparent overlapping planes' of analytical cubism.

Rowe and Slutzky explain their distinction between a 'literal' and 'phenomenal' transparency by comparing and contrasting Constructivist and Cubist painting (as seen by them), concluding that 'literal transparency ... tends to be associated with the *trompe l'oeil* effect of a translucent object in a deep, naturalistic space; while phenomenal transparency seems to be found when a painter seeks the articulated presentation of frontally displayed objects in a shallow, abstracted space' (p. 32).

In architecture, literal transparency is easily achieved with a sheet of glass, but phenomenal transparency is 'so difficult to discuss that generally critics have been willing to associate transparency in architecture exclusively with a transparency of materials' (p. 33), hence Giedion's pairing of the glass wall at the Bauhaus with Picasso's *L'Arlessienne*, in which 'a transparency of overlapping planes is very obviously to be found', but that is not enough for Rowe and Slutzky:

> 'Picasso offers planes apparently of Celluloid, through which the observer has the sensation of looking; and in doing so, no doubt his sensations are somewhat similar to those of a hypothetical observer of the workshop wing of the Bauhaus. In each case a transparency of materials is discovered. But in the laterally constructed space of his picture, Picasso, through the compilation of larger and smaller forms, offers the limitless possibilities of alternative readings, while the glass wall at the Bauhaus, an ambiguous space, seems to be singularly free of this quality. Thus for evidence of what we have designated phenomenal transparency, we shall be obliged to look elsewhere' (pp. 34-5).

They found what they were looking for in Le Corbusier's Villa Stein at Garches, which is not entirely surprising given Le Corbusier's own interest in Cubism, his identification with 'Ozenfant's sort of Cubism' (Hitchcock and Johnson) and Rowe's familiarity with the building — it had played a starring role in his first major article, 'The Mathematics of the Ideal Villa' in 1947. Leaving a description of the building to the authors, they conclude that throughout the Villa at Garches:

> 'there is that contradiction of spatial elements which Kepes recognises as a characteristic of transparency. There is a continuous dialectic between fact and implication. The reality of deep space is constantly opposed to the inference of shallow space; and by means of the resultant tension, reading after reading is enforced' (p. 41).

In the same way, the authors look at an unbuilt design of Le Corbusier's — his League of Nations project of 1927, compare that with the Bauhaus, and conclude that Gropius has 'exteriorised the opposed movements of space, has al-

lowed them to flow away into infinity; and by being unwilling to attribute to either of them any significant difference of quality, he has prohibited the possibilities of potential ambiguity' (p. 43). By contrast, Le Corbusier's scheme displays a series of stratifications, 'devices by means of which space becomes constructed, substantial and articulate, (and) are the essence of that phenomenal transparency which has been noticed as characteristic of the central post-cubist tradition. They have never been noticed as characteristic of the Bauhaus, which obviously manifests a completely different conception of space' (p. 52).

That is all very well, but using the Bauhaus as a foil to point out all the areas in which Garches and the League project are 'better' and truer to Cubist principles is disingenuous, given that noone has ever claimed any links between Gropius and Cubism. Gropius cannot be criticised for not achieving what he did not set out to achieve, though Giedion himself may have erred in proposing a direct relationship between the Bauhaus and *L'Arlessienne*. This flaw in their argument, however, does not detract from Rowe and Slutzky's achievement.

Distribution and later publication of the Transparency article made a major contribution to the re-assessment of the works of Le Corbusier under way in America at the time. It could be argued that the 'New York School' of Eisenman, Graves, Gwathmey, Hejduk, and Meier might have taken a different form without such a reassessment (Hejduk, incidentally, taught at Austin with Rowe and Slutzky). In his introduction to the 1972 survey of their work 'Five Architects', Rowe claimed that the five 'recognise that certain changes are so enormous as to impose a directive which cannot be resolved in any individual life span'. These changes particularly concerned 'the plastic and spatial inventions of Cubism and the proposition that, whatever may be said about these, they possess an eloquence and a flexibility which continues now to be as overwhelming as it was then' ('Five Architects', 1972, p. 7).

As mentioned above, Rowe and Slutzky had begun a second article on the theme of transparency as early as 1955, but this was not published until 1971 in *Perspecta*, 13/14, by which time Rowe had already moved on, the main text of 'Collage City' being completed by December 1973. The second article weakens the arguments of the first by concentrating attention 'not upon the three dimensional or spatial aspects of phenomenal transparency, but as far as possible upon its two dimensional manifestations — upon phenomenal transparency as pattern' (*Perspecta*, 13/14), particularly the pattern of Michaelangelo's proposed facade for San Lorenzo, and concluding that phenomenal transparency 'is neither a new, nor even a post-Cubist manifestation'. Not surprisingly, Part II is not included in Rowe's collected essays, nor in Hoesli's 1968 edition, which aimed to be *the* contribution of the still inexhaustible possibilities of the Cubist aesthetic' (Oechslin, p. 11).

What is disappointing about this 1997 English edition is the absence of any reaction, contemporary or otherwise, to the original articles, and, apart from footnotes to Oechslin's introduction, no exploration of the influence of the work on the profession. Both Hoesli's and Oechslin's contributions have an air of hagiography about them and the omission of any critical analysis of the original article is damning. Reviewing the Swiss edition 'Transparenz' in 1970, for example, Stanislaus von Moos spoke of the 'almost compulsive fetishism driving this word "transparency"' (cited by Oechslin in a footnote) and a review by Rosemarie Haag-Bletter of both parts in *Oppositions*, 13 in 1978 can only be described as a well informed hatchet job, and well worth study as a reaction to Rowe and Slutzky's thesis. To be a real contribution to scholarship, the current publication should perhaps have included all contributions to the topic, including Haag-Bletter's: that would have been a truly unique book.

Important as their impact was at the time, the Transparency texts were created for a generation preoccupied by Le Corbusier; to a generation less obsessed, the work is still interesting, but a broader view is required. Take away the Cubist emphasis, for example, and the question of 'multiple readings' of the same form is equally served by Venturi's concept of 'both-and' as opposed to 'either-or' architecture in *Complexity and Contradiction in Architecture*', written in 1962 and published in 1966. Not nearly as rigourous in its analysis of individual works, Venturi's book is a near-contemporary of the Transparency texts, and is more user friendly, yet it is not even granted a footnote in the 1997 publication.

Slutzky cooperated with Hoesli's 1968 edition, but Rowe did not. Hoesli's 1982 addendum (included in the present publication) includes the teasing assertion that: 'Concepts of space are inventions. They have their usefulness, life span and history' (p. 89), but he does not seem to realise that this aphorism applies to his own Transparency project. In his attempt to establish phenomenal transparency as a design tool, which was never intended, he dilutes the impact of the initial concept.

Elsewhere Rowe has summed up the problem of theoretical texts being reprinted long after their conception, and should perhaps have the last word: 'The sense of what was said some fifty years ago prohibits repetition; but then the repetition of what was said persists' ('Five Architects', p. 6).

EVAN A. FERGUSON